DEC   2014

D0196279

Life After the Military

Military Life

Military Life is a series of books for service members and their families who must deal with the significant yet often overlooked difficulties unique to life in the military. Each of the titles in the series is a comprehensive presentation of the problems that arise, solutions to these problems, and resources that are of much further help. The authors of these books—who are themselves military members and experienced writers—have personally faced these challenging situations, and understand the many complications that accompany them. This is the first stop for members of the military and their loved ones in search of information on navigating the complex world of military life.

1. *The Wounded Warrior Handbook: A Resource Guide for Returning Veterans* by Don Philpott and Janelle Hill (2008).
2. *The Military Marriage Manual: Tactics for Successful Relationships* by Janelle Hill, Cheryl Lawhorne, and Don Philpott (2010).
3. *Combat-Related Traumatic Brain Injury and PTSD: A Resource and Recovery Guide* by Cheryl Lawhorne and Don Philpott (2010).
4. *Special Needs Families in the Military: A Resource Guide* by Janelle Hill and Don Philpott (2010).
5. *Life After the Military: A Handbook for Transitioning Veterans* by Janelle Hill, Cheryl Lawhorne, and Don Philpott (2011).

Life After the Military

A Handbook for Transitioning Veterans

Janelle Hill, Cheryl Lawhorne-Scott,
and Don Philpott

ROWMAN & LITTLEFIELD PUBLISHERS, INC.
Lanham • Boulder • New York • Toronto • Plymouth, UK

650.1086
HIL

Published by Rowman & Littlefield Publishers, Inc.
A wholly owned subsidary of The Rowman & Littlefield Publishing Group, Inc.
4501 Forbes Boulevard, Suite 200, Lanham, Maryland 20706
www.rowman.com

10 Thornbury Road, Plymouth PL6 7PP, United Kingdom

Distributed by National Book Network

Copyright © 2011 by Government Institutes
First Rowman & Littlefield paperback edition 2013

All rights reserved. No part of this book may be reproduced in any form or by any electronic or mechanical means, including information storage and retrieval systems, without written permission from the publisher, except by a reviewer who may quote passages in a review.

The reader should not rely on this publication to address specific questions that apply to a particular set of facts. The author and the publisher make no representation or warranty, express or implied, as to the completeness, correctness, or utility of the information in this publication. In addition, the author and the publisher assume no liability of any kind whatsoever resulting from the use of or reliance upon the contents of this book.

British Library Cataloguing in Publication Information Available

Library of Congress Cataloging-in-Publication Data

The hardback edition of this book was previously cataloged by the Library of Congress as follows:

Hill, Janelle.
 Life after the military : a handbook for transitioning veterans / Janelle Hill, Cheryl Lawhorne-Scott, and Don Philpott.
   p. cm.
 Includes bibliographical references and index.
 1. Veterans—Services for—United States—Handbooks, manuals, etc. 2. Retired military personnel—United States—Handbooks, manuals, etc. 3. Veterans—Employment—United States—Handbooks, manuals, etc. 4. Retired military personnel—Employment—United States—Handbooks, manuals, etc. 5. Career changes—United States—Handbooks, manuals, etc. I. Lawhorne, Cheryl, 1968- II. Philpott, Don, 1946- III. Title.
 UB357.H55 2011
 650.1086'970973—dc22

2011001080

ISBN 978-1-60590-740-6 (cloth : alk. paper)
ISBN 978-1-60590-741-3 (electronic)

ISBN 978-1-4422-2133-8 (pbk. : alk. paper)

♾™ The paper used in this publication meets the minimum requirements of American National Standard for Information Sciences—Permanence of Paper for Printed Library Materials, ANSI/NISO Z39.48-1992.

Printed in the United States of America

Contents

Acknowledgments   vii

1 Leaving the Service   1

2 Developing Your Own Individual Transition
Plan (ITP)   21

3 Transitioning to a New Career   61

4 The Entrepreneurial Spirit   97

5 Finding a Home   133

6 Going Back to School   149

7 Health and Insurance   161

8 Transition Benefits   177

9 Finances   245

Appendix 1 Useful Websites   259

Appendix 2 Transition Checklists Used as Part of the Recovery
Care Coordinator Program   267

Appendix 3 Guide to Entrepreneurship   279

Appendix 4 VA Facilities   283

Index   311

About the Authors   315

Acknowledgments

As with all the titles in the Military Life series, the aim is to produce a one-stop guide that, hopefully, covers all the information you need on a specific subject. We are not trying to reinvent the wheel, simply to gather information from as many sources available as possible so that you don't have to. Almost all the information in this book comes from federal and military websites and is in the public domain. These include the Department of Defense, American Forces Press Service, U.S. Army Medical Department, Department of Veterans Affairs, Department of Health and Human Services, and the websites of all branches of the U.S. military. We have tried to extract the essentials. Where more information might be useful we have provided websites and resources that can help you.

1

Leaving the Service

The key to a smooth transition is to be prepared well before you separate from the military. Start early. Make connections and build networks that will help you transition smoothly into the civilian world.

OVERVIEW

There are many different sorts of transitioning—depending on whether you are single, have a family, are looking to find a civilian job, or planning on enjoying retirement as a veteran.

The transition process is also different depending on whether you are considered a first-termer, a midcareerist, or preretiree. Another distinction is between Active Duty and Reserve.

Returning to civilian life is an exciting time, one full of hope for what the next chapter in your life might bring. But the transition is also a complex undertaking. You have many steps to take and many questions to get answered. Transition assistance staff, personnel office staff, relocation specialists, education counselors, and many others can help, but only you and your family can make the critical decisions that must be made. So where should you start?

This guide will help you work through the sections listed on DD Form 2648, Preseparation Counseling Checklist. The checklist allows you to indicate the benefits and services that you wish to receive additional counseling on as you prepare your Individual Transition Plan (ITP). In those cases where the transition counselor cannot answer questions, you will be referred to subject-matter experts that will provide you the information that you need. Work through each element of the guide but take advantage of your opportunity to request the specific resources that are appropriate for you. If you are uncertain about your future plans, now is the time to obtain all the assistance and information you need. Professional guidance and counseling are available at your transition assistance office, as are workshops, publications, information resources, automated resources, and government programs. Take advantage of each one that applies to your unique situation. It is your Individual Transition Plan: It is your responsibility and your life.

The new "My Decision Points" ITP program will help you develop your personalized game plan for successfully transitioning back to civilian life. My Decision Points provides the framework to help you identify your unique skills, knowledge, desires, experience, and abilities to help you make wise choices. It is not a Department of Defense form; it is something you create by yourself, for yourself, with information found at http://www.TurboTAP.org and assistance from a transition counselor. Those who do not live near a military installation can also get assistance by telephone, e-mail, CD ROM, and so on.

As you prepare to transition into your new life, there are a number of psychological matters that have to be taken into account as well as all the other critical issues, such as finding a home, a job, getting the right health coverage, ensuring you have all the benefits you are entitled to, and so on. However, as you prepare for these life-changing events, it is a good time to consider how these will impact your life and those around you.

COPING WITH CHANGE

Transitioning back to civilian life, especially after periods of deployment, may present unique emotional and psychological challenges. It is natural to experience a sense of significant change, some stress, and feelings of ambivalence. You must reconnect with family, friends, and community while attempting to understand and cope both with deployment experiences and your changing circumstances.

Coming home represents a return to comfort and security, but the routines of home and work are markedly different from the focused, intense, and regimented life of active duty. There are several things to keep in mind for a smoother, healthier transition:

- A period of readjustment is normal. Take things slowly. It takes time to reestablish relationships.
- Things will be different. You have changed, as have your family members. Everyone needs to adapt to a new and mutually acceptable family pattern.
- Communication is key. Talk things out. Be honest, be clear, and be sure to listen.

RETURNING FROM HAZARDOUS DUTY

If you have been in harm's way or on hazardous duty, you may experience symptoms of combat stress. Most conditions related to stress during combat are normal reactions to abnormal circumstances. Reactions may be physical (such as sleep disturbances), cognitive (such as concentration or memory problems), or emotional (such as anger or depression).

Post-traumatic stress disorder (PTSD) can also become an issue for those returning from hazardous duty. PTSD is an anxiety disorder that may develop weeks, months, or even years after exposure to a terrifying event or ordeal. Not everyone who experiences a traumatic event will develop PTSD.

A person with PTSD exhibits three main types of symptoms:

- reexperiencing the traumatic event
- avoidance and emotional numbing
- increased arousal (hypervigilant or "on guard")

There are many ways to cope with these reactions. Positive coping strategies include rest, exercise, and social involvement. If these symptoms persist, consult with a trained health professional. Therapy, with or without medication, has proven extremely effective.

READJUSTMENT TO WORK

Returning to work may also be challenging. Personnel may have changed, and new projects may be underway. Request a briefing on any changes that occurred in your absence. Do not hesitate to ask for help or support. Take advantage of training opportunities that may help you to feel more confident in your work.

PRIMARY SOURCES OF INFORMATION AND SUPPORT

Military OneSource is a free support service provided by the Department of Defense (DoD), offering assistance and resources to servicemembers and their families on many different issues. Go to www.militaryonesource.com. The Transition Assistance Program website provides information for servicemembers on transitioning from military service. Visit www.TurboTAP.org.

For further information on PTSD, visit the website for the National Center for PTSD, a special center within Veterans Affairs, at www.ncptsd.va.gov.

COPING AS A COUPLE

When you first get married you do everything you can to please your partner. You buy each other little gifts, you help each other with the chores and the shopping, and you enjoy doing things together.

Once you have been married a little while, these little intimacies might become less and less frequent for a number of reasons. You might both have jobs and be so tired when you get home that all you want to do is eat and go to bed. You may have children, which are very time-consuming. You might work different shifts, and so you pass each other in the hallway—as one comes home the other is going to work. Transitioning can place additional stresses and strains on you and your spouse—not only on your marriage but also with your children, other family members, and friends.

Whatever the circumstances, you have to work at any relationship to make it successful. Your relationship is like a fire. It needs fuel to make it burn and without it, the flames will die down until there is nothing left. Despite all the other pressures on your time, you have to keep that fire burning. And there are lots of things you can do to make that fire burn strongly.

The most important thing is to find time to spend together—when the children are in bed, when the chores have been done, when there are no other distractions to stop you from focusing on each other. Set aside this time as your special time to do what you want to do together. It can be once a week or once a month, but make it happen.

Find time to honestly talk about the things that are important to you both: What are your goals and aspirations, do you both have the same dreams for the future? It is much easier to achieve these goals when you are both on the same page.

This honest talking should include your sex life as well. You both have needs—are these being met? Would you like more intimacy? Discuss what you would both like without embarrassment or guilt. Unless you talk about it, neither of you will know what is important to the other—and who knows, it could lead to all sorts of new and exciting things.

With that in mind, keep the magic alive. Just because you are married doesn't mean that you can't still go on dates with your partner. Go to your special restaurant for an intimate candlelit dinner, hold hands. Do not spoil the occasion by talking about work, problems, or the children. Talk about each other, funny things that have happened to you, things you'd like to do, where you would like to go on holiday, and so on. It is all about you as a couple. If your budget is tight, have an intimate dinner at home. Light some candles, dress up for the occasion, play your favorite music—and have fun.

Like a good bottle of wine, a marriage changes as it ages. If handled correctly a fine bottle of wine becomes more complex yet more harmonious, and so it is with a good marriage. The honeymoon may be over, but the love, like the wine, should be nurtured so that it develops and grows into something more beautiful. Remember the little things—the kiss as you leave for work or when you come home, the hug for no other reason than to show that you care, sending flowers even though it is not a birthday or anniversary. It is these little things that show you still care.

If you ask couples who have been happily married for a long time they will often say that they are not just lovers but best friends as well. They are able to talk to each other about anything, they share jokes, and they enjoy doing things together as a couple. Sharing a common interest—everything from jogging to bird watching and singing in the church choir to being on the same trivia team at the local pub helps cement that bond and develop a much broader relationship. Find things that you enjoy doing together—from volunteering to gardening—and really enjoy doing them together.

At the same time, everyone needs their own space, time to do their own thing. It is important that you make time for this as well.

Never take anything for granted, especially in a relationship. We all need reassuring from time to time. If you suddenly stop saying "I love you," your partner may well wonder why but be afraid to ask. It is so easy to prevent those situations from arising by simply saying those three small but important words.

Disagreements Do Happen

At some time or other every couple has an argument. How they handle that argument is a testament to how strong their marriage is. If one partner loses control and storms out of the house, that is not a good sign.

One piece of advice that used to be handed down to newly married couples was "Never go to bed angry," which means kiss and make up so that whatever you were arguing about doesn't fester overnight and resurface in another row.

You are bound to have disagreements, and sometimes they are over the silliest little things, although at the time they may not have appeared to be so silly and little. The important thing is that when you do have an argument you have to make sure that it does not escalate and get out of control.

There are several ways of doing this. First, stay in control of your emotions. Something has clearly annoyed you or your partner, so try to discuss it objectively. Never make it personal, with name-calling or deliberately hurtful remarks. No matter how much you want to hurt your partner in the heat of that particular moment, words spoken can never be taken back. Apologies afterward for saying such things don't work, and your partner will remember exactly what you said and may come to resent you for it.

If you do have a disagreement, argue only about what has upset you. Don't use it as an excuse to bring in all sorts of other issues you may have with your partner. Stay in control of your words and actions—don't sneer, don't shout or point fingers. If things are getting too heated, leave the room—don't storm out but just say that you think a time-out would be a good idea. It gives you both a chance to cool down.

Apologies for having the argument, however, are a good idea provided they are sincere. It allows you both to kiss and make up and having cleared the air, move on. If there are still issues to be resolved, set a time to talk about them. Some couples prefer to do this on "neutral" territory—at a café or while going for a walk. Practice the skills mentioned in the communications section above. Listen carefully to what your partner is saying, respect his or her position, and then let him or her know how you feel and perhaps suggest ways you can work together to resolve the problem.

Sometimes couples have issues that they cannot sort out themselves, and they should then seek help. You can approach a trusted mutual friend, a chaplain, or seek advice from the Family Service Center.

Marriage and Stress

All marriages undergo stress from time to time. This can be a result of emotional strains, work or financial problems, children, and so on. For military families there are many other situations that can be very stressful—coping with deployment and separation and frequent moves being at the top of the list.

When people are stressed they react differently. It is difficult for them to eat and sleep. They become irritable and short-tempered. They may say things in the heat of the moment they would not otherwise say. As couples tend to react differently under stress, one partner may be affected far more than the other and so the relationship gets out of kilter. The answer is to identify the source of stress and see what can be done about it. First, you must accept that you are under stress and that this is causing problems in the relationship. Then sit down together and talk about the issues. That alone is often enough to relieve some of the stress. Whatever the cause of the stress, it is not likely to be resolved easily or quickly, but just recognizing it and having some sort of plan to tackle it is reassuring. Much more important, by sitting down with your partner and talking about it you can work together to resolve it. There is a lot of truth in the saying "A problem shared is a problem halved."

Talking about the problem is half the battle; showing that you care is the other half. Be supportive and loving. Buy your partner something special—it doesn't have to be expensive—but it does show that you are thinking of them and are there for them.

Transitioning does impose additional stresses and strains on relationships, but being strong and loving together helps you overcome them as you move forward.

TRANSITIONING ASSISTANCE

Joint Transition Assistance

The Departments of Veterans Affairs, Defense, and Labor launched a new and improved website for wounded warriors—the National Resource Directory (NRD). This directory (www.nationalresourcedirectory.gov) provides access to thousands of services and resources at the national, state, and local levels to support recovery, rehabilitation, and community reintegration. The NRD is a comprehensive online tool available nationwide for wounded, ill, and injured servicemembers, veterans, and their families.

The NRD includes extensive information for veterans seeking resources on Veterans Administration (VA) benefits, including disability benefits, pensions for veterans and their families, VA health care insurance, and the GI Bill. The NRD's design and interface is simple, easy to navigate, and intended to answer the needs of a broad audience of users within the military and veteran and caregiver communities.

Transition from Military to VA

VA has stationed personnel at major military hospitals to help seriously injured servicemembers returning from Operations Enduring Freedom and Iraqi Freedom (OEF/OIF) as they transition from military to civilian life. OEF/OIF servicemembers who have questions about VA benefits or need assistance in filing a VA claim or accessing services can contact the nearest VA office or call 1-800-827-1000. The following programs are provided by the VA.

Transition Assistance Program: The Transition Assistance Program (TAP) consists of comprehensive three-day workshops at military installations designed to help servicemembers as they transition from military to civilian life. The program includes job search, employment, and training information as well as VA benefits information for servicemembers who are within twelve months of separation or twenty-four months of retirement. A companion workshop, the Disabled Transition Assistance Program, provides information on VA's Vocational Rehabilitation and Employment Program as well as other programs for the disabled. Additional information about these programs is available at www.dol.gov/vets/programs/tap/tap_fs.htm.

TAP consists of four essential components:
- preseparation counseling
- DoL TAP Employment Workshops
- VA benefits briefings
- Disabled Transition Assistance Program (DTAP)

Predischarge Program: The Predischarge Program is a joint VA and DoD program that affords servicemembers the opportunity to file claims for disability compensation and other benefits up to 180 days prior to separation or retirement.

The two primary components of the Predischarge Program, Benefits Delivery at Discharge (BDD) and Quick Start, may be used by all separating servicemembers in the contiguous United States (CONUS) on active duty, including members of the Coast Guard, and members of the National Guard and Reserves (activated under Titles 10 or 32).

BDD is offered to accelerate receipt of VA disability benefits, with a goal of providing benefits within sixty days after release or discharge from active duty.

To participate in the BDD program, servicemembers must:

1. have at least 60 days, but not more than 180 days, remaining on active duty
2. have a known date of separation or retirement
3. provide the VA with service treatment records, originals or photocopies
4. be available to complete all necessary examinations prior to leaving the point of separation

Quick Start is offered to servicemembers who have less than sixty days remaining on active duty or are unable to complete the necessary examinations prior to leaving the point of separation.

To participate in the Quick Start Program, servicemembers must:

1. have at least one day remaining on active duty
2. have a known date of separation or retirement
3. provide the VA with service treatment records, originals or photocopies

Servicemembers should contact the local transition assistance office or Army Career Alumni Program Center to schedule appointments to attend VA benefits briefings and to learn how to initiate a predischarge claim. Servicemembers can obtain more information by calling the VA toll free at 1-800-827-1000 or by visiting www.vba.va.gov/predischarge.

Federal Recovery Coordination Program

The Federal Recovery Coordination Program, a joint program of DoD and VA, helps coordinate and access federal, state, and local programs for benefits and services for seriously wounded, ill, and injured servicemembers and their families through recovery, rehabilitation, and reintegration into the community.

Federal Recovery Coordinators (FRCs) have the delegated authority for oversight and coordination of the clinical and nonclinical care identified in each client's Federal Individual Recovery Plan (FIRP). Working with a variety of case managers, FRCs assist their clients in reaching their FIRP goals. FRCs remain with their clients as long as they are needed regardless of the client's location, duty, or health status. In doing so, they often serve as the central point of contact and provide transition support for their clients.

In coordination with the Department of Defense and the Department of Health and Human Services, the joint Federal Recovery Coordinator Program is designed to cut across bureaucratic lines and reach into the private sector as necessary to identify services needed for seriously wounded and ill servicemembers, veterans, and their families.

A key recommendation of a presidential commission chaired by former senator Bob Dole and former Health and Human Services secretary Donna Shalala, the recovery coordinators do not directly provide care but coordinate federal health care teams and private community resources to achieve the personal and professional goals of an individualized "life map" or recovery plan developed with the servicemembers or veterans who qualify for the federal recovery coordinator program. Although initially based in military facilities, their work seamlessly extends into the patient's civilian life after discharge. To ensure these severely injured persons do not get lost in the system, the coordinators actively link the veteran with public and private resources that will meet his or her rehabilitation needs.

Participating patients include those with seriously debilitating burns, spinal cord injuries, amputations, visual impairments, traumatic brain injuries, and post-traumatic stress disorder. While initially focused on early stages for current military hospital inpatients, the FRCP involvement is expected to be a lifetime commitment to veterans and their families. The coordinators will maintain contacts by phone, visits, and e-mail. When a veteran settles in a remote area, the VA will use multimedia systems that integrate video and audio teleconferencing so that veterans may visit a federal clinic or private center near their homes and link up with their case coordinator for a meeting.

To get into the Federal Recovery Coordination Program, you must be seriously wounded, ill, or injured and be referred. You are referred into the program by a member of your multidisciplinary team, your commander, the wounded warrior program, or through self-referral.

An assigned Federal Recovery Coordinator will develop a Federal Individualized Recovery Plan with input from the servicemember or veteran's multidisciplinary heath care team, the servicemember or veteran, and their family or caregiver. They track the care, management, and transition of a recovering servicemember or veteran through recovery, rehabilitation, and reintegration.

Preseparation Counseling

Servicemembers may receive preseparation counseling twenty-four months prior to retirement or twelve months prior to separation from active duty. These sessions present information on education, training, employment assistance, National Guard and Reserve programs, medical benefits, and financial assistance.

Verification of Military Experience and Training

The Verification of Military Experience and Training (VMET) Document, DD Form 2586, helps servicemembers verify previous experience and training to potential employers, negotiate credits at schools, and obtain certificates or licenses. VMET documents are available only through Army, Navy, Air Force, and Marine Corps transition support offices and are intended for servicemembers who have at least six months of active service. Servicemembers should obtain VMET documents from their transition support office within twelve months of separation or twenty-four months of retirement.

Transition Bulletin Board

To find business opportunities, a calendar of transition seminars, job fairs, information on veterans' associations, transition services, training and education opportunities, as well as other announcements, visit the website at www.turbotap.org.

DoD Transportal

To find locations and phone numbers of all transition assistance offices as well as minicourses on conducting successful job-search campaigns, writing resumes, using the Internet to find a job, and links to job search and recruiting websites, visit the DoD Transportal at www.veteranprograms.com/index.html.

EDUCATIONAL AND VOCATIONAL COUNSELING

The Vocational Rehabilitation and Employment (VR&E) Program provides educational and vocational counseling to servicemembers, veterans, and certain dependents (U.S.C. Title 38, Section 3697) at no charge. These counseling services are designed to help an individual choose a vocational direction, determine the course needed to achieve the chosen goal, and evaluate the career possibilities open to them.

Assistance may include interest and aptitude testing, occupational exploration, setting occupational goals, locating the right type of training program, and exploring educational or training facilities that can be used to achieve an occupational goal.

Counseling services include, but are not limited to, educational and vocational counseling and guidance; testing; analysis of and recommendations to improve job-marketing skills; identification of employment, training, and financial aid resources; and referrals to other agencies providing these services.

Eligibility: Educational and vocational counseling services are available during the period the individual is on active duty with the armed forces and is within 180 days of the estimated date of his or her discharge or release from active duty. The projected discharge must be under conditions other than dishonorable.

Servicemembers are eligible even if they are only considering whether or not they will continue as members of the armed forces. Veterans are eligible if not more than one year has elapsed since the date they were last discharged or released from active duty. Individuals who are eligible for VA education benefits may receive educational and vocational counseling at any time during their eligibility period. This service is based on having eligibility for a VA program such as Chapter 30 (Montgomery GI Bill); Chapter 31 (Vocational Rehabilitation and Employment); Chapter 32 (Veterans' Education Assistance Program—VEAP); Chapter 33 (Post-9/11 GI Bill); Chapter 35 (Dependents' Education Assistance Program) for certain spouses and dependent children; Chapter 18 (Spina Bifida Program) for certain dependent children; and Chapters 1606 and 1607 of Title 10.

Veterans and servicemembers may apply for counseling services using VA Form 28-8832, Application for Counseling. Veteran's and servicemembers may also write a letter expressing a desire for counseling services.

Upon receipt of either type of request for counseling from an eligible individual, an appointment for counseling will be scheduled. Counseling services are provided to eligible persons at no charge.

Veterans' Workforce Investment Program

Recently separated veterans and those with service-connected disabilities, significant barriers to employment, or who served on active duty during a period in which a campaign or expedition badge was authorized can contact the nearest state employment office for employment help through the Veterans' Workforce Investment Program. The program may be conducted through state or local public agencies, community organizations, or private, nonprofit organizations.

State Employment Services

Veterans can find employment information, education and training opportunities, job counseling, job search workshops, and resume preparation assistance at state Workforce Career Centers or One-Stop Centers. These offices also have specialists to help disabled veterans find employment.

Unemployment Compensation

Veterans who do not begin civilian employment immediately after leaving military service may receive weekly unemployment compensation for a limited time. The amount and duration of payments are determined by individual states. Apply by contacting the nearest state employment office listed in your local telephone directory.

Veterans' Preference for Federal Jobs

Since the time of the Civil War, veterans of the U.S. armed forces have been given some degree of preference in appointments to federal jobs. Veterans' preference in its present form comes from the Veterans' Preference Act of 1944, as amended, and now codified in Title 5, United States Code. By law, veterans who are disabled or who served on active duty in the U.S. armed forces during certain specified time periods or in military campaigns are entitled to preference over others when hiring from competitive lists of eligible candidates, and also in retention during a reduction in force (RIF).

To receive preference, a veteran must have been discharged or released from active duty in the U.S. armed forces under honorable conditions (honorable or general discharge). Preference is also provided for certain widows and widowers of deceased veterans who died in service; spouses of service-connected disabled veterans; and mothers of veterans who died under honorable conditions on active duty or have permanent and total service-connected disabilities. For each of these preferences, there are specific criteria that must be met in order to be eligible to receive the veterans' preference.

Recent changes in Title 5 clarify veterans' preference eligibility criteria for National Guard and Reserve members. Veterans eligible for preference include National Guard and Reserve members who served on active duty as defined by Title 38 at any time in the armed forces for a period of more than 180 consecutive days, any part of which occurred during the period beginning on September 11, 2001, and ending on the date prescribed by presidential proclamation or by law as the last date of OEF/OIF. The National Guard and Reserve servicemembers must have been discharged or released from active duty in the armed forces under honorable conditions.

Another recent change involves veterans who earned the Global War on Terrorism Expeditionary Medal for service in OEF/OIF. Under Title 5, service on active duty in the armed forces during a war or in a campaign or expedition for which a campaign badge has been authorized also qualifies for veterans' preference. Any Armed Forces Expeditionary medal or campaign badge qualifies for preference. Medal holders must have served continuously for twenty-four months or the full period called or ordered to active duty.

As of December 2005, veterans who received the Global War on Terrorism Expeditionary Medal are entitled to veterans' preference if otherwise eligible. For additional information, visit the Office of Personnel Management (OPM) website at www.opm.gov/veterans/html/vetguide.asp#2.

Veterans' preference does not require an agency to use any particular appointment process. Agencies can pick candidates from a number of different special hiring authorities or through a variety of different sources. For example, the agency can reinstate a former federal employee, transfer someone from another agency, reassign someone from within the agency, make a selection under merit promotion procedures or through open, competitive exams, or appoint someone noncompetitively under special authority, such as a Veterans Readjustment Appointment or special authority for 30 percent or more disabled veterans. The decision on which hiring authority the agency desires to use rests solely with the agency.

When applying for federal jobs, eligible veterans should claim preference on their application or resume. Veterans should apply for a federal job by contacting the personnel office at the agency in which they wish to work. For more information, visit www.usajobs.opm.gov/ for job openings or help creating a federal resume.

Veterans Employment Opportunities Act: When an agency accepts applications from outside its own workforce, the Veterans Employment Opportunities Act of 1998 allows preference-eligible candidates or veterans to compete for these vacancies under merit promotion procedures.

Veterans who are selected are given career or career-conditional appointments. Veterans are those who have been separated under honorable conditions from the U.S. armed forces with three or more years of continuous active service. For information, visit www.usajobs.opm.gov or www.fedshire vets.gov.

Veterans Recruitment Appointment: Allows federal agencies to appoint eligible veterans to jobs without competition. These appointments can be converted to career or career-conditional positions after two years of satisfactory work. Veterans should apply directly to the agency where they wish to work. For information, visit www.fedshirevets.gov/.

Small Businesses

VA's Center for Veterans Enterprise helps veterans interested in forming or expanding small businesses and helps VA contracting offices identify veteran-owned small businesses. For information, write the U.S. Department of Veterans Affairs (OOVE), 810 Vermont Avenue, N.W., Washington, DC 20420-0001, call toll free 1-866-584-2344, or visit www.vetbiz.gov/.

Small Business Contracts: Like other federal agencies, VA is required to place a portion of its contracts and purchases with small and disadvantaged businesses. VA has a special office to help small and disadvantaged businesses get information on VA acquisition opportunities. For information, write the U.S. Department of Veterans Affairs (OOSB), 810 Vermont Avenue, N.W., Washington, DC 20420-0001, call toll free 1-800-949-8387, or visit www.va.gov/osdbu/.

REMEMBER: HELP IS AVAILABLE TO YOU!

Preseparation Time Line

Two Years Prior to Separation (Retirees Only)

- Schedule your preseparation counseling appointment.
- Review the DD Form 2648, Preseparation Counseling Checklist. Identify individual service providers who will provide assistance.

Eighteen Months Prior to Separation (Retirees Only)

- Attend a transition assistance program workshop. If your service-connected disability makes you eligible, attend the Disabled Transition Assistance Program workshop.
- Develop your Individual Transition Plan (at home, self-directed). Seek assistance from your Army Career Alumni Program (ACAP) Center counselor, if needed.
- Make fundamental life decisions (continue working, change careers, volunteer, etc.) and determine future goals.

- Capitalize on current career stability to prepare for future career goals. Identify training, education, and/or certification requirements and determine how to achieve goals (e.g., use tuition assistance). Start classes.
- Evaluate family requirements (college tuition, elder care for parents, etc.).
- Determine postretirement income requirements. Project retirement take-home pay. Identify if you need to supplement retirement take-home pay.

Twelve to Twenty-four Months Prior to Separation (Retirees Only)

- Continue training/education needed to qualify for your objective career/ pursuit.
- Investigate health and life insurance alternatives, including long-term health care coverage.
- Consider whether you will take terminal leave or cash in unused leave.
- Consider retirement locations.
- Identify medical/dental problems and arrange treatment for yourself and/ or your family.
- Begin networking. Track potential network contacts you have lost or may lose contact with.
- Research your Survivor Benefit Plan (SBP) options.
- Consider spouse education and career desires.
- Update legal documents (will, powers of attorney, etc.).

Twelve Months Prior to Separation (Retirees and Separatees)

- Continue training/education needed to qualify for your objective career/ pursuit.
- Schedule your preseparation counseling appointment.
- Review the DD Form 2648, Preseparation Counseling Checklist. Identify individual service providers who will provide assistance.
- Develop your Individual Transition Plan (at home, self-directed). Seek assistance from your ACAP Center counselor, if needed.
- Attend a transition assistance program workshop. If your service-connected disability makes you eligible, attend the Disabled Transition Assistance Program workshop.
- Establish a financial plan to make ends meet during your transition to civilian life.
- Assess your job skills and interests. To determine how they relate to today's job market, take a vocational interest inventory. Contact your installation's Education Center and ACAP Center.

- Begin researching the job market. Develop a career plan, including a list of possible employers in your career field.
- If you need additional educational or vocational training to compete in the job market, explore your options for adult education.
- Learn about the education benefits you are eligible for under the Montgomery GI Bill (MGIB). If you enrolled in the Vietnam-era GI Bill, learn how you can convert to MGIB. Contact your local Department of Veterans Affairs (VA) representative for details.
- Visit the Education Center to take academic entrance exams, college admission tests, or challenge exams. Remember, this is free to service-members on active duty.
- Discuss with your family possible options about your career and where to live next.
- If you need help with your finances, explore the options.
- Review and make a copy of your personnel records.
- Start developing a resume.
- Join a professional association in your chosen career field and become involved in it.
- **(Retirees Only)** Schedule Part I of your separation physical. Part II will be scheduled upon completion of Part I.

180 Days Prior to Separation (Retirees and Separatees)

- Continue training/education needed to qualify for your objective career/ pursuit.
- Research specific job possibilities, job markets, and the economic conditions in the geographic areas where you want to live.
- Contact friends in the private sector who may help you find a job. Actively network.
- Seek assistance from your ACAP counselor after completing the first draft of your resume.
- Attend job fairs to connect with potential employers.
- Develop an alternate plan in case your first career plan falls through.
- Review and copy your medical and dental records. Get a certified true copy of each.
- Schedule medical/dental appointments, as needed.
- Visit your ACAP Center to request your DD Form 2586, Verification of Military Experience and Training document.

150 Days Prior to Separation (Retirees and Separatees)

- Continue training/education needed to qualify for your objective career/ pursuit.

- Start actively applying for jobs. Make contact with employers who you will interview with.
- Start assembling a wardrobe for interviewing. Check with the ACAP Center for Dress for Success information.
- Seek help if the stress of your transition to civilian life becomes too much to handle.
- If you are separating prior to fulfilling eight years of active service, you must satisfy your obligations by becoming a member of the Reserves.
- Start posting resumes to career websites.
- Research websites for posting resumes and conducting online job searches (e.g., http://www.careers.org.)
- Schedule your separation physical examination.

120 Days Prior to Separation (Retirees and Separatees)

- Complete training/education needed to qualify for your objective career/ pursuit.
- If you are considering federal employment, check online at http://www .usajobs.opm.gov to determine the appropriate documents to submit. Explore special federal programs and hiring opportunities for veterans.
- Consider using Resumix, an automated tool that allows you to use an online application to create a resume for applying for federal jobs. You can print the resume for your use and save it to the system to retrieve and edit for future use. For some federal jobs, you may be able to submit your resume electronically. You may obtain more information from the USAJOBS website at http://www.usajobs.opm.gov/.
- Continue to network aggressively.
- Visit the Relocation Assistance Program Office located at your Army Community Service Center to learn about relocation options, entitlements, and assistance.
- If you live in government housing, arrange for a preinspection and obtain termination information.
- Contact appropriate offices at your installation to discuss extended medical care (if eligible) or conversion health insurance. Learn about your options for transitional health care. If you have specific questions about veterans' medical care, contact the VA, use the VA website, or make an appointment with your local VA counselor.
- Research Reserve programs to continue to receive part-time benefits, earn a future retirement, and continue to grow and train in your field. Even if you have fulfilled eight years of military service, you may want to explore the option of joining the Reserves or National Guard.
- Consult the Department of Veterans Affairs website containing valuable information for veterans: http://www.va.gov.

- Start a subscription to a major newspaper in the area to which you plan to move. Begin replying to want ads.
- Visit and evaluate the area to which you plan to move. Attend job interviews there. Visit a private employment agency or executive recruiter in the area.
- Send out resumes and make follow-up phone calls to check if they arrived. Submit your resume through the DoD Job Search website at http://dod.jobsearch.org.

Ninety Days Prior to Separation (Retirees and Separatees)

- Continue to post resumes to websites. Conduct an automated job search for you and your spouse using ACAP Online, Transition Bulletin Board, DoD Transportal, DoD Job Search, the Federal Job Opportunities Listing, http://goDefense.com, and other available employment data banks.
- Continue to expand your network.
- Consult this website for information on locating a home, a realtor, or a neighborhood (database of homes for sale): http://www.realtor.com.
- Once you have chosen where you will live next, arrange for transportation counseling. Learn about your options for shipment and storage of household goods.
- Schedule a final dental examination.
- Determine if you are eligible for separation pay.
- If you would like to update your will or if you have legal questions or problems, obtain free legal advice.

Sixty Days Prior to Separation (Retirees and Separatees)

- Begin planning additional visits to the area to which you plan to move.
- Continue to send out your resume. Include in your cover letter the date you plan to move to the area.
- Continue to network at all levels.
- Choose your transitional health care option: use military medical facilities or sign up for TRICARE, if eligible.
- For detailed information about disability compensation, benefits, and programs, call the VA at 1-800-827-1000.
- **(Retirees Only)** Complete Survivor Benefit Plan paperwork.

Thirty Days Prior to Separation (Retirees and Separatees)

- Continue to network.
- Review your DD Form 214, Certificate of Release or Discharge from Active Duty worksheet.

- Several government agencies offer special loans and programs for veterans. Check with your local VA office.
- If you are unemployed, you may qualify for unemployment compensation once you are a civilian. See your local state employment office for eligibility.
- Decide whether to sign up for the optional Continued Health Care Benefit Program medical coverage.
- Complete your Veterans Affairs Disability Application (VA Form 21-526) and turn it in to the appropriate office. Check with your local ACAP Center or VA representative.
- Consider converting your Servicemen's Group Life Insurance to Veterans' Group Life Insurance (optional).
- Consult this website for worldwide relocation information on major military and associate installations for use by military personnel and their families who are relocating: http://www.militaryhomefront.dod.mil/, then go to "military installations."
- Consult the website on the Military Health System: http://www.tricare.osd.mil.

Developing Your Own Individual Transition Plan (ITP)

The ITP will help you identify the actions and activities associated with your transition. Consulting with a transition assistance counselor and using the DD Form 2648-1, Preseparation Counseling Checklist for Reserve Component Service Members Released from Active Duty, will help you determine your options. The Transition Guide will help you work through the major headings listed on the DD Form 2648 checklist. The checklist will allow you to identify the benefits and services that will help you prepare your ITP. If you require further assistance with any of the topics covered on the Transitioning Counseling Checklist, please refer to the appropriate chapter of the "Transition Guide for Guard and Reserve" or online resources found at http://www.TurboTAP .org. If you still need assistance, contact Military OneSource at 1-800-342-9647.

If you are uncertain about your future plans, now is the time to get all the assistance and information you need. Professional guidance and counseling is available at a transition assistance office, as are workshops, publications, information resources, automated resources, and government programs. Take advantage of each one that pertains to your unique situation. It is your Individual Transition Plan: It is your responsibility and your life.

"MY DECISION POINTS"

A carefully thought out Individual Transition Plan (ITP) is your game plan for a successful transition to civilian life—it is not an official form, but something you create by yourself, for yourself. Your Transition Assistance Office will give you a head start with your DD Form 2648, Preseparation Counseling Checklist, which can serve as an outline for your ITP. On this checklist, you indicate the benefits and services for which you want counseling. Your transition assistance office will furnish additional information and emphasize certain points for you to consider. These selected items will help you formulate your ITP. Your Transition/ACAP or Command Career Counselor (Navy) will then refer you to subject experts or other resources to get answers to your questions or additional information.

"You may be whatever you resolve to be."

–Stonewall Jackson

CREATE YOUR OWN INDIVIDUAL TRANSITION PLAN

You ITP should identify likely actions and activities associated with your transition. You can determine what these might be through consultation with a Transition/ACAP or Command Career Counselor as well as with a VA representative or DoL representative. Remember, as stated above, be sure to use the DD Form 2648-1. Your military service has samples of ITPs that can help you. Check with your nearest military installation Transition/ACAP or Command Career Counselor (Navy) to review them. You can start developing your ITP by making decisions based on these ten not-so-simple questions:

1. What are your goals after leaving the military?
2. Where do you plan to live?
3. Do you need to continue your education or training?
4. Will the job market where you plan to relocate provide you the employment you're seeking?
5. Do you have the right skills to compete for the job(s) you're seeking?
6. Will your spouse and family goals be met at your new location?
7. Are you financially prepared to transition at this time?
8. What do you plan to do for health care?
9. How will you address the need for life insurance?
10. Which benefits arc you planning to use?

In addition, The TurboTAP website gives you the opportunity to develop your own ITP online through "My Decision Points." My Decision Points is a personalized, printable ITP that you can revise at any time. Learn more at http://www.TurboTAP.org.

LEAVING THE SERVICE

Next stop: civilian life! But before you go, make sure your military records are in order and double check them for errors. It is much easier to resolve problems before you leave the service. The following section will provide information on topics ranging from how to ensure the accuracy of your records to the dos and don'ts of wearing your uniform after you leave the military. Make a copy of your complete medical records and take them with you.

Keep Important Documents in a Safe Place

You should keep your performance ratings; service-issued licenses or certifications; DD Form 2586, Verification of Military Experience and Training; and other service documents (such as your security clearance) in a safe and permanent file. Never give away the original copy of any of these documents.

DD Form 214, Certificate of Release or Discharge from Active Duty: This form is one of the most important documents the service will ever give you. It is your key to participation in all Department of Veterans Affairs (VA) programs as well as several state and federal programs. Keep your original in a safe, fireproof place and have certified photocopies available for reference. You can replace this record, but that takes a long time—time that you may not have. Be safe. In most states, the DD Form 214 can be registered/recorded just like a land deed or other significant document. So, immediately after you separate, register your DD Form 214 with your county recorder or town hall. If you register your documents, they can later be retrieved quickly for a nominal fee. You should check whether state or local law permits public access to the recorded document. If public access is authorized and you register DD Form 214, others could obtain a copy for an unlawful purpose (e.g., to obtain a credit card in your name). If public access is permitted and you choose not to register your DD Form 214, you still should take steps to protect it as you would any other sensitive document (wills, marriage and birth certificates, insurance policies). You may wish to store it in a safe deposit box or at some other secure location.

In addition, your local Vet Center can certify your DD Form 214 and have a copy placed on file. Find your nearest Vet Center online at http://www1 .va.gov/directory/guide/vetcenter.asp.

Other military service papers: Documents associated with any military service should be kept in your permanent file at home. This includes those documents mentioned above.

VA papers: All VA forms and correspondence also should be kept in your file, including certificates of eligibility for loans, VA file number records, and other VA papers.

Family records: Documents such as marriage licenses, birth and death certificates, and divorce and adoption papers are permanent records you will need on a recurring basis. Keep these in your permanent file as well.

Health records: You and your family members should know the location of your health records, including medical history and individual immunization records. Keep a copy in a file at home and know where the original is kept (usually in a military medical facility or doctor's office). Don't forget to keep your family current with shots and immunizations as you transition.

Insurance documents: Insurance policies and premium payment records should be kept in your permanent file at home.

Wills: All service members and their spouses should have a will. Once prepared by your local legal services office or through your own private attorney, it should be placed in a safe location with your other important documents.

Need to Correct Your Military Record?

Each branch of the military has its own procedures for correcting the military records of its members and former members. Correction of a military record may result in eligibility for VA and other benefits—such as back pay and military retirement—that the veteran (or survivors) could not otherwise get. Generally, a request for correction must be filed within three years after the discovery of the alleged error or injustice.

If you believe there is an error in your military record, apply in writing to the appropriate service using a DD Form 149, Application for Correction of Military or Naval Record. The form can be submitted by the veteran, a survivor, or a legal representative. Get a copy from any VA office listed in the local telephone directory or download the form from http://www.archives .gov/veterans/military-service-records/correct-service-records.html.

Replacing a Lost DD Form 214, Certificate of Release or Discharge

You or your next-of-kin can request a copy of your DD Form 214 online by going to the National Personnel Records Center website: http://www .archives.gov/veterans/military-service-records/. Or, you can request the DD Form 214 by mail by sending an SF 180, Request Pertaining to Military Records,* or a letter to the National Personnel Records Center. Include the following information in your letter:

- your full name
- Social Security number
- current phone number (including area code)
- approximate dates of service

---

*To obtain an SF 180 you can download it from http://www.archives.gov/veterans/military-service-records/ or request the form by fax by calling the Fax-on-Demand System at (301) 837-0990 **from a fax machine**, using the handset. Follow the voice instructions, and request document number 2255. For immediate assistance you can call 314-801-0800.

- place of discharge
- return address
- reason for request

Send this request to:

National Personnel Records Center
Attention: [Your Service, e.g., Army] Records
9700 Page Avenue
St. Louis, MO 63132-5000

Or you can fax your request to 314-801-9195.

WHERE ARE YOU?

When you leave the military, you are likely to have a change of address. During this time of transition, people—including prospective employers—will be trying to contract you. Tracking you down will be a slow or impossible task unless you provide the service with a forwarding address indicating where you can be reached up to 120 days following your separation. If you do not have a reliable forwarding address, provide the permanent address of a parent or trusted friend.

Voting

As you leave the service and locate permanently in a community, make registering to vote a top priority. For more information, including contact information for your local election official and primary and general election dates, please visit http://www.canivote.org/.

HOW TO GET A REVIEW OF YOUR DISCHARGE

The Department of the Army, Air Force, Navy (including the Marine Corps), and the Coast Guard have their own discharge review boards. These boards have the authority to change or correct any discharge or dismissal from the service, unless it was the result of a general court-martial. A discharge board has no authority to address medical discharges.

If you feel your discharge decision was not fair or did not consider all the facts in the case, you may request a discharge review. Use an Application for Review of Discharge or Separation from the Armed Forces of the United States, DD Form 293, Application for the Review of Discharge or Dismissal from the Armed Forces of the United States (available at http://www.veterans.ocgov.com/forms/DD-293.pdf).

You may obtain a copy from your nearest VA office. Written application should be submitted by the veteran, next of kin, or a legal representative. Application must be made within fifteen years after discharge.

WEARING YOUR UNIFORM: DOS AND DON'TS

- **Always proper:** After separation, it is appropriate to wear your uniform during Reserve duty.
- **Sometimes proper:** Under certain conditions, you may wear your uniform as a civilian. Generally, if you served honorably, you may wear your uniform:
  - for military weddings, funerals, memorial services, or inaugural ceremonies.
  - for patriotic parades on national holidays and for any military parades.
  - for ceremonies in which a U.S. Active or Reserve unit is taking part.
- **Never proper:** Never wear the uniform under circumstances that would detract from its prestige or tend to discredit the Armed Forces (such as attending a totalitarian or subversive function or while engaging in a business activity). Also, it is against the law for unauthorized persons to wear a uniform of the U.S. Armed Forces.

MISSING MEDALS, RIBBONS, OR AWARDS

Before you separate, look over your collection of military awards, medals, ribbons, badges, and other distinguished insignia.

If awards you have earned are missing: Speak with your unit personnel officer about obtaining replacements. You may also purchase lost ribbons and medals from the military exchange. **Note:** Once you have left the service you may request issuance or replacement of military service medals, decorations, and awards through the specific branch of the military in which you served. Use the Standard Form (SF) 180, Request Pertaining to Military Records, for requesting medals and awards. SF 180 can be downloaded from http://www.archives.gov/veterans/military-service-records/.

If you believe you are eligible for awards that you did not receive: Ask your unit personnel office for the service regulation outlining the eligibility requirements or get the number of the service regulation and pursue it yourself. No one knows better than you when or where you were assigned, what special training you took, or when you received special recognition. Replacement medals and ribbons can be obtained for a small fee from:

National Personnel Records Center
Attention: Military Personnel Records
9700 Page Avenue
St. Louis, MO 63132-5000
See http://www.archives.gov/veterans/military-service-records/replacement-medals.html for more information.

YOUNG MEN MUST BE REGISTERED FOR SELECTIVE SERVICE

Currently, young men must register under the Selective Service system within thirty days before or after their eighteenth birthday. This is true even if the draft is not currently in effect. If you failed to register before entering the service, now is the time to do so.

If you were born in 1960 or later and did not register before entering active service, you are still required to register for Selective Service after you separate, even if you are in a Reserve unit. You will find the necessary forms at the main branch of your local post office. Failure to register may disqualify you from enrolling in certain federal job and training programs.

MILITARY FUNERAL HONORS

You are about to depart from the military service, and you are entitled to a number of benefits, one of which is military funeral honors. Each veteran who desires military funeral honors when they die should brief their family members on this benefit. Veterans are eligible for military funeral honors if they served in the active military and were discharged under conditions other than dishonorable, or if they were a member or former member of the Selected Reserve. Upon request of the next of kin or authorized representative, the funeral director requests the honors from the military service in which the veteran served. The military service will provide the military funeral honors to the eligible beneficiary, consisting of the ceremonial folding and presentation of the American flag and the sounding of "Taps." The ceremony is normally provided by two uniformed members of the Armed Forces, at least one of whom will be from the service in which the veteran served. The military services, based on their traditions and resources, may render additional elements of military funeral honors. The nation is grateful for every veteran's service to the country. This is the Department of Defense's time-honored way to recognize those who faithfully served. For additional information on veterans' burial benefits, go to http://www.va.gov or the Department of Defense website at http://www.militaryfuneralhonors.osd.mil.

Chapter 2

THE OBAMA PLEDGE

A Sacred Trust

Barack Obama and Joe Biden are committed to creating a twenty-first century Department of Veterans Affairs that provides the care and benefits our nation's veterans deserve. They will:

- **Allow All Veterans Back into the VA:** Reverse the 2003 ban on enrolling modest-income veterans, which has denied care to a million veterans.
- **Strengthen VA Care:** Make the VA a leader of national health care reform so that veterans get the best care possible. Improve care for polytrauma vision impairment, prosthetics, spinal cord injury, aging, and women's health.
- **Combat Homelessness among Our Nation's Veterans:** Establish a national "zero tolerance" policy for veterans falling into homelessness by expanding proven programs and launching innovative services to prevent veterans from falling into homelessness.
- **Fight Employment Discrimination:** Crack down on employers who commit job discrimination against guardsmen and reservists.

Help for Returning Service Members

Obama and Biden will improve the quality of health care for veterans, rebuild the VA's broken benefits system, and combat homelessness among veterans. They will:

- **Ensure a Seamless Transition:** Demand that the military and the VA coordinate to provide a seamless transition from active duty to civilian life.
- **Fully Fund VA Medical Care:** Fully fund the VA so it has all the resources it needs to serve the veterans who need it, when they need it. Establish a world-class VA Planning Division to avoid future budget shortfalls.
- **Fix the Benefits Bureaucracy:** Hire additional claims workers and improve training and accountability so that VA benefit decisions are rated fairly and consistently. Transform the paper benefit claims process to an electronic one to reduce errors and improve timeliness.

Improved Treatment for Mental Health and TBI

Obama and Biden will improve mental health treatment for troops and veterans suffering from combat-related psychological injuries. They will:

- **Improve Mental Health Treatment:** Recruit more health professionals, improve screening, offer more support to families, and make PTSD benefits claims fairer.

- **Improve Care for Traumatic Brain Injury:** Establish standards of care for traumatic brain injury, the signature injury of the Iraq War.
- **Expand Vet Centers:** Expand and strengthen Vet Centers to provide more counseling for vets and their families.

SOME DEFINITIONS

Discharge: Complete severance from all military status gained by the enlistment or induction concerned.

Separation: A general term that includes discharge, release from active duty, release from custody and control of the Armed Forces, transfer to the Individual Ready Reserve, and similar changes in Active or Reserve status.

Transition Benefits: Benefits provided to assist servicemembers during the transition process. Eligibility for certain types of transition benefits will depend on the nature and characterization of your discharge.

Transition Services: For active component servicemembers, this includes mandatory preseparation counseling, voluntary attendance to a Department of Labor employment workshop, voluntary attendance to a VA benefits briefing, and a VA Disabled Transition Assistance Program (DTAP) briefing. Active component servicemembers are eligible and begin the transition process one year prior to separation, and retirees can begin the transition process two years prior to retirement. Eligibility for services is not affected by length or character or service.

Disabled Transition Assistance Program (DTAP): DTAP provides separating and retiring service members—including eligible National Guard and Reserve servicemembers being released from active duty—with specialized information about the Department of Veterans (VA) Vocational Rehabilitation and Employment (VR&E) Program and eligibility and how to apply for benefits. Active duty servicemembers who believe they have a service-connected disability are strongly encouraged to request admission to the DTAP class through their Transition/ACAP/Command Career Counselor (or unit commander). For National Guard and Reserves, DTAP is available on a DTAP CD and online at www.vetsuccess.gov. Eligible service members (Active, National Guard, and Reserves) who are pending a medical separation or medical retirement and who have an **employment handicap** may begin to receive VR&E services prior to separation or release from active duty if they meet the following criteria:

- must be on active duty
- must have a need for rehabilitative services
- must have applied for and received a VA Memorandum Rating of at least 20 percent

STEPS FOR TRANSITIONING

Step 1. Schedule Your Preseparation Counseling Appointment. You may schedule your preseparation counseling appointment at your installation's transition assistance office any time within a year before your planned separation date. However, since it takes time to prepare for an effective transition, be sure to contact your transition assistance office at least 180 days before your separation. By law, preseparation counseling (completion of DD Form 2648, Preseparation Counseling Checklist) must occur no later than ninety days prior to separation; therefore, if you have not had an appointment ninety days before separation, call the transition assistance office or your Navy Command Career Counselor and schedule a visit immediately. However, it is strongly recommended that you set up your preseparation counseling appointment at least 180 days prior to separation.

    Step 2. Review the Preseparation Counseling Checklist. Your transition counselor or command career counselor will walk you through the preseparation counseling checklist, which helps ensure that you will receive the necessary assistance and advice to benefit fully from the wide range of services and entitlements available to you. The checklist is required by law to be filed in the official military personnel record of each servicemember receiving the counseling.

    At this meeting, the transition assistance office or command career counselor will:

- assist you in developing an individual needs assessment
- identify helpful relocation resources
- offer immediate and long-range career guidance
- provide benefits counseling
- refer you to other service providers for any additional assistance you may require

    Step 3. Draft Your Individual Transition Plan Information. Help on developing your My Decision Points Individual Transition Plan (ITP) is available through the transition assistance office and online at http://www .TurboTAP.org. You may choose to use your Transition Counseling Checklist as a guide for developing your own unique ITP. Once you have created your ITP, review it with your spouse or another adult family member and get their feedback. It is recommended that you consult with a VA counselor and a DoL CareerOneStop staff member to review your ITP. They will provide you with further assistance or refer you to a subject-matter expert to assist you.

Full participation in this process by you and your spouse or family member is encouraged. Each transition has three key decision points that must be considered when creating your ITP. As you proceed through the transition process, it is important to consider the following major decision points:

1. **Money Decisions:** Deciding how to best manage your finances will help you deal with changes in pay, compensation, and living expenses. This guide will give you information on your financial benefits, life insurance, thrift savings plan, and creating a household budget.
2. **Benefit Decisions:** Choosing which of the available benefits to apply for and deciding when and where to start. This guide will help you explore your benefits, such as the GI Bill, VA home loans, health care, and more.
3. **Job Decisions:** Weighing your career options and choosing whether to pursue your current career path or start over and go back to school. This guide has information to help you learn about everything from writing resumes to exploring your employment opportunities to how to start a small business.

PHASES OF INDIVIDUAL TRANSITION PLANNING

All military personnel transitioning out of the service go through the same fundamental stages. These stages can be divided into the following seven different phases: self-assessment, exploration, skills development, intern programs, job search, job selection, and support.

Phase One: Self-Assessment

Ask yourself: Who am I? What are my talents and experiences? Why would someone want to hire me?

In this phase, document your portfolio of knowledge, experience, skills, talents, and abilities. For starters, create a list using your personal DD Form 2586, Verification of Military Experience and Training. Your VMET outlines the training and experience you received during your military career. It is designed to help you, but it is not a resume.

To get your verification document, go to the VMET website at http://www .dmdc.osd.mil/vmet. All separating military personnel can electronically download and print their VMET document and personal cover letter from your military service from the VMET website. Simply click the "Request Document" and "Request Cover Letter" tabs and print each of these documents after the download.

You can get your verification document online as long as you have a current DoD Common Access Card (CAC) or have a current Defense Finance, Accounting Service (DFAS) myPay Personal Identification Number (PIN). However, you should retrieve it within 120 days prior to your separation. If you have problems getting your VMET and need assistance, check with your local transition counselor. Add anything else you can think of to this list. In essence, you are now creating an "asset bank" from which you can draw later when called upon to write a resume or attend a job interview. If you need help, use the professional guidance available through your local installation transition assistance office or education center, or refer to the self-help section of your local library or bookstore for useful career-planning books.

In addition, you can get an official transcript of your education and training credits from your service branch. Each branch has their own system for recording your military (and civilian) education and experience. The following explains each branch's system:

Army

The Army's AARTS (Army/American Council on Education Registry Transcript System) automatically captures your military training, your Military Occupational Specialty (MOS), and college-level examinations scores with the college credit recommended. AARTS website: http://aarts.army.mil/.

Navy and Marines

The Navy and Marine Corps use the SMART system. This system automatically captures your training, experience, and standardized test scores. SMART website: https://www.navycollege.navy.mil/transcript.html.

Air Force

The Community College of the Air Force (CCAF) automatically captures your training, experience, and standardized test scores. Transcript information may be viewed at the CCAF website: http://www.au.af.mil/au/ccaf/.

Coast Guard

The Coast Guard Institute (CGI) requires each servicemember to submit documentation of all training (except correspondence course records), along with an enrollment form, to receive a transcript. Transcript information can be found at the Coast Guard Institute website: http://www.uscg.mil/hq/cgi/.

Veterans

Under most circumstances, veterans are eligible to use their former service branch's transcript program. However, if you are not eligible for AARTS, SMART, CCAF, or CGI systems, you will need to fill out DD Form 295, 'Application for the Evaluation of Learning Experiences during Military Service and provide your DD Form 214, Certificate of Release or Discharge from Active Duty to receive credit for your experience. The investment you make now in conducting your assessment is crucial. It will bring the "professional you" into clearer focus, and it will have a major impact on your career decisions.

Phase Two: Exploration

Ask yourself: What are the current and emerging occupational areas that are attractive to me? Do these jobs coincide with my values and aptitudes? How do I find these jobs?

With your assessment in hand, you probably have some ideas about what you want to do. Now is not the time to limit your opportunities. Expand the list of job titles and career paths that appeal to you. Broaden your geographic horizons to include several places where you might like to pursue your career. Many resources are available to help you explore your expanded set of options.

The Employment Assistance Hub of the TurboTAP website can help you focus on jobs that employers need to fill today and will need to fill in the near future. CareerOneStop Center staff can help you identify the geographic areas that have opportunities in your fields of interest. Your state employment office is another good resource during this phase, offering such services as job interviewing; selection and referral to openings; job development; employment counseling; career evaluation; referral to training or other support services; and testing. Your state office can also lead you to information on related jobs nearby and introduce you to their state job banks, which have listings of jobs in your state. To look for jobs across the nation, you should check the job banks available on the TurboTAP website under the Employment Assistance Hub: http://www.transitionassistanceprogram.com/portal/transition/resources/Employment_Hub. And don't forget your local library's reference section. Most of them are full of helpful publications relating to job searches.

Phase Three: Skills Development

Ask yourself: How do I prepare myself to be an attractive candidate in the occupational areas that I have chosen? Do I need additional education or training?

As you continue through the exploration phase, you may find some interesting opportunities for which you feel only partially qualified. Your local transition assistance office and education center can help you determine the academic credentials or vocational training programs you will need and how to get them.

Phase Four: Intern Programs

Ask yourself: Do I have the aptitude and experience needed to pursue my occupational interests? Are there internships, volunteer jobs, temporary services, or part-time jobs where I might try out the work that interests me?

To learn about intern programs, inquire at your transition assistance office, your local civilian personnel office, or the state employment office. Some government-sponsored programs, such as obtaining teaching credentials, can provide income and training in exchange for guaranteed employment. Check local and base libraries and the education office for books containing intern program information.

Temporary agencies are also a great way to become familiar with a company or industry. Explore internship possibilities with private employers: Many companies have such programs but do not advertise them. Don't necessarily turn down an interesting volunteer position. Volunteering increases your professional skills and can sometimes turn into a paid position.

Phase Five: The Job Search

Ask yourself: How do I identify job requirements and prospective companies, find networks and placement agencies, and generally increase my knowledge and experience in the job market? How do I write a resume, develop leads, conduct an interview, and complete a job application?

Once you have selected your future career, you must now begin the challenge of finding work. Millions of people are hired all across the country every year. Employee turnover opens up existing positions, and entirely new jobs are created every day. Nevertheless, the job market is competitive. The best way to improve your odds is to play your best hand: Seek the opportunities for which you are best prepared.

Work hard at finding a job. Network! The vast majority of jobs are filled by referrals, not the want ads. Use your network of friends, colleagues, and family as well as the job listings provided by your installation's transition assistance office, the local personnel office, or even the nearest community college. Take advantage of job-hunting seminars, resume-writing workshops, and interviewing techniques classes, too. Attend job fairs and talk to as many company representatives as possible.

Phase Six: Job Selection

Ask yourself: How do I select the right job?

Although it might be tempting, you don't have to take the first job that comes along. Consider the type of work, location, salary and benefits, climate, and how the opportunity will enhance your future career growth. Even if you take the first job offer, you are not necessarily locked into it. Some experts say employers are biased against hiring the unemployed. A shrewd move might be to look for a job from a job. Take a suitable position—and then quickly move on to a better one.

Phase Seven: Support

Ask yourself: How do I make a smooth transition to a new career?

For your transition to be truly successful, you should manage the personal affairs side of your career change with the same professionalism and care as your job search. Things like out-processing, relocation, financial management, taking care of your family, and coping with the inevitable stress are important, too.

Your transition assistance office can offer support as you go through this process. In addition, your ITP provides an opportunity to integrate these issues with the career-oriented activities that are the central focus of your transition effort. **Note:** You are eligible for continued transition assistance for up to 180 days after separation, and you can access www.TurboTAP.org for life.

EFFECTS OF A CAREER CHANGE

You have been in the military for a number of years, and you are now making the transition back to civilian life. Understanding stress, and coping with it, are essential skills you will need to get through this difficult time. The following information and resources will help you prepare for a successful transition.

Leaving the Military Challenges Your Identity

You have worked hard to become a captain, sergeant, or petty officer. When asked what you do, you probably replied, "I'm in the Army (Air Force, Navy, Coast Guard, or Marines)." Now you must start over as a civilian. Now you are just another civilian.

Changing careers is a stressful undertaking, perhaps even more so for those leaving military service after many years. A servicemember may have worked for thirty years to achieve a rank or grade, but upon leaving the Armed Forces, he or she leaves this rank behind—and with it, a large portion of his or her identity. Some people find it easier than others to adopt new identities. Transition is traumatic and stressful, but it also opens up a whole range of possibilities. If you approach your transition as an opportunity to grow, you will have already taken a giant step toward reestablishing your identity.

What Is Stress?

Everybody knows what stress feels like. But what is it really? The experts tell us that stress is a state of being. It is not an attitude; it is not a sign of being unable to handle things. Stress is a physical response, which, left unchecked, can lead to mental and physical exhaustion and illness.

Natural stress in our lives is considered good. It allows our bodies to respond to danger. You know the expression, "fight or flight." *Unnatural* stress comes from continued threats or dangers over which we have no control. The body is alert for long periods of time with no chance to relax. It is important to remember that the body, like any good machine, begins to wear out if it runs in high gear for too long.

Life's Most Stressful Events

In his book, *Winning Life's Toughest Battles*, Dr. Julius Segal outlines three broad categories of very stressful events. These include the following:

- events that lead to the loss of a special relationship, such as divorce
- events you cannot control that make you feel helpless, such as an accident
- events with lasting consequences, such as a terminal illness or the loss of your job

Transitioning from the military can have aspects of all three categories. In a sense, you lose many special relationships by losing the daily interaction with your co-workers. If you are transitioning involuntarily, you may be in a situation that is beyond your control. Transition, obviously, has permanent consequences, and being involuntarily separated may bring on some unforeseen stresses. When you change jobs, your life changes.

The Stress-Health Connection

It is important to look for signs of stress overload. Here are some of the symptoms:

- Constant fatigue
- Headaches
- Trouble sleeping or sleeping too much

- Stomach problems
- More frequent colds or other illnesses
- Smoking or drinking more than usual
- Feeling nervous
- Being irritable or angrier than you want to be
- Desire to be alone, away from other people
- Inability to eat or eating more than usual

If you are suffering from any of these symptoms, it is likely they are stress related.

Coping with Transition-Related Stress

The experiences of thousands of servicemembers who have recently separated suggest that this transition is likely to be stressful for you and your family. Those that have transitioned in the past have found several tactics extremely important in dealing with the stress related to separation from the military:

- **Get going:** It is your transition; no one can do it for you. Work through the transition process and do not procrastinate. Put your situation in perspective and get on with your life. After all, you are not the first person to go through transition, and you will not be the last. You'll do okay, too.
- **Sell yourself:** You have a great product—YOU! So sell yourself! Now is not the time to be modest about your accomplishments. No one will come looking for you unless they know you are available. Once you let them know, you will find many people who will help you.
- **Work at it:** Work at planning your transition as if it were a job. However, if you spend every waking hour working on it, you will burn out. Take time for yourself and your family.
- **Lighten up:** This is probably the most important piece of advice. Do not lose your sense of humor. An upbeat disposition will see you through.
- **Keep your family involved:** Your family has a large stake in your transition. They are experiencing many of the same feelings, worries, and uncertainties as you are. Do not keep your plans to yourself; get your family involved in this process. Let them in on your plans and ask for their input throughout the process. It's their life, too.
- **Volunteer:** Consider doing volunteer work. Your charitable actions will help others and assist you in getting to know the community beyond the military installations and enhance your networking.
- **Take a change-management course:** Consider taking a change-management course before stress appears, or at the first signs of stress.

THE "GRIEVING PROCESS" IS NORMAL

Research has shown that most people go through major life changes in stages. These stages are present in a wide variety of major life traumas:

- Denial: "This is not really happening," or "This is not happening to me."
- Anger: Directed either at yourself or at others.
- Depression: Often accompanied by a sense of helplessness.
- Acceptance: The turning point, when you begin to accept your situation.
- Resolution: Begin to take the steps necessary to return to a normal state.

Proceeding through each step is normal, and the process should not be rushed. Often, however, people may progress out of a stage and then drop back into it. If uncontrolled, the bouncing back and forth between stages can continue for a long time. As you make your transition to civilian life, look for these stages in yourself and acknowledge your movements from one step to the next.

WHERE TO GO FOR HELP

We all deal with stress every day. However, during a major life transition stress can manifest itself in unforeseen and undesirable ways. Fortunately, help is only a phone call away. Various agencies on and off base provide counseling for personal issues, marital issues, parent-child conflicts, stress-related concerns, and alcohol and drug abuse. Remember, while you are on active duty, these services are free on military installations.

For information, assistance, and referrals, contact any of the following resources:

- Local assistance at a family center, chaplain's office, or a military mental health care facility can be found online at: http://www.nvti.cudenver.edu/resources/militarybasestap.htm.
- The Department of Veterans Affairs, 1-800-827-1000 (VA locator website: http://www1.va.gov/directory/guide/home.asp?isFlash=1).
- Military OneSource 24/7 Support at 1-800-342-9647 or http://www.militaryonesource.com.
- Marine for Life at https://www.m4l.usmc.mil/Public/m4lx/start.aspx.
- Military Family Network at www.emilitary.org.

TRANSITIONING FOR A WOUNDED
WARRIOR INTO THE VA

All branches of the military have recovery care programs to assist wounded warriors in transitioning into civilian life. The program ensures that all appropriate care coordination activities, both medical and nonmedical, are completed prior to transition so that the wounded warrior continues to receive the treatment and care required. This process includes:

- Notification to the appropriate VA point of contact (such as a transition patient advocate) when the Recovering Service Member (RSM) begins the physical disability evaluation process, as applicable.
- Scheduling initial appointments with the Veterans Health Administration system.
- Transmitting the RSM's military service record and health record to the VA. The transmittal includes:
  - The RSM's authorization (or that of an individual legally recognized to make medical decisions on behalf of the RSM) for the transmittal in accordance with Public Law 104-191 (Reference [k]). The RSM may have authorized release of his or her medical records if he or she applied for benefits prior to this point in the transition. If so, a copy of that authorization shall be included with the records.
  - The RSM's address and contact information.
  - The RSM's DD Form 214, Certificate of Release or Discharge from Active Duty, which shall be transmitted electronically when possible, and in compliance with Reference (d).
  - The results of any PEB.
  - A determination of the RSM's entitlement to transitional health care, a conversion health policy, or other health benefits through the Department of Defense, as explained in section 1145 of Title 10, United States Code (U.S.C.) (Reference [l]).
  - A copy of requests for assistance from the VA, or of applications made by the RSM for health care, compensation, and vocational rehabilitation, disability, education benefits, or other benefits for which he or she may be eligible pursuant to laws administered by the Secretary of Veterans Affairs.
- Transmitting the RSM's address and contact information to the department or agency for veterans' affairs of the state in which the RSM intends to reside after retirement or separation.

- Updating the Comprehensive Recovery Plan for the RSM's transition that shall include standardized elements of care, treatment requirements, and accountability for the plan. The CRP shall also include:
  - Detailed instructions for the transition from the DoD disability evaluation system to the VA disability system.
  - The recommended schedule and milestones for the RSM's transition from military service.
  - Information and guidance designed to assist the RSM in understanding and meeting the schedule and milestones.
  - The RCC and RT shall:
    - Consider the desires of the RSM and the family or designated caregiver when determining the location of the RSM's care, treatment, and rehabilitation.
    - Coordinate the transfer to the VA by direct communication between appropriate medical and nonmedical staff of the losing and gaining facilities (e.g., MCCM to accepting physician).

Transition from DoD Care and Treatment to Civilian Care, Treatment, and Rehabilitation

- Prior to transition of the RSM to a civilian medical care facility, the RCC (assisted by the RT) shall ensure that all care coordination activities, both medical and nonmedical, have been completed, including:
  - Appointment scheduling with civilian medical care facility providers.
  - Transmittal of the RSM's health record to the civilian medical care facility. The transmittal shall include:
    - The RSM's authorization (or that of an individual legally recognized to make medical decisions on behalf of the RSM) for the transmittal in accordance with Reference (i).
    - A determination of the RSM's entitlement to transitional health care, a conversion health policy, or other health benefits through the Department of Defense, as explained in section 1145 of Reference.
- Transmittal of the RSM's address and contact information.
- Preparation of detailed plans for the RSM's transition, to include standardized elements of care, treatment requirements, and accountability of the CRP.
- The RCC and RT shall:
  - Consider the desires of the RSM and the family or designated caregiver when determining the location of the RSM's care, treatment, and rehabilitation.
  - Coordinate the transfer by direct communication between appropriate medical and nonmedical staff of the losing and gaining facilities (e.g., RCC to FRC, MCCM to accepting physician).

Upon medical retirement, the RSM receives the same benefits as other retired members of the military departments. This includes eligibility for participation in TRICARE and to apply for care through the VA.

An RSM who is enrolled in the RCP and subsequently placed on the temporary disability retired list shall continue to receive the support of an RCC, including implementation of the recovery plan, until such time as the wounded warrior program determines that the services and resources necessary to meet identified needs are in place through non-DoD programs.

TRANSITION SUPPORT

Transition from DoD Care

The RT shall provide transition support to the RSM and family or designated caregiver before, during, and after relocation from one treatment or rehabilitation facility to another or from one care provider to another. Transition preparation will occur with sufficient advance notice and information that the upcoming change in location or caregiver is anticipated by the RSM and family or designated caregiver and will be documented in the CRP.

You and the Department of Veterans Affairs

The Department of Veterans Affairs is responsible for ensuring that you, as a disabled veteran, receive the care, support, and recognition that you have earned. The following information will help you gain access to the benefits and services you deserve.

Disabled Transition Assistance Program (DTAP)

DTAP is a briefing sponsored by the Department of Veterans Affairs, in conjunction with the Department of Defense. It may be offered following a VA benefits briefing, a Department of Labor employment workshop, or separately. Contact your local Transition/ACAP office or command career counselor to find out when a DTAP briefing is scheduled on your installation. If DTAP briefings are not available at your facility, the transition office or family center staff will refer you to other sources where similar information is available.

DTAP provides separating servicemembers with specialized information about the Department of Veterans Affairs (VA) Vocational Rehabilitation and Employment (VR&E) Program, eligibility, and how to apply for benefits. Separating servicemembers who believe they have a service-connected disability are strongly encouraged to request admission to the DTAP class through their unit commander. DTAP is also available online at http://www.vetsuccess.gov/.

Some servicemembers who are pending medical separation may be eligible to receive VR&E services prior to separation.

Servicemembers being separated with a service-connected disability or being referred to a Physical Evaluation Board or being placed in a "medical hold" status by their service should attend DTAP.

VA Vocational Rehabilitation Program

Vocational Rehabilitation and Employment (VR&E) is a program whose primary function is to help veterans with service-connected disabilities become suitably employed, maintain employment, or achieve independence in daily living.

The program offers a number of services to help each eligible disabled veteran reach his or her rehabilitation goal. These services include vocational and personal counseling, education and training, financial aid, job assistance, and, if needed, medical and dental treatment. Services generally last up to forty-eight months, but they can be extended in certain instances.

If you need training, VA will pay your training costs, such as tuition and fees, books, supplies, equipment, and, if needed, special services. While you are in training, VA will also pay you a monthly benefit to help with living expenses, called a subsistence allowance. For details, visit http://www.vetsuccess.gov/.

Eligibility

Usually, you must first be awarded a monthly VA disability compensation payment. In some cases, you may be eligible if you aren't getting VA compensation. For example, if you are awaiting discharge from the service because of a disability you may be eligible for vocational rehabilitation.

Eligibility is also based on you meeting the following conditions:

- You served on or after September 16, 1940; *AND*
- Your service-connected disabilities (SCD) are rated at least 20 percent disabling by VA; *AND*
- You need vocational rehabilitation to overcome an employment handicap; *AND*
- *It has been less than twelve years since VA notified you of your qualified SCD.* **Note:** You may be entitled to Vocational Rehabilitation (VR) services if you are rated 10 percent disabled; however it must be determined that you have a serious employment handicap (SEH).

Regardless of your SCD rating percentage, you may have longer than twelve years to use your VR benefit if certain conditions prevented you from participating in a VR program or it is determined that you have an SEH.

How to Apply

You can apply by filling out VA Form 28-1900, Disabled Veterans Application for Vocational Rehabilitation, and mail it to the VA regional office that serves your area. You can also apply online at http://vabenefits.vba.va.gov/vonapp.

VA Disability Benefits

Recent laws passed by Congress have made several changes in veterans' eligibility for VA medical care. Basically, these laws ensure that VA care will be continued for disabled veterans with service-connected disabilities.

Veterans with non-service-connected disabilities will also continue to receive VA medical care but on a space-available basis, and a copayment may be charged. Laws are subject to change, and there are many applicable details. Contact the VA for the latest information on disability benefits.

Classifying Disabled Veterans

The VA makes an important distinction among veterans based on the nature of their disability. This distinction determines the cost and availability of VA medical services.

- **Service-connected disability:** Any veteran who was disabled by injury or disease incurred or aggravated during active military service in the line of duty will receive VA medical care on a mandatory basis. In general, this means that service will be provided as needed, at no cost to the veteran.
- **Non-service-connected disability:** Any veteran whose disability originated outside of active service will receive VA medical care on a discretionary basis. Examples of such disabilities might include disabling arthritis that you inherited from your parents, loss of the use of your legs after a fall during a ski vacation, contracting malaria, and so on. The VA generally provides medical care to those in the discretionary category on a space-available basis, so long as the veteran agrees to make a copayment.

Veterans with Service-Connected Disabilities

- If your disability is service connected, your benefits fall within the mandatory category.
- **Outpatient care:** If you have a single disability or a combined disability rating of 50 percent or more, the VA will furnish outpatient care without limitation. If your disability rating is less than 50 percent, the VA will treat at no cost only those conditions that are service connected.

- **Hospital care:** The VA is required to provide hospital care at no cost. All medical services are covered while you are hospitalized. This coverage also may include transportation under certain circumstances.
- **Nursing home care:** The VA may or may not provide nursing home or domiciliary care, depending on your income and disability. For more information, call the VA.

Veterans with Non-Service-Connected Disabilities

If your disability is not service connected, the benefits you can receive are in the discretionary category.

- **Outpatient care:** With very few exceptions, outpatient care is provided to veterans with service-connected disabilities only. Contact your local VA office for details.
- **Hospital care:** Hospital care in VA facilities may or may not be provided to veterans in the discretionary category, depending on whether space and resources are available. However, you must agree to pay a deductible of what you would pay under Medicare.
- **Nursing home care:** The VA may or may not provide nursing home care, depending on whether space and resources are available. However, you must pay a copayment. Contact the VA for details.

DEPARTMENT OF VETERANS AFFAIRS
COMPENSATION AND PENSION PROGRAMS

The Department of Veterans Affairs offers the Veteran Disability Compensation and Veteran Pension programs, which may provide you with assistance based on your personal circumstances.

Veteran Disability Compensation

If you are a military veteran with a service-related disability you may qualify for monthly benefit payments. These benefits are paid to veterans who are disabled by an injury or disease that occurred while on active duty, active duty for training, or was made worse by active military service. These benefits are tax free.

You may be eligible for disability compensation if you have a service-related disability and you were discharged under other than dishonorable conditions. The amount of compensation that can be paid through this program ranges from $115 to $2,471 per month, depending on the severity of your disabilities. Your monthly compensation rate is also based on other circumstances. For example, you may receive an increased payment if you have any of the following:

- very severe disabilities or loss of limb(s)
- a spouse, child(ren), or dependent parent(s)
- a seriously disabled spouse

You can apply for compensation benefits by filling out VA Form 21-526, Veterans Application for Compensation and/or Pension (http://www.vba .va.gov/pubs/forms/21-526.pdf). Be sure to attach copies of any of the following documents to your application:

- Discharge or separation papers (DD214 or equivalent)
- National Guard servicemembers should also include a copy of their military orders, presidential proclamation, or executive order that clearly demonstrates the federal nature of the service
- Dependency records (marriage and children's birth certificates) as applicable
- Medical evidence (doctor and hospital reports)

You can also apply online through the website at http://vabenefits.vba.va.gov/ vonapp.

Veteran Pension

If you are a wartime veteran with limited income **and** you are permanently and totally disabled **or** age sixty-five or older you may be eligible for a veteran pension. The veteran pension (also known as VA pension) is a non-service-connected benefit that provides a monthly payment to supplement your income.

You may be eligible if you meet the following criteria:

- you were discharged from service under other than dishonorable conditions; *AND*
- you served ninety days or more of active duty and at least one day of that service occurred during a period of war*; *AND*
- your countable family income is below a yearly limit set by law; *AND*
- you are permanently and totally disabled; *OR*
- you are age sixty-five or older.

*Note: Anyone who enlists after September 7, 1980, generally must have served at least twenty-four months or the full period for which he or she was called or ordered to active duty. Military service from August 2, 1990, through a date to be set by law or presidential proclamation is considered to be a period of war (Gulf War). VA pension pays you the difference between your count-able family income and the yearly income limit. This difference is generally paid in twelve equal monthly payments rounded down to the nearest dollar.

Example: Joe (a single veteran) has an annual income of $5,000. His an-nual income limit is $10,929. To determine Joe's pension, subtract his annual income of $5,000 from the $10,929 income limit, which gives him an annual pension rate of $5,929. This translates into a monthly pension check of $494.

How to Apply

You can apply for this benefit by filling out VA Form 21-526, Veterans Application for Compensation and/or Pension (http://www.vba.va.gov/pubs/forms/21-526.pdf). Be sure to attach copies of any of the following docu-ments to your application:

- Discharge or separation papers (DD214 or equivalent)
- Dependency records (marriage and children's birth certificates) as ap-plicable
- Medical evidence (doctor and hospital reports)

You can also apply online through the website at http://vabenefits.vba.va.gov/vonapp.

SOCIAL SECURITY ADMINISTRATION BENEFITS FOR WOUNDED WARRIORS

Servicemembers can receive expedited processing of disability claims from So-cial Security. Benefits available through Social Security are different than those from the Department of Veterans Affairs and require a separate application.

The expedited process is used for military servicemembers who become disabled while on active military service on or after October 1, 2001, regard-less of where the disability occurs. To learn more about this benefit, visit the Social Security Wounded Warriors website at http://www.socialsecurity.gov/woundedwarriors.

LIFE INSURANCE COVERAGE FOR SERVICE-CONNECTED DISABLED VETERANS

In addition to the extended Servicemembers' Group Life Insurance (SGLI) cov-erage and Veterans' Group Life Insurance (VGLI) programs mentioned in chap-ter 8 of the preseparation guide, veterans with service-connected disabilities are eligible for two additional life insurance programs. The following information will help you determine if you are eligible for these programs and how to apply.

Service-Disabled Veterans Life Insurance (S-DVI)

Service-Disabled Veterans Insurance is life insurance for veterans who receive a service-connected disability rating by the Department of Veterans Affairs. The basic S-DVI program, commonly referred to as RH Insurance, insures eligible veterans for up to $10,000 of coverage. Veterans who have the basic S-DVI coverage and are totally disabled are eligible to have their premiums waived. If waiver is granted, totally disabled veterans may apply for additional coverage of up to $20,000 under the Supplemental S-DVI program. Premiums for supplemental S-DVI coverage, however, cannot be waived. You are eligible for S-DVI if:

- You were released from service under other than dishonorable conditions on or after April 25, 1951; *AND*
- VA has notified you that you have a service-connected disability; *AND*
- You are healthy except for your service-related disability; *AND*
- You apply within two years of being notified of your service-connected disability.

You are eligible for supplemental S-DVI if:

- You have an S-DVI policy; *AND*
- The premiums on your basic coverage are being waived due to total disability; *AND*
- You apply within one year of being notified of the waiver; *AND*
- You are under sixty-five years of age.

The S-DVI premiums vary depending on your age, type of plan (term or permanent), and the amount of coverage you select.

You may apply for S-DVI using the following forms:

- VA Form 29-4364, Application for Service-Disabled Veterans Insurance to apply for basic S-DVI (http://www.insurance.va.gov/inForceGliSite/forms/29-4364.pdf).
- VA Form 29-357, Claim for Disability Insurance Benefits to apply for a total disability waiver of S-DVI premiums (http://www.insurance.va.gov/inforceGLISite/forms/29-357.pdf).

You can also use the Department of Veterans Affairs "Autoform" online application process, which can be found at http://www.insurance.va.gov/inforceGLISite/forms/sdviQuest/Q1a.htm.

For more information call toll free 1-800-669-8477 or go to http://www
.insurance.va.gov.

Waiver of Premiums: You may be eligible for a waiver if you become totally disabled before your sixty-fifth birthday and stay that way for at least six
consecutive months. (Premiums for supplemental S-DVI can't be waived.)

Veterans' Mortgage Life Insurance (VMLI)

Veterans' Mortgage Life Insurance is an insurance program that provides up
to $90,000 in mortgage life insurance coverage on the home mortgages of
veterans with severe service-connected disabilities who:

- Receive a specially adapted housing grant from VA for assistance in
  building, remodeling, or purchasing an adapted home; *AND*
- Have title to the home; *AND*
- Have a mortgage on the home.

The insurance is payable only to the mortgage lender, not to family members. VMLI coverage is available on a new mortgage, an existing mortgage,
a refinanced mortgage, or a second mortgage.

VMLI premiums are determined by:

- The insurance age of the veteran; *AND*
- The outstanding balance of the mortgage at the time of application; *AND*
- The remaining length of the mortgage.

Note: Now you can determine your premium rate online at https://insurance
.va.gov/inForceGliSite/VMLICalc/VMLICalc.asp. Veterans can apply by
submitting VA Form 29-8636, Veterans' Mortgage Life Insurance Statement
(http://www.insurance.va.gov/inforceGLISite/forms/29-8636.pdf). For more
information on the VMLI program call toll free 1-800-669-8477 or go to
http://www.insurance.va.gov.

CHAMPVA: MEDICAL CARE FOR
FAMILY MEMBERS AND SURVIVORS

The Civilian Health and Medical Program of the Department of Veterans Affairs (CHAMPVA) helps pay for medical services and supplies that veterans'
family members and survivors obtain for civilian sources.

To qualify, family members and survivors must *not* be eligible for Medicare or TRICARE. The following are eligible for CHAMPVA:

- the spouse or child of a veteran who has a permanent and total service-connected disability
- the surviving spouse or child of a veteran who died as a result of a service-connected condition
- the surviving spouse of child of a person who died while on active military service in the line or duty

For details and submitting new health care claims, contact:
VA Health Administration Center
CHAMPVA
P.O. Box 65024
Denver, CO 80206-9024
Toll free: 1-800-733-8387
The CHAMPVA website is http://www.va.gov/hac/forbeneficiaries/champva/champva.asp.

DISABILITY COMPENSATION

The VA pays monetary benefits to veterans who were disabled by injury or disease incurred or aggravated during active military service in the line of duty. Filing a claim with the VA (VA Form 21-256, Application for Disability Compensation or Pension Benefits) is very important. It serves to notify the VA about your health problems so that service-connected disabilities can be evaluated.

Note: Servicemembers who are medically separated from the military with severance pay and who are subsequently awarded disability compensation from the VA will have their disability compensation offset until their severance pay has been recouped. Call the VA for details: 1-800-827-1000.

DisabilityInfo.gov: The Online Disability Resource

The federal government has created the http://www.disabilityinfo.gov/ website, which is designed to give people with disabilities and many others access to the information and resources they need to live full and independent lives in the workplace and in their communities. Managed by the U.S. Department of Labor's Office of Disability Employment Policy (http://www.dol.gov/odep), DisabilityInfo.gov offers a broad range of valuable information not only for people with disabilities but also their family members, health care professionals, service providers, and many others.

Easy to navigate, DisabilityInfo.gov is organized by subject areas that include benefits, civil rights, community life, education, employment, health, housing, technology, and transportation. By selecting a category from the tabs at the top of the home page, users are directed to valuable information covering state and local resources, news and events, grants and funding, laws and regulations, and more. Several sections of the site link to disability-related programs geared toward veterans and the military community.

With twenty-one federal agencies contributing content to this website, DisabilityInfo.gov contains extensive, frequently updated information on a host of cross-cutting topics. Areas of particular interest to the military community and their families include information on the availability of assistive technologies for DoD employees and servicemembers with disabilities, links to employment programs for transitioning wounded servicemembers in addition to information on benefits, compensation, and health care programs, links to relocation and employment services as well as special needs programs for military families, and many other Department of Defense programs serving troops and their families.

DisabilityInfo.gov also offers a free subscription service where you can sign up to receive *Disability Connection*, the quarterly newsletter, as well as other e-mail alerts covering information tailored to your individual interests. Just visit http://service.govdelivery.com/service/user.html?code=USODEP to sign up.

VETERAN CENTERS

Vet centers provide readjustment counseling and outreach services to all veterans who served in any combat zone. Services are also available for their family members for military-related issues. Veterans have earned these benefits through their service, and all are provided at no cost to the veteran or family.

Readjustment counseling is a wide range of services provided to combat veterans in an effort to make a satisfying transition from military to civilian life. Services include:

- Individual counseling
- Group counseling
- Marital and family counseling
- Bereavement counseling
- Medical referrals
- Assistance in applying for VA benefits
- Employment counseling
- Guidance and referral
- Alcohol/drug assessments

- Information and referral to community resources
- Military sexual trauma counseling and referral
- Outreach and community education

VA's readjustment counseling is provided at community-based vet centers located near veterans and their families. There is no cost for vet center readjustment counseling. Find your nearest vet center in the online Vet Center Directory at http://www1.va.gov/directory/guide/vetcenter.asp or check your local blue pages.

The vet center staff is available toll free during normal business hours at 1-800-905-4675 (Eastern) and 1-866-496-8838 (Pacific).

TRANSITIONING FOR A NONWOUNDED, RETIRING WARRIOR

All those years of service will now be paid back with extra benefits and programs. As a retiree you are eligible for all the same benefits as any other veteran or disabled veteran, in addition to the following retiree benefits.

Servicemembers who remain on active duty or serve in the Reserves or Guard for a sufficient period of time may retire and receive retired pay. Retirees also retain the privilege to use base facilities, such as the commissary and gym. Those members who entered service on or after August 1, 1986, and who will qualify for an active duty retirement may choose between two of the current three systems. Members who become disabled while on duty may be medically retired and receive a disability retirement. See the Disability Compensation Programs section below for further details.

Did You Know? Military enlisted retirees can work for virtually whomever they want (except for foreign governments) and work on any project or subject matter for their new employer. However, a conflict of interest may exist if you begin to interact with certain departments or agencies of the federal government. For example, if you worked for procurement during your military career, you may be prohibited from working for a company that sells supplies to your former base.

Military Retirement Pay

Retirement Pay and Compensation

Servicemembers who remain on active duty or serve in the Reserves or National Guard for twenty years or longer may retire and receive retirement pay.

There are currently three retirement systems to choose from. Your Pay and Compensation Administrative Officer within your command can provide more information on these system options. Also, visit DoD's online Retirement Pay Calculators to see how each retirement system will affect payouts: http://www.defenselink.mil/militarypay/retirement/calc/index.html.

Nondisability Retirement Pay Options

- Final Pay: The Final Pay retirement system only applies to members who first entered service before September 8, 1980.
- High-3: The High-3 Year Average retirement system applies to members who first entered service on or after September 8, 1980, and before August 1, 1986. High-3 also applies to members who first entered the service on or after August 1, 1986, and chose to revert to the High-3 retirement plan by not accepting the Career Status Bonus (CSB).
- CSB/REDUX: This system applies only to members who first entered service after July 31, 1986, and chose to receive the Career Status Bonus (CSB) and the REDUX retirement plan.

Disability Retirements

Servicemembers who become wounded, ill, or injured may be medically retired. They may receive either a permanent or temporary disability retirement. A Physical Examination Board (PEB—Medical Board) determines the percent disability and recommends whether the disability is permanent or needs reexamination every eighteen months up to five years, at which time a final retirement system determination is made.

See your Pay and Compensation Administrative Officer in your command or at your military treatment facility (MTF) for additional information and referrals. Visit the DoD's online Retirement Calculators to learn more about your retirement pay options: http://www.defenselink.mil/militarypay/retirement/calc/index.html.

Health Care for Retirees

As a retiree you have several health care benefits to choose from. These include VA-provided medical benefits, TRICARE, and other supplemental health care insurance options.

Care at VA Facilities

Retirees continue to be eligible for Department of Veterans Affairs (VA) medical care on a space-available basis. There are many limitations and eligibility requirements. VA medical care should *not* be relied on as your only source of health care.

TRICARE

Retirees and their families remain eligible to use civilian health care facilities under TRICARE. TRICARE eligibility remains in force until you are sixty-five years old. Upon reaching age sixty-five, TRICARE ends and you become eligible for TRICARE for Life. For information on TRICARE, contact the beneficiary service representative or health benefits advisor at your nearest military treatment facility. You can also learn more about TRICARE at http://www.tricare.osd.mil. Go to this website to find out more about TRICARE benefits for retirees age sixty-five and older.

TRICARE Retiree Dental Plan

The TRICARE Retiree Dental Program (TRDP) provides comprehensive dental coverage for uniformed services retirees and their family members. Under contract with the U.S. Department of Defense, the federal services division of Delta Dental Plan of California administers the TRDP. The TRDP is a voluntary dental benefits program with enrollee-paid premiums.

Covered services under the TRDP are offered throughout the fifty United States, the District of Columbia, Puerto Rico, Guam, the U.S. Virgin Islands, American Samoa, the Commonwealth of the Northern Mariana Islands, and Canada. Visit the TRICARE Retiree Dental Plan website at http://www.trdp .org for further information.

Supplemental Health Insurance for Retirees

One short stay in the hospital could offset the cost of several years of supplemental health insurance. Even though you are covered by TRICARE, a supplemental insurance policy is a good idea for retirees.

Here's why:

- TRICARE does not cover all costs.
- TRICARE has a yearly deductible to be paid.
- TRICARE has a yearly cap on noncovered expenses; the cap is extremely high, and you are responsible for the cost of noncovered items up to that amount.

If you are covered by health insurance with your new employer, you may use TRICARE as your supplemental insurance for that policy. Check with your TRICARE advisor concerning your particular circumstances.

The Supplemental Health Insurance Test

Private supplemental health insurance makes sense in a variety of situations:

- **Unemployed?** If you remain unemployed after retirement, you should ask yourself, "Do I have sufficient health insurance coverage for me and my family?"
- **Underinsured?** After retirement, did you accept a job that does not provide full medical coverage for you or your family?
- **Not insured?** Do you rely on limited VA medical benefits as your only source of medical care?

If you answered *yes* to any of these questions, you should consider obtaining supplemental health insurance.

Shopping for Supplemental Health Insurance

There are many places to obtain supplemental health insurance. Several fraternal associations and many commercial insurance companies offer such plans, but you should look carefully for the one that is best for you. Insurance plans vary greatly with which medical procedures are covered and the percentage the policy will pay.

When shopping for health insurance, first consider the benefits you may have as a retiree or veteran. Then purchase supplemental insurance. The trick is to find a supplemental insurance plan that covers all your anticipated needs *without* paying for benefits that duplicate what you already have.

There are five basic types of health insurance coverage:

- **Hospital expense insurance** pays for hospital bills either in part or in full. Watch out for policies that do not pay for the first eight to ten days of a hospital stay (the average hospital stay is fewer than eight days).
- **Surgical expense insurance** covers surgeon fees. Beware: for major surgeries, all of the fees may not be covered. Read the policy carefully before you sign.
- **Medical expense insurance** covers doctor's visits in the hospital, in the doctor's office, or house calls.
- **Major medical insurance** pays practically every form of hospital and outpatient care as long as a licensed physician provides the care. Most people choose major medical because it is so comprehensive. However, the payments for this type of coverage are high.
- **Disability insurance** pays a percentage of your normal income if a disability prevents you from doing your job.

When looking at your health insurance coverage, take a moment to review your insurance on your automobile, personal property, real estate, and loan payments. Insurers sometimes offer discounts to customers who purchase several types of insurance from the same company.

Disability Compensation Programs

Military retirees who have service-connected disabilities are eligible for disability compensation. The type and amount of disability compensation eligibility is based on several factors, including the nature of the service-connected disability and the nature of your retirement. You may qualify for more than one program; however, you may not receive benefits from more than one program at a time. The following will help you to determine which of these benefits you qualify for and which best suit your needs.

Veteran Disability Compensation

If you are a military retiree with a service-related disability you may qualify for monthly benefit payments. These benefits are paid to retirees who are disabled by an injury or disease that occurred while on active duty, active duty for training, or was made worse by active military service.

As a military retiree you may be required to waive a portion of your military retirement to receive these tax-free benefits. This reduction in military retirement pay is commonly referred to as a VA disability offset. Certain disabled military retirees may be eligible for one of the following programs that restore some or all of the VA disability offset.

Concurrent Retirement and Disability Pay (CRDP)

Concurrent Retirement and Disability Pay (CRDP) is a program that provides certain military retirees a monthly restoration of some or all of their VA disability offset. Qualified military retirees are those with twenty or more years of service who have a service-connected disability of 50 percent or more. When the CRDP program is fully implemented such members will no longer have their military retirement pay reduced by the amount of their VA disability compensation.

Unlike the Combat-Related Special Compensation (CRSC), CRDP is being phased in (except for those retirees that have a VA-rated, service-connected disability rating of 100 percent). The program began in 2004, and the phase-in will be complete in 2014. The phase-in is progressive. In 2007, the restoration of the offset pay was approximately 50 percent; by 2009 it will be nearly 85 percent complete.

You are eligible for CRDP if you meet the following criteria:

- You must be a military retiree with twenty or more years of service, including:
  - Chapter 61 medical retirees with twenty years or more.
  - National Guard and Reserve with twenty or more good years (after drawing a retirement check at age sixty).
  - Temporary Early Retirement Authority (TERA) retirees with less than twenty years of service.
- Have a service-related VA disability rating of 50 percent or higher.

Your CRDP payment is a restoration of retired pay. It is taxed and, if applicable, subject to collection actions for alimony, child support, community property, garnishment, and government debt just as your retired pay.

Your monthly CRDP amount cannot exceed the lesser of your monthly gross retired pay or VA waiver amount. If you are a disability retiree whose retired pay is calculated using a percentage of disability rather than your years of service, your CRDP cannot exceed the amount your gross retired pay would currently be had it been calculated at retirement using your years of service.

Fortunately, you do not need to apply; CRDP is automatic. If you qualify you will automatically see an increase in your monthly retirement check.

Additional information is also available at the Defense Finance and Accounting Service (DFAS) website, http://www.dfas.mil/retiredpay.html, or the Office of the Secretary of Defense for Personnel Readiness website, http://www.defenselink.mil/prhome/mppveterans.html.

As noted above, your personal CRDP payment rate is determined by several factors. If you have questions, you can contact the DFAS by calling toll free 1-800-321-1080 to learn about your personal CRDP payment rate.

Combat-Related Special Compensation (CRSC)

Combat-Related Special Compensation (CRSC) provides military retirees a monthly compensation that replaces their VA disability offset. Qualified military retirees are those with twenty or more years of service who have "combat related" VA-rated disability. Such members are now entitled to a payment that makes up for their military retirement pay being reduced by the amount of their VA disability compensation.

Combat-Related Special Compensation includes disabilities incurred as a direct result of:

- Armed Conflict
- Hazardous Duty
- Conditions Simulating War
- An Instrumentality of War

Unlike Concurrent Retirement and Disability Pay (CRDP), CRSC has no phase-in period. Once a military retiree has been determined to be qualified they will receive their reduced retirement pay plus an additional sum that makes up for part or all of their offset retired pay.

Your CRSC payment is based on the percentage of your disability that your service determines to have been combat related, as described above. This percentage may be less than your overall VA disability rating, and consequently the CRSC payment may be less than your offset retired pay. Your CRSC payment is not a restoration of retired pay. It is a special entitlement payment and is not taxed.

Your monthly CRSC amount cannot exceed the lesser of your monthly gross retired pay or VA waiver amount. If you are a disability retiree whose retired pay is calculated using a percentage of disability rather than your years of service, your CRSC cannot exceed the amount your gross retired pay would currently be had it been calculated at retirement using your years of service.

Unlike CRDP, CRSC is not automatic; you will need to apply to your military service. If you qualify your service will advise you of your status.

Retired veterans with combat-related injuries must meet all of the following criteria to apply for CRSC:

- Receiving military retired pay (This includes Chapter 61 Medical, Temporary Early Retirement [TERA] Retirees, and Temporary Disabled Retirement List [TDRL] retirees.)
- Have 10 percent or greater VA-rated disability due to injury
- Military retired pay is reduced by VA disability payments (VA Waiver); *AND*
- You must be able to provide documentary evidence that your injury was a result of one of the following:
  - Training that simulates war (e.g., exercises, field training)
  - Hazardous duty (e.g., flight, diving, parachute duty)
  - An instrumentality of war (e.g., combat vehicles, weapons, Agent Orange)
  - Armed conflict (e.g., gunshot wounds [Purple Heart], punji stick injuries)

To learn more about the specific eligibility criteria and how to apply, visit one of the following websites:

AIR FORCE CRSC
United States Air Force
Disability Division (CRSC)
550 C Street West, Suite 6
Randolph AFB TX 78150-4708
Phone: 1-800-616-3775
Website: http://www.afpc.randolph.af.mil/library/combat.asp

ARMY CRSC
Department of the Army
U.S. Army Physical Disabilities Agency/
Combat Related Special Compensation (CRSC)
200 Stovall Street
Alexandria, VA 22332
Phone: 1-866-281-3254
E-mail: crsc.info@us.army.mil
Website: http://www.CRSC.army.mil

COAST GUARD CRSC
Commander (adm-1-CRSC)
U.S. Coast Guard
Personnel Command
4200 Wilson Boulevard
Arlington, VA 22203-1804
Phone: 1-800-772-8274
Website: http://www.uscg.mil/hq/cgpc/adm/adm1.htm

NAVY and MARINE CORPS CRSC
Secretary of the Navy Council of Review Boards
Attn: Combat-Related Special Compensation Branch
720 Kennon Street SE, Suite 309
Washington Navy Yard, DC 20374
Website: http://www.hq.navy.mil/ncpb/CRSCB/combatrelated.htm

Additional information is also available at the Defense Finance and Accounting Service (DFAS) website, http://www.dfas.mil/retiredpay.html, or the Office of the Secretary of Defense for Personnel Readiness website, http://www.defenselink.mil/prhome/mppveterans.html.

SURVIVOR BENEFIT PLAN

All retirees may choose to participate in the Survivor Benefit Plan or the Reserve Components Survivor Benefit Plan. The Survivor Benefit Plan is designed to provide ongoing income for your spouse and minor children should you die before them. Videos on preretirement planning and the Survivor Benefit Plan may be available for viewing at home. Check with your installation's transition program office.

The Survivor Benefit Plan can be very confusing. You and your spouse will need to learn as much as possible before making your final decision. In addition, your spouse's signature is required on the form.

The Defense Accounting and Finance Service (DAFS) offers a great resource to help you learn more about the cost and benefits of the SBP. Visit http://www.dod.mil/dfas/retiredpay/survivorbenefits.html to learn more.

LEGAL ASSISTANCE

Retirees should obtain legal assistance on most personal legal matters such as wills, powers of attorney, filing federal and state income taxes, and reviewing contracts. Military legal office priority is given to active duty personnel. Retirees residing overseas may have restrictions on privileges based upon Status of Forces agreements.

NATIONAL RETIREE COUNCILS

The Military Retiree Councils provide a link between members of the military retiree community—retirees, family members, and surviving spouses living throughout the world—and the leaders of their respective military service branches.

Each National Retiree Council is comprised of a board that consists of both senior NCO and officer retirees. The members represent geographic areas within the continental United States and at least one at-large representative.

The Retiree Councils meet annually to discuss retiree benefit issues. Upon conclusion of the meeting, they report their findings directly to the appropriate member of their respective service branch. These annual reports reflect the issues of most significance to the retiree community that year.

Note: Rather than issuing an annual report, the Air Force Retiree Council issues letters to various air staff offices requesting support for specific items of concern. These letters are not normally made available to the public.

Visit each of the National Retiree Councils to view their annual reports:

- The Army Chief of Staff's Retiree Council website: http://www.armyg1 .army.mil/rso/RetireeCouncil.
- The Secretary of the Navy's Navy and Marine Corps Retiree Council website: https://secnavretireecouncil.lifelines.navy.mil/CouncilInformation/ tabid/254/Default.aspx.
- The Air Force Retiree Council website: http://www.retirees.af.mil/council/.
- Coast Guard Commandant's Retiree Council website: http://www.uscg .mil/hq/g-w/g-wp/g-wpm/g-wpm-2/retiree/retiree.htm.

3

Transitioning to a New Career

PREPARATION

You can start the transition process twelve months prior to separation or twenty-four months prior to retirement. The sooner you start the better. There is a lot of information to absorb, and you need time to plan and decide what is in the best interest for yourself and your family. A dedicated and highly trained transition staff is available to assist you.

The Transition Assistance Program demonstrates the Department of Defense, the Department of Labor, the Department of Veterans Affairs, and the Department of Homeland Security's continued commitment to our men and women in uniform.

Special transition benefits information, employment workshops, automated employment job-hunting tools and job banks, veteran benefits information, disabled veterans benefits information, and many other types of transition and other related information is available to you. AND IT'S ALL FREE. Take full advantage of TAP and all it has to offer.

GENERAL INFORMATION

The Department of Defense Transition Assistance Program (TAP) for active component servicemembers (including AGR, AR, and FTS) consists of four components:

1. Preseparation Counseling—mandatory and conducted by the military services

2. Department of Labor (DOL) Transition Assistance Program Employment
3. Workshops—facilitated and sponsored by DOL
4. Veterans Benefits Briefings—facilitated and sponsored by VA
5. Disabled Transition Assistance Program (DTAP)—facilitated and sponsored by VA

The transition process begins with the completion of the DD Form 2648, Preseparation Counseling Checklist. This is a legal requirement, and a copy of your DD Form 2648 is required to be filed in your personnel file.

The Preseparation Guide was developed primarily to augment the four components of TAP with special emphasis on the preseparation counseling component. The guide provides information on the various services and benefits available to separating and retiring servicemembers and their families. Information contained in the guide may also be used by Department of Defense civilian employees affected by downsizing, reductions in force (RIFs), base closures, and base realignments.

All separating and retiring servicemembers should make an appointment to see their local transition counselor for information on transition services and benefits. Transition counselors are located in the following offices at local military installations:

- Army: Army Career and Alumni Program (ACAP)
- Air Force: Airman and Family Readiness Center
- Navy: Fleet and Family Support Center
- Marine Corps: Career Resource Management Center (CRMC)/Transition and Employment Assistance Program Center
- Coast Guard: Work-Lfe Division—Coast Guard Work-Life staff can be found at the nearest Integrated Support Command.

Information Accuracy: The material contained in the guide is current as of May 2007. Subsequent changes in laws, policies, and regulations are not addressed herein. It is important to check with your local counselor to ensure you have the most up-to-date information.

Supplementation: Supplementing the Preseparation Guide or establishing military, command, or local forms is prohibited without prior approval from the Office of the Under Secretary of Defense for Personnel and Readiness. Requests to supplement the guide or produce additional forms should be forwarded through military service chain of command to the address below the section on "Comments and Suggestions."

A transition counselor is a person responsible for conducting the transition program. Personnel may be military, civilian, or a contractor. Transition counselors may be assigned to family centers, Army Career and Alumni Program Centers, military personnel offices, on ships, and transition centers. The term *transition counselor* is used throughout the guide. Individual military services may use a different title (see below) for a transition counselor.

- Army: ACAP Transition Counselor
- Air Force: Transition Assistance Staff or Career Consultant
- Navy: Command Career Counselor
- Marine Corps: Career Resource Management Center Specialist
- Coast Guard: Work-Life Staff

The Coast Guard has its own version of the Preseparation Guide. Coast Guard personnel should contact the nearest Work-Life Transition and Relocation Manager for a copy of the Coast Guard guide.

Comments and Suggestions: Comments, suggestions, and recommendations from active duty military personnel must be forwarded through the respective service's chain of command. Specific comments concerning websites listed in this document should be sent to the address listed below.

Office of the Under Secretary of Defense (Personnel and Readiness)
ATTN: DoD Transition Assistance Program Manager
4000 Defense Pentagon, Washington, DC 20301-4000

PROCESSES

Preseparation Counseling: Your Best Beginning

Your first step in the separation process is to go to your installation's transition assistance office. Each service has its own way of doing things; so too with the transition assistance offices. In most cases, you will find the transition assistance office located inside your installation's Family Center. Listed below is the name of each service's Transition Assistance Program:

- Army: The Army Career and Alumni Program (ACAP) is a military personnel function, and the centers are found under the Director of Human Resources (DHR) or the Military Personnel Office (MILPO) at http://www.acap.army.mil/.

- Air Force: Airman and Family Readiness Center. You can find the nearest office using the military installation finder at http://www.military installations.dod.mil.
- Navy: Fleet and Family Support Center. Navy personnel should make an appointment with their Command Career Counselor for a preseparation counseling interview and the Navy CONSEP (Career Options and Skills Evaluation Program) self-assessment at least 180 days prior to separation. https://www.nffsp.org/.
- Marines: Career Resource Management Center (CRMC)/Transition and Employment Assistance.
- Coast Guard: Work-Life Division—Transition Assistance. Coast Guard Work-Life staffs can be found at your nearest Integrated Support Command. http://www.uscg.mil/worklife/.

The Transition Assistance Program (TAP) was developed by the Department of Defense (DoD) to help separating and retiring servicemembers and their families make a smooth transition from a military career to the civilian sector. For the Marine Corps, the program consists of five important components:

1. **Preseparation Interview:** This mandatory component is the beginning of USMC TAMP process. The preseparation interview is conducted by the Unit Transition Counselor (UTC) and shall consist of an explanation of the transition requirements for separating and retiring servicemembers, including obtaining the Verification of Military Experience and Training (VMET). https://www.dmdc.osd.mil/appj/vmet/loginDisplay.do.
2. **Preseparation Counseling Brief:** This briefing typically takes one full day and includes subject-matter experts outlining the benefits and entitlements available to transitioning servicemembers. This brief is mandatory and must be completed before a servicemember can separate or retire.
3. **Transition Assistance Program (TAP) Employment Workshop:** Mandatory. Qualified comprehensive workshops conducted by the Department of Labor or TAMP personnel. In the workshop personnel will learn how to write a resume and cover letter, get information on skills assessment, job search techniques, and other important information about career and job services available through DoL. Servicemembers will learn how to access the DoL CareerOneStop Center in their local community to continue their job search if they have not found a job prior to separation or retirement.
4. **Veterans Affairs Benefits Briefing:** A briefing conducted by the Department of Veterans Affairs personnel outlining VA benefits and

entitlements available to transitioning servicemembers. This component of TAP is sponsored by VA. All separating and retiring servicemembers should attend a VA benefits briefing to learn about all the VA benefits they are or may be entitled to, the procedures for applying for benefits, information on the Montgomery GI Bill, and where to go to get VA assistance (health care, VA counseling at a Vet Center, etc.).

5. **Disabled Transition Assistance Program (DTAP):** Specifically for individuals who have or *THINK* they have a potential disability claim. DTAP is also sponsored by VA. All servicemembers separating or retiring with a service-connected disability must attend this briefing. They will learn about eligibility for Chapter 31, Vocational Rehabilitation and Employment Service benefits, by VA.

FINDING A JOB

Finding a job might be your top priority. The sections below offer resources for several stages of job searching: Many servicemembers have never written a resume, filled out a job application, or attended a job interview. Fortunately, these skills can be learned. The following section will give you the resources and information you need to launch your new civilian career.

Labor Needs in the Twenty-first Century

Today's job market demands increasingly sophisticated and technological skills—skills that are well suited for those leaving military service. American veterans are superbly qualified and capable of meeting the needs of the current and future civilian labor force. Today's defense occupations are diverse and numerous: senior management, executives, civil engineers, medical specialists, auditors, caseworkers, nuclear engineers, food service managers, mechanics, heavy equipment operators, qualified and skilled people in information technology and telecommunications, to name a few.

Most positions correspond closely to private sector occupations. It is true that a few military specialties have no direct application. However, the training and discipline required to master those specialties clearly demonstrate the potential to learn and master other skills required in the private sector. Look at it from an employer's point of view:

- Today's soldiers, sailors, Airmen, Marines, and Coast Guard members are the highest-quality military personnel in our nation's history.
- The men and women serving the Department of Defense (DoD) and Department of Homeland Security are competent, positive, selfless, and oriented toward mission accomplishment.

- They perform skillfully using today's sophisticated military equipment: computers, electronics, avionics, and so on.
- They demonstrate their ability to learn sophisticated skills on short notice. Look at yourself. You have several things going for you. You are well trained, healthy, disciplined, and team oriented. What employer wouldn't want an employee like you?

The following programs and services are available to all transitioning servicemembers.

Transition Assistance Offices

You might be reluctant to start your transition because you dread the thought of finding a job. Career changes are, however, a common part of American life. Most people change careers at least three times in their lives.

Transition assistance offices have programs and counselors to assist you and your family members in seeking employment in government and the private sector. Examples of some employment assistance services available at your transition assistance office are listed below:

- **Counseling:** The transition staff provides individual career development counseling, comprehensive assessment of employment skills, and identification of employment opportunities.
- **Services:** Transition assistance offices offer computerized listings of jobs, career workshops and training opportunities, as well as automated resume writing. Many transition assistance offices also provide access to a minireference library, word processing, and copying equipment to assist in job-search preparation.
- **Job banks:** Job banks provide information and referrals on temporary, permanent, part-time, and full-time positions in the federal, state, and private sectors. Separating servicemembers are strongly encouraged to start their job search by using the following websites:
  ○ http://www.TurboTAP.org—look for job banks/boards under the employment hub
  ○ DoD Transportal at http://www.dodtransportal.org/
  ○ Transition Bulletin Board at http://www.dmdc.osd.mil/ot
  ○ http://www.usajobs.com
  ○ http://www.go-defense.com/

Whatever you do, start by putting your resume online in the Department of Labor's job bank under the DoD Job Search Website. Employers who are registered with the Department of Labor's job bank and are looking to hire former military personnel go to this website to search for resumes.

You can also visit these websites for more employment assistance: http://www.careeronestop.org and the Army Career and Alumni Program (ACAP) website, http://www.acap.army.mil.

Workshops and seminars: A variety of workshops and seminars are available through your transition assistance office to help you and your spouse become more competitive in the job market. Topics include enhancing job search skills, goal setting, and preparation of standard and optional forms for federal civil service employment, resumes, and interviewing techniques. One of the most popular job-hunting workshops is sponsored by the Department of Labor. Their two-and-a-half day Transition Assistance Employment Workshop is one component of the overall Transition Assistance Program (TAP). You can sign up for this important workshop through your Transition/ACAP Office or through your command career counselor.

Training: Some locations offer occupational skills training for those seeking entry-level classes in typing, word processing, and data entry. In addition, you'll find helpful articles about writing resumes, dressing for success, interviewing techniques, and how to work a job fair at http://www.military.com/careers.

Employment Assistance and Credentialing Programs

Army and Navy COOL. The Army and Navy both offer Credentialing Opportunities Online (COOL). These programs give you the opportunity to find civilian credentials related to your rating or military occupational specialty. You can learn what it takes to get the credentials and learn about programs that will help pay credentialing fees. Check out the Army COOL website at https://www.cool.army.mil/ or Navy COOL website at https://www.cool.navy.mil/ to learn more.

Helmets to Hardhats. The Helmets to Hardhats (H2H) program lets your military service speak for itself. The program will help you find career opportunities that match your military background. Congressionally funded, H2H is the fastest, easiest way for transitioning military, Reservists, and Guards members to find a rewarding career in the construction industry. Visit: http://helmetstohardhats.org/ to learn more.

USMAP. USMAP (United Services Military Apprenticeship Program) is available to members of the Navy, Marine Corps, and Coast Guard. Those who participated in this program are eligible to receive a Department of Labor (DoL) Certificate of Completion, which gives them a definite advantage in getting better civilian jobs since employers know the value of apprenticeships. Visit https://usmap.cnet.navy.mil to learn more.

Library

Your local public and military libraries can be an excellent source of job-search information. Most information of interest to job seekers is located in the reference section. Most public and military libraries offer access to the Internet. Helpful library resources include the following:

- **Occupational Information Network: The Dictionary of Occupational Titles (O*NET):** This provides detailed descriptions of most occupations. Available online at http://online.onetcenter.org/.
- **The Encyclopedia of Associations:** This lists the addresses of professional and industry associations: http://library.dialog.com/bluesheets/html/bl0114.html.
- **Dun and Bradstreet and Standard and Poor's Register of Corporations:** Both documents offer information on individual companies and organizations. No website available for this resource. Check the reference section of your local library.
- **The Occupational Outlook Handbook:** This book addresses the projected needs for various occupations. It may help you choose a career or open the door to a new one. You can also view the handbook online at http://www.bls.gov/oco/home.htm.

Libraries also offer newspapers, trade journals, magazines, audio and video cassettes, and computer software packages that aid in career identification and planning. You also may find information on state training, employment, and apprenticeship programs as well as statistics regarding employment availability, economic climate, and cost of living. Your librarian can show you where to find these resources and how to use them.

Fraternal Military Associations and Veterans Services Organizations

Fraternal military associations and veterans services organizations are good sources of employment information, assistance, and services. Many provide their own job referral and registration services; others sponsor events such as job fairs to expose you to prospective employers. All provide networking opportunities to learn about job requirements and opportunities.

Your transition counselor can help you locate local Veteran Service Organization offices. In addition, lists of Military and Veteran Service Organizations can be found at http://www.military.com/benefits/resources/military-and-veteran-associations.

Industry Associations

Industry associations are a source of industry-specific information. You can learn what an industry is all about from material provided by these associations. You can also learn the jargon and get insight into how people in the industry think. You also may find salary ranges, qualification requirements, locations of jobs, and the names and addresses of individual companies through these associations. More information can be found at http://www.BLS.GOV.

THE "HIDDEN" JOB MARKET

More than 70 percent of the jobs in the United States are never advertised or listed with employment agencies. They are simply announced (and filled) by word of mouth. This is the "hidden" job market.

Following are some steps you can take to tap this market.

Step 1. Make a list. List everyone you know who might have a job lead for you—friends of the family, people you went to school or church with, clubs you belong to, and so on. Your friends who have recently left the military are likely to be a step ahead in the job-hunting process and may know who is hiring. Your colleagues may even have leads on job openings that would suit you perfectly.

Step 2. Send your resume. Send your resume to each person on your list and attach a cover letter explaining that you are looking for a job in your area of interest. Ask them to keep their eyes and ears open. They will help you; they are your friends.

Step 3. Make calls. Call each person to whom you send a resume and ask for his or her suggestions and guidance.

Step 4. Follow up. After you call, send each person a letter thanking him or her for the help. Call them periodically to see if they have heard of anything. Using this approach, you will have dozens of people helping you find the right job.

Step 5. Develop and maintain a network. The preceding steps have helped you develop a network. Networking is the most effective way to land the job you want.

ASSESSING YOUR SKILLS

To find a good civilian job, you need to clarify your skills. Skills assessment helps you answer the question "What do I do best?" A skills assessment can:

- Help you determine the types of jobs in which you are likely to excel (manager, mechanic, nurse, salesperson, teacher, etc.)

- Help you prepare a focused resume (one that only includes the aspects of your background that specifically relate to the job or career you are looking for)
- Help you answer job interview questions such as, "What do you like to do in your spare time?"

Translating military experience into civilian language is one of the most common stumbling blocks in the skills assessment process. One way to tackle this problem is to talk to friends who have already left the service. Ask them to tell you the dos and don'ts of what civilian employers want to hear. You should also consider attending workshops and seminars. Here's a good approach to assessing skills:

Step 1. Assignments. List the projects you have worked on, problems you have solved, situations you have helped clarify, and challenges you have met.

Step 2. Actions. List the actions you have taken to carry out these tasks.

Step 3. Results. List the results that your actions helped to achieve.

The skills that appear on these three lists should be incorporated into your resume and job interviews. Skill assessment for many servicemembers and their families requires assistance. The staffs at the transition assistance office and education center can provide that assistance.

For more assistance in skills assessment, go to http://www.dol.gov/vets/ and http://www.Military.com/careers.

RESUME WRITING FOR THE NEW MILLENNIUM

In the current job market, managers receive dozens of resumes. They do not have time to read lengthy listings of skills and complete life histories. For them, "less is more." Here are some tips on creating the most effective resumes:

- **Know the goal:** The goal of your resume should be to motivate employers to call you in for an interview. *Then* during your interview, you can discuss your background in as much detail as the employer desires.
- **Focus on skills:** Employers are more interested in what you *can* do than in what you want to do. Today's resume emphasizes skills, allowing the employer to compare your skills to those required for the job. (Remember, volunteering is considered real work experience, so don't forget to include appropriate volunteer work when preparing your resume.)

Writing a skills-oriented resume is easier after you have completed your skills assessment.

- **Don't fuss over format:** Don't get hung up on which type of resume to use—functional, chronological, or whatever. Most employers appreciate a job history that tells them what you did and when. You should also state your accomplishments. Again, performing a skills assessment will help you do this.
- **Create a "scannable" resume:** More and more, companies are scanning—rather than reading—resumes, especially if they get a great number of them. There are many books available to help you design a "scannable" resume. Research the company. Use their language where you can. There is no "perfect" resume, but you have to feel comfortable with the format you choose and be familiar with what you have written. The employer will use your resume as the basis for asking detailed questions during your interview.

Create a one-minute verbal resume that quickly highlights your experience and skills. Then, practice delivering your one-minute resume aloud until you're comfortable. This will give you the confidence to answer the "Tell me something about yourself . . ." interview question.

RESUME SAMPLES

Resume samples model the basic formats and principles of resume writing. Draw the best from each to help style your resume.

A template is a tool for crafting your resume. It isn't a fill-in-the-blank form, but it can help you get started. Ultimately, your resume should be unique to you and tailored to your particular strengths and experience.

The samples and templates below are organized by resume type. Choose the one that best matches your skills and qualifications.

Chronological Resume

- Emphasizes work history—where you worked and when
- Easy for employers to scan
- Often used by job seekers with steady work experience in their desired career field

Chronological Sample

Elizabeth DuShane
5555 Lakewood Road
Warren, OH 44481
(330) 555-5555
OBJECTIVE: Mechanical Engineer
ENGINEERING EXPERIENCE:
Industrial Engineer **1998–Current**
Tool Incorporated, Warren, OH

- Designed a plant layout for the shipping department
- Developed a multistep shipping process improvement plan

Design Engineer **1995–1998**
Mechanical Systems, Columbus, OH

- Developed a complete safety package for a robot loader
- Designed hydraulic double-stack lift
- Redesigned dairy open-style conveyor
- Trained ten engineers on AutoCAD Rev. 12
- Evaluated and purchased machine components

HVAC Engineer Assistant **1990–1995**
Engineering Consultants, Columbus, OH

- Prepared building and equipment bid specifications
- Evaluated HVAC equipment options
- Incorporated EPA and OSHA regulations into safety procedures
- Created working drawings on AutoCAD Rev. 1

MANAGEMENT EXPERIENCE:
Supervisor **1987–1990**
College Police Department, Cincinnati, OH

- Supervised more than fifty student security personnel
- Maintained security accounts and budgets
- Interviewed, hired, field trained, and conducted performance appraisals
- Prepared a twenty-five-page monthly report

Manager **1986–1988**
Building Management Co., Cincinnati, OH

- Maintained and performed building improvements

EDUCATION:
Bachelor of Science Degree: Mechanical Engineering 1986–1990
Minor: Engineering Management
University of Cincinnati, Cincinnati, OH
Coursework: Thermodynamics, Heat Transfer, HVAC,
Machine Design, Fluid Power, IBM Compatible
AutoCAD 12, FORTRAN, Lotus, and Quattro Pro

Chronological Template

First and Last Name
Address Line 1
Address Line 2
City, State Zip Code
(555) 555-5555
OBJECTIVE: Include objective here
WORK EXPERIENCE:
Job Title **Dates**
Employer, City, State

- List your responsibilities, accomplishments, and skills

Job Title **Dates**
Employer, City, State

- List your responsibilities, accomplishments, and skills

Job Title **Dates**
Employer, City, State

- List your responsibilities, accomplishments, and skills

EDUCATION:
LICENSES AND CERTIFICATIONS:
AWARDS:
PROFESSIONAL MEMBERSHIPS:

Functional Resume

- Groups work experience and skills by skill areas or job function
- Deemphasizes lack of experience in a field
- Useful for first-time job seekers, those reentering the workforce, and career changers

Functional Sample

Charles Lopez
1234 Circle Drive
Minneapolis, Minnesota 55404
(612) 555-5555

OBJECTIVE

Dependable, enthusiastic worker with more than ten years of experience seeking a Welding or Building Maintenance position. Self-starter, dedicated to achieving high-quality results.

SUMMARY OF QUALIFICATIONS

Welding—

Developed extensive experience in a wide variety of welding styles and positions including:

MIG	TIG	ARC	Heliarc
Oxyacetylene	Air ARC	Cutting and Gouging	Automatic Seam
Plasma Cutting	Underwater	Water Cooled Spot Welding	

Fabrication—

Skilled in layout and design of sheet metal and pipe. Developed extensive knowledge of sheet rollers and brakes. Followed Manufacturer's Operating Processes (MOP) to detail.

Equipment Operator—

Experienced forklift operator on various sizes and styles of forklifts. Skilled in the use of a variety of power tools and metal fabrication equipment, including: drills, drill press, edge planer, end mill, benders, power saws, sanders, and grinders.

Equipment Maintenance—

Performed general maintenance on welding equipment and production machinery. Maintained high production levels through onsite machine repairs and preventive maintenance.

Building Maintenance—

Acquired experience in general construction, including basic electrical repairs, carpentry, concrete, glass, spray and roller painting, plumbing, patching, and Sheetrock.

SUMMARY OF EXPERIENCE

Lead Welder

- Maintained strict performance, quality, and production standards
- Trained new employees and monitored their performance during probationary period

EDUCATION
Certificate:
Welding and Blueprint Reading
Minneapolis Community and Technical College—Minneapolis, MN
Diploma:
Central High School—Saint Paul, MN

Functional Template

FIRST AND LAST NAME
Address Line 1
Address Line 2
City, State Zip Code
(555) 555-5555
OBJECTIVE
Include objective here
SUMMARY OF QUALIFICATIONS
Qualification—
Short summary of skills, accomplishments, or responsibilities for this specific qualification.
Qualification—
Short summary of skills, accomplishments, or responsibilities for this specific qualification.
Qualification—
Short summary of skills, accomplishments, or responsibilities for this specific qualification.
SUMMARY OF EXPERIENCE
Job Title (can include employer and/or dates)

* Main responsibilities or accomplishments

Job Title (can include employer and/or dates)

* Main responsibilities or accomplishments

EDUCATION
LICENSES AND CERTIFICATIONS
AWARDS OR PROFESSIONAL MEMBERSHIPS

Combination Resume

* Combines the knowledge, skills, and abilities as highlighted in a functional resume with a shorter, chronological work summary

- Easily incorporates other experiences, like volunteering or internships
- Often used by job seekers with a varied employment history and by career changers

Combination Sample

SHIRLEY ADAMS
1234 56th Avenue
Apartment #203
Tucson, AZ 85725
(520) 555-5555
SUMMARY
Dependable **General Office Worker** with more than ten years of transferable experience. Proven clerical, customer service, and communication skills in a variety of settings. Upbeat, positive attitude with a history of producing quality results and satisfied customers. Computer literate.
SELECTED SKILLS
General Office

- Organized and implemented group activities in an efficient manner
- Scheduled appointments and assured timely arrival
- Maintained accurate financial records and paid all invoices on time
- Answered phones and took accurate messages
- Prepared reports and created documents using MS Word and WordPerfect
- Located desired information using the Internet

Customer Service

- Welcomed customers and visitors in a friendly and courteous manner
- Provided customers/clients with desired information in a timely manner
- Listened, calmed, and assisted customers with concerns
- Established friendly and lasting relationships

Communication

- Used Internet e-mail as an effective communication tool
- Answered phones in a courteous and professional manner
- Established rapport with diverse individuals and groups
- Demonstrated ability to express ideas in a team environment and influence action

RELATED VOLUNTEER EXPERIENCE

General Office Volunteer	Salvation Army—Tucson, AZ	5 Years
Elected Secretary	Parent Teachers Association (ISD 01)—Tucson, AZ	5 Years
Event Coordinator	Neighborhood Involvement Program—Phoenix, AZ	3 Years
Group/Activities Leader	Girl Scouts of America— Phoenix, AZ	4 Years
Family Manager	Self-employed—Tucson, AZ	7 Years

EDUCATION
GED: Maricopa County Action Program, Phoenix, AZ

Combination Template

First and Last Name
Address Line 1
Address Line 2
City, State Zip Code
(555) 555-5555
SUMMARY OR OBJECTIVE
Include employment objective and/or summary of qualifications here.
SUMMARY OF SKILLS AND/OR EXPERIENCE
Skill or Experience

- Description
- Description

Skill or Experience

- Description
- Description

Skill or Experience

- Description
- Description

EMPLOYMENT HISTORY
Job Title

Employer   City, State   Dates

Job Title

Employer   City, State   Dates

EDUCATION
Type of Award or Degree:
Degree or Certification Name (GPA if relevant)
Minor if applicable
School Name—City, State
LICENSES
PROFESSIONAL MEMBERSHIPS OR ORGANIZATIONS

Text Format

- A plain-text version of a typical resume
- Allows a computer to scan for certain terms and keywords more effectively

Text Format Sample

IRMA PARKER
Phone: (763) 555-5555
Email: jobhunter@success.com

OBJECTIVE: Registered Medical Laboratory Technician requiring extensive experience with success in pediatrics and at a trauma emergency hospital.

SUMMARY OF SKILLS AND EXPERIENCE

LAB TECHNICIAN—Highly skilled lab technologist with experience serving ER, Urgent Care, and Stab-Room Trauma Unit. Processed cultures in microbiology, gram stains, urinalysis, and various manual tests.

PHLEBOTOMY—Inpatient and outpatient, preop and postop, blood draws. Recognized for exceptional skill in serving hard-to-draw patients and children.

INSTRUMENT MAINTENANCE—Skilled in troubleshooting and maintenance of technical equipment.

TEACHING—Responsible for training staff on equipment operation and procedures.

QUALITY CONTROL—Maintained high quality standards with an emphasis on accuracy. Maximized performance through organization, equipment testing, and procedures development.

EMPLOYMENT HISTORY

MEDICAL LABORATORY TECHNICIAN, ASCP
May 1995 to September 2006 Hennepin County Medical Center
*Increased lab efficiency through improved processing procedures, development of technical equipment, lab layout, and design.
*Maintained peak lab performance. Blood samples from Stab-Room Trauma Unit had to be accurately processed within two minutes!
*Assisted medical staff in the research and development of "Kiss of Life" mask used in respiratory emergency care.

PHLEBOTOMIST
August 1989 to March 1995 Minneapolis Children's Medical Center

EDUCATION

CERTIFIED: American Society of Clinical Pathologists
MEDICAL LABORATORY TECHNICIAN (GPA 3.5)
College of St. Catherine 1987
BIOLOGY/CHEMISTRY (117 credits)
Mankato State University 1985

Source: Creative Job Search, a publication of the Minnesota Department of Employment and Economic Development.

WORKSHOPS HELP SEPARATEES "TAP" INTO GOOD JOBS

The Department of Labor–sponsored Transition Assistance Program Employment Workshops are sponsored in conjunction with the installation transition assistance staffs. The DoL TAP Employment Workshops normally run two-and-a-half days. However, some local installations may combine this workshop with other specialty workshops. During your first visit to the transition assistance office or with your command career counselor, you should ask to be scheduled to attend the next available workshop (your spouse should attend if space is available). You should plan to attend employment workshops at least 180 days prior to separation. TAP addresses such useful subjects as the following:

• Employment and training opportunities
• Labor market information

- Civilian workplace requirements
- Resume, application, and standard forms preparation
- Job analysis, job search, and interviewing techniques
- Assistance programs offered by federal, state, local, military, and veterans' groups
- Procedures for obtaining verification of job skills and experience
- Obtaining loans and assistance for starting a small business
- Analysis of the area where you wish to relocate, including local employment opportunities, the local labor market, and the cost of living (housing, child care, education, medical and dental care, etc.)

At the TAP workshops, you will receive a participant manual. Among other valuable information, this manual contains points of contact around the nation for many of the services you will need after your separation.

Note: Not all installations and bases offer the Department of Labor TAP Employment Workshop. If the workshops are not available at your installation or base, the transition counselor will refer you to other sources where similar information is available.

MILITARY EXPERIENCE AND TRAINING HELP YOU WIN THAT JOB

Verification of your military experience and training is useful in preparing your resume and establishing your capabilities with prospective employers. Verification is also helpful if you are applying to a college or vocational institution. These institutions want information on your military training and experience as well as how this might relate to the civilian world.

As a servicemember, you have had numerous training and job experiences, perhaps too many to recall easily and include on a job or college application. Fortunately, the military has made your life a little easier in this regard. The DD Form 2586, Verification of Military Experience and Training, is created from your automated records on file. It lists your military job experience and training history, recommended college credit information, and civilian equivalent job titles. This document is designed to help you, but it is not a resume!

Obtain Your Verification of Military Experience and Training Document

To get your verification document, go to the VMET website at http://www .dmdc.osd.mil/vmet. All separating military personnel can electronically download and print their VMET document and personal cover letter from your military service from the VMET website. Simply click the "Request Document" and "Request Cover Letter" tabs and print each of these documents after they are downloaded.

You can get your verification document online as long as you have a current DoD Common Access Card (CAC) or have a current DFAS myPay PIN; however, you should retrieve it within 120 days prior to your separation. If you have problems getting your VMET and need assistance, check with your local transition counselor.

Once You Receive Your Verification Document

Identify the items that relate to the type of work or education you are pursuing and include them in your resume. If there are problems with information listed on the form, follow the guidance indicated below for your respective service:

- Army: Review and follow the guidance provided by the Frequently Asked Questions (FAQs) listed on the VMET website.
- Air Force: Follow the instructions in the verification document cover letter or contact your transition counselor.
- Navy: Contact your command career counselor or review and follow the guidance provided by the Frequently Asked Questions (FAQs) listed on the VMET website.
- Marine Corps: Follow the instructions in the verification document cover letter. If you need further assistance, contact your administrative office.

RETURNING TO PREVIOUS EMPLOYMENT

If you left a civilian job to fulfill Reserve or National Guard duty, you are entitled to return to the job after demobilization if you have:

- given advance notice of military service to your employer (except when precluded by military necessity);
- not exceeded five years cumulative absence from the civilian job (with some exceptions);
- submitted a timely application for reemployment; and
- not received a dishonorable or other punitive discharge.

The Uniformed Services Employment and Reemployment Rights Act (USERRA) prohibits employers from denying any benefit of employment due to military service and protects employee rights when reclaiming civilian employment after an absence due to military service or training. These rights include the following:

- Upon completion of military service, employers must provide prompt re-employment. Your right to return to your job is protected by federal law.
- Individuals returning from military service are entitled to the seniority and seniority-based benefits held prior to military service and are also entitled to any additional seniority and seniority-based benefits that would have accrued had they not been called to active duty.
- You are entitled to required retraining, employer-provided health care plans, and employer-provided pension plans.
- If you can no longer perform the job, your employer must use reasonable efforts to help you upgrade or update your skills.
- You are entitled to special protection against discharge, except for cause.

Failure to report to work or make timely application to return to work does not automatically result in the loss of reemployment rights. However, it does subject you to the rules of conduct, policies, and general practices established by your employer, which may result in loss of USERRA protections.

If you believe that your rights under USERRA have been violated, there are options for resolving the issue:

- Speak directly with the employer. More often than not, discussions with employers can lead to acceptable solutions.
- Speak with your unit commander. Unit commanders may be able to discuss or articulate the issue with the employer in a different manner or they may be able to suggest compromises and alternatives.
- If the first two options are not successful, contact Employer Support for the Guard and Reserve (ESGR). ESGR is a DoD organization that promotes cooperation between Guard and Reserve component members and their employers.

DOD JOB SEARCH

The Department of Defense (DoD) and the Department of Labor activated a new veterans and servicemember website called DoD Job Search. This website features job announcements, resume writing, and referral systems geared to transitioning military personnel and their spouses, DoD federal civilian employees and their spouses, and the spouses of relocating active-duty members. There are over one million jobs available on this website. Check out the website at http://www.dod.jobsearch.org for additional information and assistance.

DOD TRANSPORTAL

DoD has created a web portal for military transitioners. This website is sponsored by the Department of Defense and is designed specifically to assist servicemembers and their spouses leaving active duty. While DoD Transportal contains valuable information and resources, you should use this site as part of a comprehensive program of transition and employment assistance. The best place to start is your installation's transition assistance office. The DoD Transportal is another tool to assist you in your transition back into the civilian community. You can access this website at http://www.dodtransportal .org. This website has three features that can be accessed using the buttons on the left of the web page screen:

- **Transition Assistance:** This feature is a brief overview of the DoD Transition Assistance Program. Here you will find a general discussion of all benefits and services available to you.
- **At Your Service:** This feature provides the locations and phone numbers of all transition assistance offices as well as links to transition assistance–related websites.
- **Your Next Career:** This feature provides:
  - Getting ready: A minicourse on conducting a successful job search campaign, including instructions on creating winning resumes.
  - Tips on using the Internet: A minicourse on using the Internet to find a job, including instructions on creating electronic resumes and avoiding Internet scams.
  - Internet career links: Links to the best job search websites on the net.
  - Websites with up to 1.5 million job listings.
  - Websites where you can post your resumes for employers to view.
  - Links to state job search websites.
  - Corporate recruiting websites: Links to recruiting websites operated by Fortune 500 companies.
  - Links to one hundred corporate recruiting sites selected among the Fortune 500 companies.
  - Suggested reading: A list of books that you can use as job search resources.

PUBLIC AND COMMUNITY
SERVICE (PACS) REGISTRY PROGRAM

The 1993 National Defense Authorization Act, P. L. 102-484 [10 USC, 1143 a(c)], requires the Secretary of Defense to maintain a registry of public and community service organizations. Servicemembers selecting early retirement under the Temporary Early Retirement Act (TERA) are registered on the Public and Community Service Personnel Registry prior to release from active duty. Servicemembers looking for employment in the public and community service arena and including those retiring under TERA can access the PACS Organization Registry to see which organizations have registered for the purpose of hiring separating military personnel in public and community service jobs. In addition, servicemembers with approved retirement under TERA earn additional credit toward full retirement at age sixty-two by working in a public or community service job. Employers who wish to advertise job openings in the public and community service arena on the DoD Operation Transition Bulletin Board (TBB) at http://www.dmdc.osd.mil/ot will complete the DD Form 2581, Operation Transition Employer Registration, and DD Form 2581-1, Public and Community Service Organization Validation. Then, the organization will be included in the Operation Transition employer database and also be listed on the PACS organization registry. Completing the DD forms is a requirement for posting employment opportunities (want ads) on the TBB.

PACS employers hiring servicemembers who retired under the TERA program are required to complete both DD Forms 2581 and 2581-1. TERA retirees who are employed by approved PACS organizations during their enhanced retirement qualification period (ERQP) enables them to earn additional retirement credit and enhanced retirement pay beginning at age sixty-two. Retirees interested in gaining the additional credit toward full retirement can go to the TBB to look for PACS employment opportunities as well as see a list of approved PACS organizations. Please refer to the website at http://www.dmdc.osd.mil/ot.

The Public and Community Service organizational registry program is just another tool separating servicemembers can use to get their names in front of nonprofit, public, and community service organizations such as schools, hospitals, law enforcement agencies, social service agencies, and many more for employment opportunities.

TRANSITION BULLETIN BOARD (TBB)

Searching through the employment section of the newspaper is not the only way to find work. Internet websites provide a quick and easy way to find the latest job openings and up-to-the-minute information useful to your job search. DoD's Transition Bulletin Board lists jobs as well as registered Public and Community Service (PACS) organizations and a list of business opportunities. Search ads are listed by job type and/or location; jobs are located both stateside and overseas. In addition, individuals retiring under the Temporary Early Retirement Authority (TERA) can fulfill the mandatory requirement to register for Public and Community Service (PACS) online at the TBB. Simply log on to the Operation Transition/TBB website and click "TERA Individual Registration for PACS."

Accessing the TBB

Your access to this resource is through any computer having Internet access. Access TBB from your home, office, library, or your transition assistance office. You can perform your own automated job search tailored to your individual needs.

How to Use the TBB

Once you find a position that interests you, pursue the opportunity by following the employer's instructions listed in the TBB ad. Call or write the employer directly and send a copy of your full resume. To access the TBB, go to http://www.dmdc.osd.mil/ot. Click "Login as a Job Seeker." Enter your Social Security Number, last name, and date of birth and click "Login." At the moment you click "Login," the information entered is encrypted, so it is protected as it is transmitted over the Internet. Your information is matched against up-to-date personnel information at the Department of Defense.

TROOPS-TO-TEACHERS PROGRAM

Background: Troops to Teachers (TTT) was established in 1994 as a Department of Defense program. The National Defense Authorization Act for fiscal year 2000 transferred the responsibility for program oversight and funding to the U.S. Department of Education, but continued operation is by the Department of Defense.

The No Child Left Behind Act provides for the continuation of TTT as a teacher recruitment program. TTT is managed by the Defense Activity for Nontraditional Education Support (DANTES), Pensacola, Florida.

Goals and Objectives: Reflecting the focus of the No Child Left Behind Act, the primary objective of TTT is to help recruit quality teachers for schools that serve students from low-income families throughout America. TTT helps relieve teacher shortages, especially in math, science, special education, and other critical subject areas and assists military personnel in making successful transitions to second careers in teaching.

Function: TTT assists eligible military personnel to transition to a new career as public school teachers in targeted schools. A network of state TTT offices has been established to provide participants with counseling and assistance regarding certification requirements, routes to state certification, and employment leads. Pending annual appropriation of funds, financial assistance is available to eligible individuals as stipends up to $5,000 to help pay for teacher certification costs or as bonuses of $10,000 to teach in schools serving a high percentage of students from low-income families. Participants who accept the stipend or bonus must agree to teach for three years in targeted schools in accordance with the authorizing legislation. The TTT link (http://www.proudtoserveagain.com) leads to the home page, which provides information and resource links, including links to state Departments of Education, state certification offices, model resumes, programs leading to teacher certification, and job listing sites in public education. An Internet Referral System has been established to enable participants to search for job vacancies online and post resumes for view by school districts searching for teachers. A "Mentor Connection" site provides access to TTT participants who have made the transition to teaching and are available to respond to questions from prospective teachers.

Eligibility: Military personnel within several years of retirement are encouraged to register with Troops to Teachers. Counseling and guidance is available to help individuals assess academic background, identify programs that will lead to state teacher certification, and identify potential employment opportunities.

Financial Assistance: Individuals eligible for immediate financial assistance are:

- Retired military personnel, Active and Reserve
- Personnel within one year of retirement
- Active duty personnel separating with six years active duty and joining a Selected Reserve component unit
- Current Reserve component members with ten+ years of active and/or Selected Reserve service creditable toward retirement
- Veterans separated due to a service-connected disability

Educational Requirements: Those interested in elementary or secondary teaching positions must have a bachelor's degree from an accredited college. Individuals who do not have a baccalaureate degree but have experience in a vocational/technical field may also submit an application. There is also a growing need for teachers with backgrounds in areas such as electronics, construction trades, computer technology, health services, food services, and other vocational/technical fields.

Self-Determination Eligibility Guide: A guide to determining eligibility is available at http://www.proudtoserveagain.com.

Registration: Registration forms may be downloaded from the Troops to Teachers link at http://www.proudtoserveagain.com.

Current Information: The Troops to Teachers website is updated as new or revised information becomes available. The website also provides a standard PowerPoint briefing and other promotional materials.

REEMPLOYMENT

Under certain circumstances, veterans have the right to return to their preservice jobs after discharge or release from active duty. Your former employer must rehire you if you meet all of the following requirements:

- You must have left other-than-temporary employment to enter military service; *AND*
- You must have served in the armed forces (either voluntarily or involuntarily) no more than five years, unless at the request of and for the convenience of the government; *AND*
- You must have been discharged or released under honorable conditions; *AND*
- You must still be qualified to perform the duties of the job. If you became disabled while in military service, you must be able to perform some other job in your employer's organization (with comparable seniority, status, and pay).

Contact the U.S. Department of Labor, Veterans' Employment and Training Service (VETS), for assistance under the Uniformed Services Employment and Reemployment Rights Act of 1994. A complete list of VETS state directors is available online at http://www.dol.gov/vets/.

Your reemployment rights also protect you against being discharged by your employer without cause for one year (six months in the case of a reservist or national Guard member returning from training).

PRIVATE EMPLOYMENT AGENCIES

Overall, private employment agencies are responsible for approximately 3 to 5 percent of all hires nationally. If your skills and experience match those fields in which the agency specializes, you can expect some assistance. For example, a separatee with computing skills should seek an agency specializing in computer-related placements.

Most private employment agencies are reputable. They possess an extensive list of employers, and they charge those employers a fee for their services. Before registering with a private agency, confirm that all fees will be paid by the employer, and not by you.

FINDING FEDERAL EMPLOYMENT OPPORTUNITIES

Opportunities for employment with the U.S. government are available in all parts of the nation as well as overseas. Here are some ways to find out about different types of federal job listings.

- **Government jobs near you:** Openings may be available at the installation from which you are separating. You can find out about these from your local civilian personnel office.
- **Opportunities overseas:** To assist you in finding out about federal job opportunities elsewhere in the world, the Office of Personnel Management (OPM) maintains federal job information/testing offices in each state. A listing of these offices is located on the Transition Bulletin Board.
- You can view federal employment opportunities online at http://www.usajobs.com. You can also call OPM at 912-757-3000. Call the OPM Computer Bulletin Board at 912-757-3100.

Unique positions: OPM maintains an automated job referral system for hard-to-fill jobs. This system, to be expanded in the future, presently focuses on those positions requiring special skills. Applicants may register directly with the OPM computer center in Macon, Georgia. Write to:
Office of Personnel Management
Staffing Service Center
Macon, Georgia 31297

Other Federal Employment Websites:
Fed World: http://www.fedworld.gov
Federal Employment Portal: http://www.opm.gov
DoD Civilian Employment: http://www.go-defense.com
Army Civilian Personnel Online: http://www.cpol.army.mil/

WORKING FOR THE DOD

The Department of Defense (DoD) welcomes veterans to join the DoD civilian workforce and continue serving the defense mission! The DoD is the nation's number-one employer of veterans, offering nearly seven hundred challenging occupations.

As a DoD civilian, you can serve with the Army, Navy, Air Force, Marines, or any one of the many other defense agencies. Career opportunities exist in research laboratories, manufacturing facilities, office complexes, hospitals, military bases, and schools in almost every major population center in the United States and in numerous countries throughout the world.

The Department offers preference in employment to eligible veterans along with world-class benefits and many opportunities for personal and professional growth, travel, and advancement.

You have served our nation with honor and distinction. Now, the Department of Defense invites you to become part of the Department's rich and proud tradition of civilian service.

goDefense.com

The Department of Defense (DoD) website, http://www.goDefense.com, offers veteran job seekers assistance with pursuing DoD civilian careers by providing online career opportunity information and resources. In addition, Recruitment Assistance Division (RAD) career counselors are available Monday through Friday, 7:00 a.m. to 5:00 p.m. EST to provide assistance with completing required forms and advisory guidance on how to respond to vacancy announcements. For more information visit http://www.goDefense.com or call toll free 1-888-DOD4USA (1-888-363-4872), TTY for Deaf/Hard of Hearing 703-696-5436, or send request by e-mail to daao@cpms.osd.mil.

APPLYING FOR FEDERAL JOBS

You apply for most federal jobs by preparing and submitting the documents requested in the federal job announcement. If you have any questions, contact the civilian personnel office and/or the point of contact listed on the job announcement. If you believe your veterans' preference rights have been violated when applying for federal jobs, contact the U.S. Department of Labor, Veterans Employment and Training Service for assistance under the Veterans Employment Opportunities Act of 1998. A complete list of VETS state directors is available online at http://www.dol.gov/dol.vets.

EMPLOYMENT PREFERENCES

Involuntarily and Certain Voluntarily Separated Members: Under Chapter 58, Section 1143 (d) of Title 10, U.S. Code, eligibility applies to members of the armed forces and their dependents who were on active duty on September 30, 1990, and who were involuntarily separated under honorable conditions on or after October 1, 1990. Preference-eligible veterans shall be identified by possession of a DD Form 1173, Uniformed Services Identification and Privilege Card, overstamped with "TA."

HOW FEDERAL JOBS ARE FILLED

Many federal agencies fill their jobs like private industry does by allowing applicants to contact the agency directly for additional job information and in understanding the application process. Most federal agencies will accept the Optional Application for Federal Employment, Form OF-612, from individuals applying for federal employment. As an applicant you may submit the OF-612 or a resume.

While the process may be similar to that in private industry, there are still significant differences due to the many laws, executive orders, and regulations that govern federal employment.

Competitive, Excepted, and Senior Executive Service

Federal jobs in the executive branch fall into three categories: 1) those that are in the *competitive service*, 2) those that are in the *excepted service*, and 3) those that are in the *senior executive service*.

Competitive service jobs are under OPM's jurisdiction and are subject to the civil service laws passed by Congress to ensure that applicants and employees receive fair and equal treatment in the hiring process. These laws give selecting officials broad authority to review more than one applicant source before determining the best-qualified candidate based on job-related criteria. A basic principle of federal employment is that all candidates must meet the qualification requirements for the position for which they receive an appointment.

Excepted service positions are excepted by law, by executive order, or by action of OPM placing a position or group of positions in excepted service Schedules A, B, or C. For example, certain entire agencies such as the Postal Service and the Central Intelligence Agency are excepted by law. In other cases, certain jobs or classes of jobs in an agency are excepted by OPM. This includes positions such as attorneys, chaplains, student trainees, and others.

Note: The excepted service is subject to the provisions of veterans' preference unless otherwise exempted. Some federal agencies such as the Central Intelligence Agency (CIA) have only excepted service positions. In other instances, certain organizations within an agency or even specific jobs may be excepted from civil service procedures.

The Senior Executive Service (SES) was established by Title IV of the Civil Service Reform Act (CSRA) of 1978. The SES was set up as a "third" service, completely separate from the competitive and excepted services. Top management positions are joined into a unified and distinct personnel system that provides for considerable agency authority and flexibility. SES positions are classified above GS-15 or equivalent. All SES vacancies are advertised on OPM's USAJOBS. From this site, you may download announcements for vacancies of interest to you. Veterans do not receive hiring preference for SES positions because 5 USC 2108(3), which defines the term *preference eligible*, provides that this term does not include applicants for, or members of, the Senior Executive Service.

Vacancy Announcements

A posted vacancy announcement is an agency's decision to seek qualified candidates for a particular vacancy. The agency is under no obligation to make a selection. In some instances, an agency may cancel the posting and choose to reannounce the vacancy later.

Sources of Eligibles

In filling competitive service jobs, agencies can generally choose from among four groups of candidates:

1. A *competitive list of eligibles* administered by OPM or by an agency under OPM's direction. This list consists of applicants who have applied and met the qualification requirements for a specific vacancy announcement. It is the most common method of entry for new employees.
2. A list of eligibles who have *civil service status* consists of applicants who are eligible for noncompetitive movement within the competitive service because they either now are or were serving under career-type appointments in the competitive service. These individuals are selected under agency *merit promotion procedures and can receive an appointment* by promotion, reassignment, transfer, or reinstatement.
3. A list of eligibles who qualify for a special *noncompetitive appointing authority* established by law or executive order. Examples of special noncompetitive appointing authorities include the Veterans Recruitment Appointment (VRA) and Peace Corps.
4. Agencies in the competitive service are required by law and OPM regulation to post vacancies with OPM whenever they are seeking candidates from outside their own workforce for positions lasting more than 120 days. (*Agency*, in this context, means the parent agency—i.e., Treasury, not the Internal Revenue Service.) These vacancies are posted on OPM's USAJOBS.

If you are interested in excepted service positions and do not find any posted on USAJOBS, you should contact the respective federal agency directly. The U.S. Office of Personnel Management does not provide application forms or information on jobs in the excepted service.

Preference applies to jobs graded at NF-3 and below and to positions paid at hourly rates. Preference applies to any job that is open to competition in accordance with merit staffing practices. Spouse preference may be used once for each permanent relocation of the military sponsor. The spouse must have been married to the military sponsor before relocation to the duty station.

Military Spouses: Under DoD Instruction 1404.12, Employment of Spouses of Active Duty Military Members Stationed Worldwide, eligibility applies to spouses of active duty military members of the armed forces. Under this basic policy, preferences for military spouses are the same as the involuntarily and certain voluntarily separated members, except that military spouse preference has priority over that preference.

Visit the DoD's Spouse Career Center at http://www.military.com/spouse to learn more about military spouse employment preferences.

Family Members in Foreign Areas: In accordance with DoD Instruction 1400.23 and DoD 1402.2-M, Chapter VII, family members of active duty military members and civilian employees stationed in foreign areas are eligible for job placement. Basic policy allows preference for all NAF jobs. Preferences apply when not at variance with the Status of Forces Agreements, country-to-country agreements, treaties, or as prescribed by DoD Instruction 1400.23.

FEDERAL JOBS THROUGH THE NONAPPROPRIATED FUND AND THE VETERANS READJUSTMENT ACT

Because of your military service, you may have an advantage over others when applying for federal employment. Congress provided this advantage by enacting veterans' hiring preference laws. These laws do *not* imply guaranteed placement of a veteran in every federal job. The veterans' hiring preference laws are not applicable to Nonappropriated Fund (NAF) employment. Veterans applying for NAF jobs may be given preference at the time of hire only.

If you are a Vietnam or post–Vietnam-era veteran: The Veterans Readjustment Appointment (VRA) program provides special employment opportunities and job training to veterans who were honorably discharged and who served for more than 180 days on active duty.

- If you are an eligible involuntary separatee, you and your family members are authorized a one-time employment preference for NAF positions you are qualified to perform. For details, ask your installation's transition office to refer you to the local NAF personnel office.

- Eligible Vietnam-era veterans qualify for appointments under Veterans Readjustment Appointment (VRA) until ten years after their last discharge or separation from active duty or until December 31, 1995, whichever is later.
- Eligible post–Vietnam-era veterans qualify for ten years after the date of discharge or release from active duty or until December 31, 1999, whichever is later.
- Eligible veterans with a service-connected disability of 30 percent or more have no time limit.

For information about specific VRA job opportunities, contact the personnel office at the federal agency where you would like to work.

Veterans Recruitment Appointment (VRA): The VRA is a special authority by which agencies may, if they wish, appoint an eligible veteran without competition. The candidate does not have to be on an eligibility list but must meet the basic qualification requirements for the position. The VRA is a convenient method of appointment for both the agency and the veteran. However, use of the authority is entirely discretionary, and no one is entitled to a VRA appointment.

VRA appointees initially are hired for a two-year period. Successful completion of the two-year VRA appointment leads to a permanent civil service appointment. (Please note, however, that a veteran may be employed without competition on a temporary or term appointment based on VRA eligibility. Such an appointment is not a VRA appointment and does not lead to conversion to a permanent position.)

Eligibility Requirements

The following individuals are eligible for a VRA appointment:

- Disabled veterans;
- Veterans who served on active duty in the armed forces during a war declared by Congress or in a campaign or expedition for which a campaign badge has been authorized;
- Veterans who, while serving on active duty in the armed forces, participated in a military operation for which the Armed Forces Service Medal was awarded; *AND*
- Veterans separated from active duty within the past three years.

There is no minimum service requirement, but the individual must have served on *active duty*, not active duty for training.

The Veterans' Preference Point System for Federal Employment

A "point system" is used to determine veterans' hiring preference:

- **Five-point preference:** Basically, five points are given to honorably separated veterans who have served more than 180 consecutive days of active duty before October 14, 1976 (including service during training under the six-month Reserve or National Guard programs), or during any war or expedition for which a campaign badge has been authorized (such as Desert Shield/Storm) and served continuously for twenty-four months or the full period called or ordered to active duty (including for training). Retired members of the Armed Forces above the rank of major or lieutenant commander are no longer eligible for the five-point preference. Their preference is contingent upon a disability.
- **Ten-point preference:** Ten points are given to disabled veterans and veterans who are awarded the Purple Heart and are honorably separated.

The point system program is administered by OPM. The VA issues letters to OPM indicating the degree of disability for veterans' preference purposes. The more points you have, the closer you get to the front of the line for possible job consideration with the federal government.

Hiring preference is not limited to veterans alone. It is also granted to the spouse of an unemployable disabled veteran, the unmarried widow or widower of a veteran, or the mother of a deceased or disabled veteran. Any federal agency personnel officer can give you more information on the point system. Visit the USAJOBS website at http://jobsearch.usajobs.opm.gov/veteranscenter/ to learn more about veteran employment opportunities

PRIORITY AT STATE EMPLOYMENT OFFICES

As a veteran, you receive special consideration and priority for referral, testing, and counseling from your state employment office. Your state employment office can provide many additional services, as noted below.

Veterans Employment and Training Service Office: There is at least one Veterans Employment and Training Service Office in every state (http://www.dol.gov/vets/aboutvets/contacts/main.htm). Veterans' employment representatives may also be found at local employment offices with large numbers of veteran job applicants. Their job is to monitor and oversee veterans' employment services, administer veterans' training programs, and protect the reemployment rights of veterans. They will assist you with any employment problem you may have.

Make sure you take DD Form 214, Certificate of Release or Discharge from Active Duty (certified copy), with you for your first appointment with the state employment office.

DoD Job Search: This job bank, sponsored by the Department of Defense and the Department of Labor, lists millions of jobs across the nation that are not readily filled. Check out the website at http://www.dod.jobsearch.org for further detail and assistance.

Training opportunities: State employment offices can offer you seminars on subjects such as resume writing, interviewing skills, and career changes; information on vocational training opportunities; and proficiency tests in typing and shorthand for positions requiring such certification.

Information: At your state employment office, you will find data on state training, employment, and apprenticeship programs and statistics regarding employment availability, economic climate, and cost of living. Some offices even have extensive information about the things you should know before moving to the state.

To locate state employment offices, visit http://www.naswa.org/links.cfm.

To locate the local CareerOneStop Center, visit http://www.dol.gov/vets/.

FAMILY MEMBERS GET JOB ASSISTANCE, TOO

Family members can take advantage of many of the outplacement services offered to transitioning servicemembers. Most of these services are coordinated from the transition assistance office at your installation. Family members can get help in developing their own Individual Transition Plans; they also have access to the following employment services:

Department of Labor TAP Employment Workshops: These two-and-a-half day Department of Labor–sponsored workshops are coordinated through the transition assistance and ACAP Offices and can help you with your employment objectives before you leave the military. Contact your Transition/ACAP Office or command career counselor immediately to get scheduled for an appointment. Spouses are highly encouraged to attend the DoL Employment Workshop in order to prepare themselves for the transition from an active duty lifestyle to a civilian one.

TBB: The Transition Bulletin Board is an electronic listing of job vacancies and transition information, located at http://www.dmdc.osd.mil/ot.

Career counseling: The transition assistance office will provide individual job/career development counseling, assist in assessing employment skills, and identify employment opportunities.

Job training: These services include workshops and seminars on enhancing job search skills; goal setting; preparing federal employment applications and resumes; interviewing techniques; and occupational skills training for family members.

Job banks: National job banks and local job banks provide information and referral on temporary, permanent, part-time, full-time, and volunteer positions in both the federal and private sectors. In addition, family members of separating personnel can receive a one-time priority for nonappropriated funds jobs in the federal government. Ask your local civilian personnel office for details.

WHERE TO LOOK FOR GREAT JOBS

Several places offer you the help you will need to find the job that's right for you. Check out these websites for more information:

www.careeronestop.org
www.bls.gov
http://www.dol.gov/vets/www.doleta.gov/programs
http://www.doleta.gov/

Military-Friendly Job Banks

- Veteran's Employment Resources provides multiple tools and valuable resources for all U.S. veterans—job opportunities, forms, benefits, and program information as well as training assistance for private sector employment.
- Troops to Teachers helps military personnel begin new careers in education.
- Helmets to Hardhats matches military skills to civilian jobs.
- Calendar and location of military-friendly job fairs.
- USAJobs.com has federal jobs and employment information.
- GoDefense.com is a site for civilians and veterans working for the National Defense Department.
- MilitaryConnection.com's Virtual Job Fair provides links to government and private companies recruiting veterans.

4

The Entrepreneurial Spirit

This chapter is divided into sections. The first section contains information provided by the U.S. Small Business Administration, which explains federal programs, loans, and federal contacting information. The National Veterans Business Development Corporation is a federally chartered independent 501(c)(3) nonprofit organization designed to assist veterans in starting or growing small businesses. These resources are tools created specifically to support members of the National Guard and Reserve with entrepreneurship, including fully mentored access programs and a guide to prepare businesses for deployment.

U.S. SMALL BUSINESS ADMINISTRATION

Since 1953, the U.S. Small Business Administration has helped veterans start, manage, and grow small businesses. Today, the SBA provides specific programs for veterans, service-disabled veterans, and Reserve and National Guard members, and they offer a full range of entrepreneurial support programs to every American, including veterans. Their job is to help you successfully transition from the world's finest warrior to the world's finest small business owner.

On August 17, 1999, Congress passed Public Law 106-50, The Veterans Entrepreneurship and Small Business Development Act of 1999. This law established the SBA Office of Veterans Business Development, under the guidance and direction of the Associate Administrator for Veterans Business Development, to conduct comprehensive outreach, to be the source of policy and program development, to initiate and implement the Administration, and to act as an Ombudsman for full consideration of veterans within the Administration.

In addition, this law created the National Veterans Business Development Corporation, set goals for federal procurement for service-disabled veterans and veterans, established the Military Reservists Economic Injury Disaster Loan, initiated new research into the success of veterans in small business, and brought focus to veterans in the full range of SBA capital, entrepreneurial, and government contracting programs.

SBA has established Veterans Business Outreach Centers, special loans and surety bonding programs for veterans and Reservists, government procurement programs for veterans, Veterans Business Development Officers stationed in every SBA District Office, special District Office outreach efforts, and counseling and training at more than 1,500 small business centers and SCORE chapters and online.

SPECIAL LOCALIZED PROGRAMS

Special local initiatives target veterans, service-disabled veterans, and Reserve and Guard members. Online and printed Business Planning Guides are available, including *Balancing Business and Deployment* for self-employed Reserve and Guard to prepare for mobilization and *Getting Veterans Back to Business* to assist in restarting or reestablishing your business upon return from active duty. These manuals include an interactive CD with a wealth of information on preparing your business and your employees for your absence, reestablishing a small business upon return from Title 10 activation, and information on various business assistance resources available to assist you. The CDs also contain information on loans, government procurement, and the full range of SBA's assistance to any veteran.

To learn more about the services and assistance SBA offers to veterans, service-disabled veterans, and Reservists, please explore the links below, or follow-up at the local district offices and programs located in or near the community you return home to.

THE PATRIOT EXPRESS PILOT LOAN PROGRAM

The Patriot Express Pilot Loan was created by SBA to offer financial, procurement, and technical assistance programs to the military community. Patriot Express is a streamlined loan product with enhanced guarantee and interest rate characteristics.

Patriot Express is available to veterans, service-disabled veterans, active-duty servicemembers participating in the military's Transition Assistance Program, Reservists and National Guard members, current spouses of any of the above, spouses of any servicemember and the widowed spouse of a servicemember or veteran who died during service or of a service-connected disability.

The Patriot Express Loan is offered by SBA's network of participating lenders nationwide. It features SBA's fastest turnaround time for loan approvals. Loans are available up to $500,000 and qualify for SBA's maximum guaranty of up to 85 percent for loans of $150,000 or less and up to 75 percent for loans over $150,000 and up to $500,000.

The Patriot Express Loan can be used for most business purposes, including start-up, expansion, equipment purchases, working capital, inventory, or business-occupied real-estate purchases.

Patriot Express Loans feature SBA's lowest interest rates for business loans, generally 2.25 percent to 4.75 percent over prime depending upon the size and maturity of the loan. Local SBA district offices will have a listing of Patriot Express lenders in their areas. More details on the initiative can be found at http://www.sba.gov/patriotexpress.

DISTRICT OFFICE VETERANS BUSINESS DEVELOPMENT OFFICERS (VBDOS)

As a new veteran, we realize you may not know a lot about the assistance available to you from SBA. To ensure that every veteran entrepreneur has access to the full range of SBA programs, and to receive the specific assistance and guidance you may be seeking, SBA has established a Veterans Business Development Officer (VBDO) in every one of the sixty-eight SBA district offices around the nation. These VBDO officers are responsible for providing prompt and direct assistance and guidance to any veteran or Reservist seeking information about or access to any SBA program. To identify your local VBDO, please contact your local SBA district office (see the blue pages) or contact OVBD at 202-205-6773 or visit http://www.sba.gov/VETS/reps.html.

VETERANS BUSINESS OUTREACH CENTERS

OVBD provides funding to five Veterans Business Outreach Centers (VBOC) to offer and coordinate business development assistance to veterans, service-connected disabled veterans, and Reservist entrepreneurs. Services include face-to-face and online outreach, concept development, business training, counseling, and mentoring. Please contact them directly at:

The Research Foundation of the State University of New York
41 State Street
Albany, NY 12246
518-443-5398
Website: http://www.nyssbdc.org/vboc
E-mail: brian.goldstein@nyssbdc.org

The University of West Florida in Pensacola
2500 Minnesota Avenue
Lynn Haven, FL 32444
1-800-542-7232 or 850-271-1108
Website: http://www.vboc.org
E-mail: vboc@knology.net

The University of Texas–Pan American
1201 West University Drive
Edinburg, TX 78539-2999
956-292-7535
Website: http://www.coserve.org/vboc
E-mail: vboc@panam.edu

Vietnam Veterans of California
7270 E. Southgate Drive, Suite 1
Sacramento, California 95823
916-393-1690
Website: http://www.vboc-ca.org
E-mail: cconley@vboc-ca.org

Robert Morris University
600 Fifth Avenue
Pittsburgh, PA 15219
(412) 397-6842
Website: www.rmu.edu/vboc
E-mail: vboc@rmu.edu

SMALL BUSINESS DEVELOPMENT CENTERS

SBA provides funding to one thousand Small Business Development Centers in all fifty states and U.S. territories. This program provides a broad range of specialized management assistance to current and prospective small business owners. SBDCs offer one-stop assistance to individuals and small businesses by providing a wide variety of information, guidance, linkages, training, and counseling in easily accessible branch locations, usually affiliated with local educational institutions. The SBDC Program is designed to deliver up-to-date counseling, training, and technical assistance in all aspects of small business management. SBDC services include, but are not limited to, assisting small businesses with financial, marketing, production, organization, engineering and technical problems, and feasibility studies.

To find your local SBDC: http://www.sba.gov/sbdc/sbdcnear.html or contact your district office VBDO.

SCORE "COUNSELORS TO AMERICA'S SMALL BUSINESS"

SCORE is the best source of free and confidential small business advice to help you build your business—from idea to start-up to success. The SCORE Association is a nonprofit association dedicated to entrepreneurial education and the formation, growth, and success of small businesses nationwide. More than half of SCORE's network of 10,500 retired and working volunteers are veterans, and they are experienced entrepreneurs and corporate manager/executives. They have worn the uniform, and they have succeeded in business. They provide free business counseling and advice as a public service to all types of businesses, in all stages of development.

- SCORE offers Ask SCORE e-mail advice online at http://www.score.org/. Some SCORE ecounselors specifically target veterans, service-disabled veterans, and Reserve Component members.
- Face-to-face small business counseling at 389 chapter offices.
- Low-cost workshops and seminars at 389 chapter offices nationwide.
- A great online web-based network.

SCORE provides small business counseling and training under a grant from the U.S. Small Business Administration (SBA). SCORE members are successful, retired, and active businessmen and women who volunteer their time to assist aspiring entrepreneurs and small business owners. There are SCORE chapters in every state.

Find your local SCORE chapter at http://www.score.org/findscore/chapter_maps.html.

WOMEN'S BUSINESS CENTERS

The Office of Women's Business Ownership provides women-focused (men are eligible as well) training, counseling, and mentoring at every level of entrepreneurial development, from novice to seasoned entrepreneur, through representatives in the SBA district offices and nationwide networks of women's business centers (WBCs) and mentoring roundtables. Additionally, WBC provides online training, counseling, and mentoring. Women's Business Centers represent a national network of more than one hundred centers designed to assist women start and grow small businesses. WBCs operate with the mission to level the playing field for women entrepreneurs, who face unique obstacles in the world of business. To find your local WBC: http://www.sba.gov/wbc.html.

FINANCIAL ASSISTANCE

SBA administers three separate, but equally important, loan programs. The Agency sets the guidelines for the loans while the partners (lenders, community development organizations, and microlending institutions) make the loans to small businesses. SBA backs those loans with a guaranty that will eliminate some risk to lending partners. As the Agency's loan guaranty requirements and practices change as government alters its fiscal policy and priorities to meet current economic conditions, past policy cannot always be relied upon when seeking assistance in today's market. The loan guaranty SBA provides transfers the potential risk of borrower nonpayment, up to the amount of the guaranty, from the lender to SBA. Therefore, when a business applies for an SBA loan, they are actually applying for a commercial loan, structured according to SBA requirements, but provided by our cooperating private or not-for-profit lending partner, which receives an SBA guaranty.

Basic 7(a) Loan Guaranty

The 7(a) Loan Guaranty Program serves as the SBA's primary business loan program to help qualified small businesses obtain financing when they might not be eligible for business loans through normal lending channels.

Loan proceeds can be used for most sound business purposes, including working capital, machinery and equipment, furniture and fixtures, land and building (including purchase, renovation, and new construction), leasehold improvements, and debt refinancing (under special conditions). Loan maturity is up to ten years for working capital and generally up to twenty-five years for fixed assets. SBA does target veterans specifically in some of the loan programs. To find out more, visit http://www.sba.gov/category/navigation-structure/loans-grants/small-business-loans/sba-loan-programs, or contact your district office or any of the centers or chapters mentioned previously.

Certified Development Company 504 Loan Program

The Certified Development Company 504 Loan Program is a long-term financing tool for economic development within a community. The 504 Program provides growing businesses with long-term, fixed-rate financing for major fixed assets, such as land and buildings. A Certified Development Company is a nonprofit corporation set up to contribute to the economic development of its community. CDCs work with the SBA and private-sector lenders to provide financing to small businesses. There are about 270 CDCs nationwide. Each CDC covers a specific geographic area. Typically, a 504 project includes a loan secured with a senior lien from a private-sector lender covering up to 50 percent of the project cost, a loan secured with a junior lien from the CDC (backed by a 100 percent SBA-guaranteed debenture) covering up to 40 percent of the cost, and a contribution of at least 10 percent equity from the small business being helped.

Microloan Program

Microloan Program provides very small loans and business counseling to start-up, newly established, or growing small business concerns. Under this program, SBA makes funds available to nonprofit community-based lenders (intermediaries) which, in turn, make loans to eligible borrowers in amounts up to a maximum of $35,000. The average loan size is about $13,000. Applications are submitted to the local intermediary, and all credit decisions are made on the local level.

Terms, Interest Rates, and Fees: The maximum term allowed for a microloan is six years. However, loan terms vary according to the size of the loan, the planned use of funds, the requirements of the intermediary lender, and the needs of the small business borrower. Interest rates vary, depending upon the intermediary lender and costs to the intermediary from the U.S. Treasury. Generally these rates will be between 8 percent and 13 percent.

INTERNATIONAL TRADE

The Office of International Trade works in cooperation with other federal agencies and public- and private-sector groups to encourage small business exports and to assist small businesses seeking to export. Through sixteen U.S. Export Assistance Centers, SBA district offices, and a variety of service-provider partners, we direct and coordinate SBA's ongoing export initiatives to encourage small businesses going global.

SBA'S INVESTMENT PROGRAMS

In 1958 Congress created the Small Business Investment Company (SBIC) program. SBICs, licensed by the Small Business Administration, are privately owned and managed (venture) investment firms. They are participants in a vital partnership between government and the private-sector economy. All SBICs are profit-motivated businesses. A major incentive for SBICs to invest in small businesses is the chance to share in the success of the small business if it grows and prospers. Equity (venture) capital or financing is money raised by a business in exchange for a share of ownership in the company. Ownership is represented by owning shares of stock outright or having the right to convert other financial instruments into stock of that private company. Two key sources of equity capital for new and emerging businesses are angel investors and venture capital firms. Typically, angel capital and venture capital investors provide capital unsecured by assets to young, private companies with the potential for rapid growth. Such investing covers most industries and is appropriate for businesses through the range of developmental stages. Investing in new or very early companies inherently carries a high degree of risk. But venture capital is long term or "patient capital" that allows companies the time to mature into profitable organizations.

SURETY BOND GUARANTEE PROGRAM

The Surety Bond Guarantee (SBG) Program was developed to provide increased bonding opportunities to small veteran and minority contractors to support contracting opportunities for which they would not otherwise bid. If your small construction, service, or supply company bids or performs projects requiring surety bonds, the U.S. Small Business Administration program could help make you more competitive.

A surety bond is a three-way agreement between the surety company, the contractor, and the project owner. The agreement with the SBA guarantees the contractor will comply with the terms and conditions of the contract. If the contractor is unable to successfully perform the contract, the surety assumes the contractor's responsibilities and ensures that the project is completed.

The SBA Surety Bond Guarantee Program covers four types of major contract surety bonds:

- **Bid Bond:** guarantees the project owner that the bidder will enter into the contract and furnish the required payment and performance bonds.
- **Payment Bond:** guarantees the contractor will pay all persons who furnish labor, materials, equipment, or supplies for use on the project.
- **Performance Bond:** guarantees the contractor will perform the contract in accordance with its terms, specifications, and conditions.
- **Ancillary Bond:** bonds that are incidental and essential to the performance of the contract.

The overall surety bond program has two programs:

- **The Prior Approval Program:** The SBA guarantees 80 or 90 percent (for veterans) of a surety's loss. Participating sureties must obtain SBA's prior approval for each bond.
- **The Preferred Surety Bond Program:** Selected sureties receive a 70 percent guarantee and are authorized to issue, monitor, and service bonds without the SBA's prior approval.

Program Eligibility Requirements

In addition to meeting the surety company's bonding qualifications, you must qualify as a small business concern, as defined by SBA. For federal prime contracts, your company must meet the small business size standard for the North American Industry Classification System (NAICS) Code that the federal contracting officer specified for that procurement. For more information about the Surety Bond Guarantee Program, visit http://www .sba.gov/osg/.

BUSINESS PLANNING AND DISASTER ASSISTANCE FOR SMALL BUSINESSES THAT EMPLOY OR ARE OWNED BY MILITARY RESERVISTS

All of the technical assistance programs referenced above can provide pre- and postmobilization business counseling and planning assistance to any Reservist who owns their own business or to the small business they work for. They also offer assistance to the caretaker of the business who may manage the business while the Reservist owner is activated.

The Office of Disaster Assistance also offers the Military Reservist Economic Injury Disaster Loan (MREIDL) program at very favorable rates and terms. The purpose of the MREIDL is to provide funds to eligible small businesses to meet their ordinary and necessary operating expenses that they could have met, but are unable to meet, because an essential employee was "called up" to active duty in their role as a military Reservist. These loans are intended only to provide the amount of working capital needed by a small business to pay its necessary obligations as they mature until operations return to normal after the essential employee is released from active military duty. The purpose of these loans is not to cover lost income or lost profits. MREIDL funds cannot be used to take the place of regular commercial debt, to refinance long-term debt, or to expand the business. Contact your district office or visit http://www.sba.gov/disaster_recov/loaninfo/militaryreservist.html.

GOVERNMENT PROCUREMENT

The Office of Government Contracting (GC) works to maximize participation by small, disadvantaged, woman, veteran, and service-disabled veteran-owned small businesses in federal government contract awards and large prime subcontract awards. GC also advocates on behalf of small business in the federal procurement arena.

The federal government purchases billions of dollars in goods and services each year, and it is federal policy to ensure that all small businesses have the maximum practicable opportunity to participate in providing goods and services to the government. To ensure that small businesses get their fair share of federal procurements, the government has established an annual 23 percent government-wide procurement goal to small business concerns, including small business concerns owned and controlled by service-disabled veterans, qualified HUBZone small businesses, small businesses owned and controlled by socially and economically disadvantaged individuals, and small businesses owned and controlled by women. The individual program goals are 5 percent of prime and subcontracts for small disadvantaged businesses; 3 percent of prime and subcontracts for HUBZone businesses; and 3 percent of prime and subcontracts for service-disabled veteran-owned small businesses. The SBA negotiates annual procurement goals with each federal agency and reviews each agency's results. The SBA is responsible for ensuring that the statutory government-wide goals are met in the aggregate. In addition, large business prime contractors are statutorily required to establish subcontracting goals for service-disabled and veteran-owned small businesses as part of each subcontracting plan submitted in response to a prime federal contract opportunity. GC administers several programs and services that assist small businesses in meeting the requirements necessary to receive government contracts as prime contractors or subcontractors. These include the Certificate of Competency, the Nonmanufacturer Rule Waiver, and the Size Determination programs.

The office also oversees special initiatives, such as the Women's Procurement Program, the Procurement Awards Program, and the Annual Joint Industry/SBA Procurement Conference.

Resources and Opportunities: Contact your local SBA district office or visit http://www.sba.gov/GC/indexwhatwedo.html and the Federal Agency Procurement Forecast, http://www.sba.gov/GC/forecast.html.

SBA Contacts and Representatives: A Subcontracting Opportunities Directory contains a listing of prime contractors doing business with the federal government: http://www.sba.gov/GC/indexcontacts-sbsd.html.

Procurement Technical Assistance Centers (PTACS)

The Defense Logistics Agency, on behalf of the Secretary of Defense, administers the DoD Procurement Technical Assistance Program (PTAC). PTA Centers are a local resource available to provide assistance to business firms in marketing products and services to the federal, state, and local governments. See http://www.dla.mil/db/procurem.html.

Procurement Center Representatives

SBA's Procurement Center Representatives (PCR), located in area offices, review and evaluate the small business programs of federal agencies and assist small businesses in obtaining federal contracts and subcontracts.

TPCR: Traditional Procurement Center Representative—TPCRs increase the small business share of federal procurement awards by initiating small business set-asides; reserving procurements for competition among small business firms; providing small business sources to federal buying activities; and counseling small firms.

BPCR: Breakout Procurement Center Representative—BPCRs advocate for the breakout of items for full and open competition to effect savings to the federal government.

CMRs: Commercial Marketing Representatives—CMRs identify, develop, and market small businesses to large prime contractors and assist small businesses in identifying and obtaining subcontracts. Contact your local SBA district office or visit http://www.sba.gov/GC/pcr.html.

OFFICE OF SMALL AND
DISADVANTAGED BUSINESS UTILIZATION

OSDBUs offer small business information on procurement opportunities, guidance on procurement procedures, and identification of prime and subcontracting opportunities in various federal agencies. OSDBUs also have Veteran Small Business Representatives. If you own, operate, or represent a small business, you should contact the Small Business Specialists for marketing assistance and information.

The specialists will advise you as to what types of acquisitions are either currently available or will be available in the near future. Contact your local SBA office or visit http://www.osdbu.gov/Listofmembers.htm.

GC PROGRAMS

Section 8(a) Program/Small Disadvantaged Business Certification Program

The SBA administers two particular business assistance programs for small disadvantaged businesses (SDBs). These programs are the 8(a) Business Development Program and the Small Disadvantaged Business Certification Program. While the 8(a) Program offers a broad scope of assistance, including federal contracting assistance to socially and economically disadvantaged firms, SDB certification strictly pertains to benefits in federal procurement. Companies that are 8(a) firms automatically qualify for SDB certification. Contact your local SBA Office or visit http://www.sba.gov/8abd/.

Small Disadvantaged Business

SBA certifies SDBs to make them eligible for special bidding benefits. Evaluation credits available to prime contractors boost subcontracting opportunities for SDBs.

Qualifications for the program are similar to those for the 8(a) Business Development Program. A small business must be at least 51 percent owned and controlled by a socially and economically disadvantaged individual or individuals. African Americans, Hispanic Americans, Asian Pacific Americans, Subcontinent Asian Americans, and Native Americans are presumed to qualify. Other individuals, including veterans and service-disabled veterans, can qualify if they show by a "preponderance of the evidence" that they are disadvantaged. All individuals must have a net worth of less than $750,000, excluding the equity of the business and primary residence. Successful applicants must also meet applicable SBA size standards for small businesses in their industry.

HUBZone Empowerment Contracting Program

The HUBZone Empowerment Contracting Program stimulates economic development and creates jobs in urban and rural communities by providing federal contracting preferences to small businesses. These preferences go to small businesses that obtain HUBZone (Historically Underutilized Business Zone) certification in part by employing staff that live in a HUBZone. The company must also maintain a "principal office" in one of these specially designated geographic areas. A principal office can be different from a company headquarters, as explained in our section dedicated to Frequently Asked Questions.

Contact your local SBA Office or visit https://eweb1.sba.gov/hubzone/internet/ or the Service-Disabled Veteran-Owned Small Business Concern Program website, http://www.sba.gov/gc/indexprograms-vets.html.

On May 5, 2004, the U.S. Small Business Administration issued regulations in the Federal Register as an Interim Final Rule implementing Section 36 of the Veterans Benefits Act of 2003 (Public Law 108-183).

Section 308 of PL 108-183 amended the Small Business Act to establish a procurement program for Small Business Concerns (SBCs) owned and controlled by service-disabled veterans. This procurement program provides that contracting officers may award a sole source or set-aside contract to service-disabled veteran business owners, if certain conditions are met. Finally, the purpose of this procurement program is to assist agencies in achieving the 3 percent government-wide goal for procurement from service-disabled veteran-owned small business concerns.

IMPORTANT DEFINITIONS

Veteran: A person who served in the active military, naval, or air service, and who was discharged or released under conditions other than dishonorable.
Service-Disabled Veteran: A person with a disability that is service connected and was incurred or aggravated in the line of duty in the active military, naval, or air service.
Service-Disabled Veteran with a Permanent and Severe Disability: A veteran with a service-connected disability that has been determined by the U.S. Department of Veterans Affairs to have a permanent and total disability for purposes of receiving disability compensation or a disability pension.

Permanent Caregiver: A spouse or an individual eighteen years of age or older who is legally designated, in writing, to undertake responsibility for managing the well-being of a service-disabled veteran, to include housing, health, and safety.

Service-Disabled Veteran-Owned Small Business Contracts: SDVO contracts are contracts awarded to an SDVO SBC through a sole source award or a set-aside award based on competition restricted to SDVO SBCs. The contracting officer for the contracting activity determines if a contract opportunity for SDVO competition exists.

SDVO SBC Set-Aside Contracts: The contracting officer may set aside acquisitions for SDVO SBCs if:

- The requirement is determined to be excluded from fulfillment through award to federal prison industries, Javits Wagner-O'Day programs, orders under indefinite delivery contracts, orders against federal supply schedules, requirements currently being performed by 8(a) participants, and requirements for commissary or exchange resale items.
- The requirement is not currently being performed by an 8(a) participant and SBA has consented to release of the requirement from the Section 8(a) Program.
- SBA has not accepted the requirement for performance under the 8(a) authority, unless SBA has consented to release of the requirement from the Section 8(a) Program.
- There is a reasonable expectation that at least two responsible SDVO SBCs will submit offers.
- The award can be made at a fair market price.

SDVO SBC Sole Source Contracts: A contracting officer may award a sole source contract to an SDVO SBC if the contracting officer determines that none of the SDVO SBC set-aside exemptions or provisions apply and the anticipated award price of the contract, including options, will not exceed:

- $5.5 million for manufacturing requirements
- $3.5 million for all other requirements

and provided:

- the SDVO SBC is a responsible contractor able to perform the contract
- award can be made at a fair and reasonable price

SDVO SBC Simplified Acquisition Contracts: If a requirement is at or below the simplified acquisition threshold, a contracting officer may set-aside the requirement for consideration among SDVO SBCs using simplified acquisition procedures or may award a sole-source contract to an SDVO SBC.

Contact your local SBA office or visit http://www.sba.gov/gc/indexprograms-vets.html.

NATIONAL VETERAN'S BUSINESS CORPORATION

The following information and resources will help you develop a business plan, find financing, and determine if starting a franchise is your best option. This information is provided by the National Veterans Business Development Corporation, a federally contracted program for assisting veterans in starting a business or purchasing a franchise.

Many servicemembers never consider small business ownership as a career when they transition out of the military, but you may discover that entrepreneurship is just the path for you.

What Does It Take to Be an Entrepreneur?

The skills and strengths arising from military experience, such as leadership, organization, and the ability to work under pressure, lend themselves naturally to entrepreneurship, and as a result, many veterans find themselves attracted to business ownership when they leave the military. If you are considering entrepreneurship, it is important to assess your strengths and weaknesses to determine whether you are cut out to be a business owner. Although there are no guarantees in business, successful entrepreneurs tend to share many similar characteristics. The following is a guide to help you determine if you share the entrepreneurial characteristics of other successful business owners.

Step 1: Think about why you want to be an entrepreneur.

There are many reasons people take the plunge into entrepreneurship, but not all reasons are the right reasons for opening your own business. Below are the most common reasons people consider business ownership as a career.

1. You want to be your own boss.

Although this is the number-one reason given by new entrepreneurs when making the change from employee to self-employed, there are a few important things to consider. Without a boss watching over you, do you have the self-discipline to get things done, to do them right, and to finish them on time?

Without a boss to blame, are you willing to take responsibility for mistakes and fix problems yourself? If you eliminate the demands of your boss, will you be able to handle demands from customers and clients, suppliers and vendors, partners, and even yourself?

2. You are tired of working 9 to 5.

As an entrepreneur, you can usually set your own hours, but that does not necessarily mean shorter hours. Many entrepreneurs are forced to put in twelve to eighteen hours a day, six or seven days a week. Are you ready to work that hard, and is your drive for entrepreneurial success strong enough to get you through the long hours? You may be able to sleep in and work in the comfort of your home in your fuzzy slippers on occasion, but probably not initially and probably not all the time.

3. You are looking for an exciting challenge.

Entrepreneurship is full of decisions that can affect your company's success. Every day is a new adventure, and you can learn from your mistakes as well as from your successes. Many successful entrepreneurs claim they are adrenaline junkies, motivated by the excitement of business ownership. That excitement requires risks, however, and you must know your own tolerance for risk. Entrepreneurship, as exciting as it may be, means putting everything on the line for your business. Sound too risky to you? Or maybe it sounds like just the adventure you are craving.

4. You want to make more money.

Entrepreneurship can be an escape from structured pay charts and minimal growth opportunities, and, as a small business owner, your hard work directly benefits you. Despite the potential of big payoffs, however, entrepreneurs sometimes have to work months—even years—before they begin to see those profits. Oftentimes, entrepreneurs take a pay cut when they start out on their own. Are you willing to sacrifice your current level of pay until your business becomes a success?

5. You really want to become an entrepreneur.

This is perhaps the most important reason people should enter entrepreneurship. Entrepreneurship takes time, energy, and money, but it also takes heart. It must be something you want to do in order to succeed because it takes drive and motivation, even in the face of setbacks. If you are considering entrepreneurship just because you haven't found anything else that suits you, make sure you are honest with yourself about whether or not you are ready to be an entrepreneur.

Step 2: Assess your skills.

Do your skills apply to entrepreneurial success? Many of the skills needed in entrepreneurship are those gained through military experience, including:

- Leadership
- Ability to get along with and work with all types of people
- Ability to work under pressure and meet deadlines
- Ability to give directions and delegate

- Good planning and organizational skills
- Problem-solving skills
- Familiarity with personnel administration and record keeping
- Flexibility and adaptability
- Self-direction
- Initiative
- Strong work habits
- Standards of quality and a commitment to excellence

Think about your other skills that might help you become a successful entrepreneur. Are you good with money and have a strong credit history? Do you have a high energy level? Do you see problems as challenges and enjoy trying new methods for success? Listing your skills will not only help you assess yourself as an entrepreneur but it might also tell you what kind of business you should start!

Step 3: Define your personality.

Your personality often helps determine what type of work best suits you. People preferring structure might find the corporate environment most suitable while creative types might enjoy flexible jobs with relaxed policies. Like any job, there are certain types of personalities that thrive in entrepreneurship.

- Goal-oriented
- Independent
- Self-confident
- Innovative and creative
- Strong commitment
- Highly reliable
- Competitive
- Desire to work hard
- Problem solver
- Good manager
- Organized
- Honest
- Tolerance for failure, but a drive to achieve
- Idea-oriented
- Motivated by challenge
- Calculated risk-taker
- Courageous
- Persistent
- Adaptable
- Positive

Even if you do not have all of these characteristics, you can still be a great entrepreneur. Every entrepreneur is a blend of skills and strengths. Think about the skills or traits you don't have and learn to improve them or work to overcome them on the road to entrepreneurship!

Franchise Ownership

If you are considering business ownership but are hesitant to venture out on your own, you may want to consider becoming a franchisee, or franchise owner. Becoming a business owner can be an intimidating process, but when you purchase a franchise, you get a team of support, which includes marketing assistance, HR tools, and training. Having others who are committed to your success as a business owner and who are willing and able to help when you run into problems is just one of the many advantages to franchise ownership.

Advantages of Franchises

1. Higher rate of business success.

Perhaps the number-one reason people become franchise owners is because franchises have a higher likelihood of succeeding than do traditional start-up businesses. In fact, according to the U.S. Department of Commerce, 95 percent of franchises are still in business after five years. Franchisors (the companies who sell or grant franchises to individuals) evaluate each prospective franchisee (individual franchise owners) and invest in those they think will thrive as franchise owners for their company. They look for specific skills, experience, motivation, financial capacity, and more to choose people who will be able to afford the franchise, follow the business operational model, and become successful.

2. Established brand identity.

One of the key advantages of operating a franchise is the ability to give consumers a brand they know, quality they trust, and a consistency they have come to expect. Purchasing a franchise means purchasing the reputation of the brand, an established customer base, and a set of products or services that have been successfully tested in communities. While new business start-ups must work at building a reputation and generating awareness of the product or service they offer, franchises are often preceded by their reputation and can make an immediate impact.

3. The dirty work is done.

Perhaps the most difficult thing new business owner's face when opening a business of their own is the burden of starting from scratch. The tasks of starting a business can be lengthy and expensive. In a franchise system, however, the work has already been done to develop a product or service, identify and reach a target market, build a reputation, and create a replicable business model. While many new business owners spend the first year (or longer!) testing products, sales tactics, and marketing avenues, franchise owners already know exactly what works and how to effectively reach their target audience.

4. Business support.

Business owners who start their own business take on a great deal of responsibility: they must market to new customers, provide products and services to existing customers, hire employees, and train those employees to do their jobs properly. In other words, new business owners must be sales representatives, accountants, human resource managers, marketing experts, and more. That is a lot of responsibility!

While some individuals may thrive in the multiple roles business owners must take on, others need support in some or all of the aspects of business ownership. Franchisees get the support they need in the form of training and even on-site assistance. In addition, most franchisors provide human resources tools, specialized software, marketing materials, and other valuable resources that independent business owners must find or develop for themselves.

5. Easier to finance.

If you are looking to start a business with less-than-perfect credit and need to apply for a business loan, the established history of a franchise may help you get your loan. Because new business start-ups are extremely risky, banks are often hesitant to hand out loans without a history of business management and credit management in your past. Prospective franchisees applying for a business loan have the advantage of a tested product or service, a successful business model, and a core of support from the franchisor. Banks know that franchises have a higher likelihood of success than other new businesses; as a result, it is often easier to secure a business loan for a franchise than for a business start-up.

Disadvantages of Franchises

Does owning a franchise seem too good to be true? Although there are many advantages to owning a franchise, there are downsides as well. While these disadvantages may seem minor to some, they may turn others away from the notion of franchise ownership entirely. Read on to learn the negatives of franchise ownership and decide if it is the path for you.

1. Factors beyond your control.

The value of a franchise lies in the value of the brand and the brand's reputation. When you purchase a franchise, you must take into account the reputation of the parent company and other branches of the franchise. If, over time, that reputation is damaged by factors beyond your control, the results on your business can be catastrophic. And because your franchise agreement is a long-term agreement, getting out of that franchise system may be more difficult than you thought.

2. High costs.

Many people who pursue franchise ownership do so because they believe the costs associated with franchises will be less than those of a traditional start-up business. And for some franchises, that is true; for many others, however, the costs can soar when franchise fees, capital requirements, marketing fees, royalties, and other fees add up. In fact, one of the reasons that new franchises fail is insufficient funding and a lack of working capital. There are hundreds of reputable, low-cost franchises, but you must know what to look for and be smart from the very beginning.

3. Restrictions on business.

If you are going into business to be independent, creative, and entrepreneurial, franchise ownership may not be right for you. Franchises are based on previously developed, successfully tested business ideas and plans. Most franchisors have strict regulations on how individual franchises may operate, and deviations are rarely allowed. Franchise owners, for example, must sell a specific product or service and advertise with specific marketing materials and slogans. While this may appeal to business owners who are eager for structure and support, others may find this too regimented for their individual business style.

4. Reduced profits.

One of the greatest appeals of business ownership is that you benefit personally from your hard work, and many people seek entrepreneurship as a way to increase their earnings and have greater control over their financial destiny. Franchise ownership is actually a middle step between the financial freedom of business ownership and the rigid pay structure of other jobs. As a franchise owner, your hard work will directly result in higher profits for your business, but most franchisors will require continuous monthly royalty payments equaling 5 to 10 percent of your profits.

Writing a Business Plan

Business plans are the face of your company, and can make the difference in whether or not you receive a loan or whether someone chooses to invest in your company. The importance of a good business plan cannot be overstated, as it defines your business, sets your objectives, and enhances your ability to make sound business decisions in line with your overall business goals. Although all business plans vary slightly, there are six primary sections that should be included in all plans.

Executive Summary

The executive summary is perhaps the most critical part of your business plan, as it is sometimes the only section that will be read before deciding whether or not to consider your business for a loan. If a lender or investor likes what is written in the executive summary, he or she will continue reading; otherwise, you may not get another chance to impress them with your business idea. The executive summary should describe your business and highlight the key points from each section of your business plan. For example, the executive summary would not include an exhaustive list of your competitors and their products—that is for the marketing and sales section—but it would mention how your product differs from others on the market and what you have to offer that is special. The executive summary should be no more than one or two pages, and although it comes at the beginning of your business plan, it is recommended that you write this section last to ensure you highlight the most important points of each section.

Business Opportunity

The business opportunity should answer the question, is my business idea viable? This section should first define the simple vision for your company. Provide an overview of your business, including its history, progress to date, and vision for the future. Questions to be answered in the overview of your business include: Have you started conducting business? If not, when? If so, what progress have you made? Did you acquire this business from a previous owner or start from scratch? If you acquired it, what is the history of the business previously?

Second, the business opportunity must address your product, including why it is different, why customers will buy your product, whether or not your product is already developed, and whether you hold or plan to hold any patents, copyrights, or trademarks. Questions to be answered in the overview of your product include: Have you already developed this product? If yes, have you begun selling the product, and how has it been received? If no, what are your plans and time line for development? How is this product unique, and what are the benefits to using this product instead of a competitor's product?

Marketing and Sales Plan

First, define your business and the product and/or service you are going to sell and create an overview of your market area. Identify your competition and the products or services they offer and what you can offer.

A marketing plan is critical to entrepreneurial success because it tells you who you need to reach and how you are going to reach them. Without customers, you have no business.

What have you got that the competition does not, and how will you attract customers away from the competition? Include the price of your product, how it compares to the competition's price, and why you can offer it for less money or how you plan to attract customers despite a higher price. Finally, give an overview of how you will sell your product or service (online, face to face, etc.) and how that relates to the competition's sales methods.

Next, describe your customers, including their demographics, needs, patterns, and preferences. Describe the size of your target market and what they will find attractive about your product as opposed to products currently on the market. How does your product better respond to their needs and preferences?

Third, outline your marketing strategy by identifying the methods you will use to market your product to your customers. Will you advertise only on television? Will you place ads in the newspaper or local periodicals? Would billboards be appropriate, or should you send out bulk mailings? Include in your strategy whatever ways you see appropriate to reach your customer base and identify what percentage of your total marketing dollars you will dedicate to each marketing method.

Last, create your marketing budget. Effective marketing is critical from the first day; otherwise, no one will know about your business! Research marketing costs in your area. If you plan to rent a billboard on the main interstate for three months, find out exactly how much it costs. Do not guess on marketing costs—research and determine the exact numbers it will take to market your product to your target audience. If costs seem too high, eliminate high-cost options or look for marketing strategies that reach fewer people overall but reach a higher number of people in your targeted customer base.

Management Team and Personnel

It is important to demonstrate that your management team and/or staff have the skills and qualifications to handle every facet of your business. Is there evidence of expertise in marketing, finance, operations, and development? This section of your business plan should outline the structure and key skills of your staff.

Define the positions of your staff, their role in the company, and a summary of each person's background, experience, and qualifications. Include the time commitment of each individual (e.g., full time, part time, one day a week); also include descriptions and qualifications for consultants and partners. If you have not begun hiring employees, include the structure and key skills of staff you plan to hire, a time line for hiring, and the salaries you estimate to assign to each position. Identify recruitment and training procedures, time lines for doing so, and the costs of employee training.

Operating Plan

Your business plan must include a section covering your operating capabilities and plans. The areas you should cover in this section include office space and location, production facilities, and information technology (IT) infrastructure.

Office space and location will include where you will house your office (e.g., in your home, an office building, etc.), the costs associated with this location, the benefits and disadvantages to being housed in that location, whether you rent or own the space, and (if you rent) the duration of your lease. If you have plans for upgrading your space or relocating, that should be included as well.

If your business requires you to create a product, you will have to include a paragraph on your production facilities. This should include whether you already have facilities and whether you plan to do your own production or outsource it to another company. It should describe the benefits and disadvantages to handling your own production versus outsourcing it as well as the facilities you have or need, the capacity of the facilities versus anticipated demand, and whether you plan on making an investment into enhancing your production capabilities.

Finally, this section should include a description of your IT infrastructure, including the strengths and weaknesses of your system, your plans to upgrade the system, and how your system will be used as a business tool.

Finances

The final component of your business plan should be your financial forecasts. The purpose of this section is to inform lenders and investors of how much capital you need, how secure their loans or investments are, how you plan to repay the loans, and what your projected sources of revenue and income will be. To do so, you should include detailed financial projections by month for the first year and by quarter for years two and three, as well as the assumptions upon which your projections were made, including the breakdown of anticipated costs and revenues for all three years. You should also include cash flow statements, loan applications, capital equipment and supply lists, and profit and loss statements.

Financing Your Small Business

One of the most common mistakes entrepreneurs make is underestimating the costs of their business and creating a financial plan based on low cost projections. Every entrepreneur has different costs associated with his or her business. For example, establishing a home-based business will have little to no cost for acquiring office space; renting office space will entail low to moderate costs; and building an office will require a high cost. Regardless of your specific needs, every entrepreneur must take two costs into account: start-up costs and recurring costs. Start-up costs are all of the one-time costs required to start your business, such as a security deposit on office space, furniture and equipment purchase, signage, and so on. Recurring costs are all of the costs you encounter monthly, such as salary and benefit expenses, insurance fees, monthly rent, and so on.

Once you have determined your costs, determine whether you will need to borrow money to start your business. If so, there are several different funding options to consider. Each funding source brings with it a series of pros and cons that should be weighed in order to find a lender to meet your start-up needs.

Option 1: Banks

Banks are usually the first place people look when they want to borrow money. Banks offer a variety of loans and can often advise you as to which type of loan would be best for your needs. Some loans, for example, require you to make set payments of both the principal and interest, whereas others require you to pay back only the interest with a lump payment of the entire principal at the end. The obvious advantage of approaching banks for loans is that banks are designed for just that purpose. The downside is that if you have a bad credit history or have accumulated debt, it can be difficult to get approval for a loan at most banks. The best way to determine whether bank loans are appropriate for your needs is to do your research: locate the banks in your region, find out what types of loans they offer, and learn what requirements they have for approving loans.

Option 2: Venture Capital Firms

Venture capital firms invest in small companies in return for equity. They look for companies with the potential for high growth and high profitability. Although some venture capitalists will invest in companies that are just beginning, they generally seek to fund companies that have been in business for some amount of time in order to assess progress, growth, and earned revenues. For that reason, acquiring start-up funding from venture capitalists can be very difficult; also, the earlier the stage of investment, the more equity venture capital firms require. If you are serious about acquiring venture capital funds for your business start-up, look for firms that specifically cater to business in the start-up phase. If you have a thorough, viable business plan, and your management team has extensive experience fostering rapid growth in small businesses and creating substantial profits, you will have a much higher chance of receiving venture capital funding.

Option 3: Angel Investors

Angel investors are individuals who invest their own money in entrepreneurial ventures in return for equity. Angel investors can be persons you know or persons you don't know, and can also work as an individual or be part of an angel group. Angel investors generally invest smaller amounts of money in companies than do venture capitalists, making them an ideal source for funding when you have exhausted funding from your friends, family, and self but are not yet ready to approach a venture capital firm.

Option 4: Partners

In some cases, funding can be secured by current or potential partners seeking a share of the business. The advantages to partner financing are that partners considering investment are already knowledgeable about the business idea and have confidence in its future, and the approval process may be easier than with a bank or lending firm. The decision you as an entrepreneur must make is whether or not you are willing to give up a portion of your company in order to obtain this funding or whether you would rather go to banks or other lenders and maintain your control.

Option 5: Friends and Family

Many people warn against the risks of borrowing money from friends and family, but there are also benefits to acquiring loans this way, and it is an extremely popular source of funding for small businesses. Friends and family already know you, your character, and your history of credit, debt, and financial management. Nevertheless, even friends and family considering making a loan should ask to see a business plan to make sure it is well thought out. The terms on which you must pay back loans from friends and family will likely be more relaxed, and they may not demand interest on the repayment of the loan. The obvious downside to borrowing from friends and family is the potential inability to repay the loan, damaging not only your finances but also their finances and the relationships you share with those individuals.

Option 6: Self-Financing

Self-financing is the most popular form of financing for small business owners, and it can serve to be extremely advantageous when you approach other lenders. By investing your own money and assets into your business, it demonstrates your faith that your business will succeed. Different forms of self-financing include borrowing against your retirement fund, taking out personal lines of credit, and using a home equity loan. The disadvantage to financing your business this way is that if your business flounders and you are unable to repay the money, you can lose a lot more than your business. Before putting your home on the line for your business or risking your personal credit history, carefully consider whether self-financing is the right option for you.

Entrepreneurship Resources

The Veterans Corporation

The National Veterans Business Development Corporation, doing business as The Veterans Corporation, is a federally chartered 501(c)(3) organization that was created by Public Law 106-50, the Veterans Entrepreneurship and Small Business Development Act of 1999. This Act recognized that America "has done too little to assist Veterans . . . in playing a greater role in the economy of the United States." The Corporation is charged with creating and enhancing entrepreneurial business opportunities for veterans, including service-disabled veterans. Toward this mission, TVC provides veterans with the tools and resources they need to be successful in business, including:

- access to capital
- access to business services
- entrepreneurial education
- surety bonding
- insurance and prescription coverage
- veterans business directory

Contact TVC toll free at 866-283-8267 or access them on the web at http://www.veteranscorp.org.

Small Business Administration (SBA)

The primary federal agency providing financial and business development assistance to small firms and aspiring entrepreneurs is the U.S. Small Business Administration, an independent agency chartered in 1953. SBA encourages participation by qualified veterans in all of its various financial and business development programs. A variety of special outreach programs for veterans are coordinated by SBA's Office of Veterans Business Development (OVBD), established for this and other purposes pursuant to Public Law 106-50. OVDB supports Veterans Business Outreach Centers, and it further leverages its resources and extends its outreach efforts throughout the nation by the use of designated Veterans Business Development Officers in each of SBA's seventy district offices. SBA provides financial assistance, business development counseling, procurement assistance, and other support to veteran entrepreneurs. Contact SBA toll free at 800-827-5722 or access them on the web at http://www.sba.gov.

Center for Veterans Enterprise (CVE)

The Department of Veterans Affairs established the Center for Veterans Enterprise (CVE) in 2001. CVE is dedicated to helping veterans succeed in business and specializes in assisting with procurement opportunities. To help coordinate prime and subcontracting business opportunities with veterans for government and private-sector buyers, CVE maintains an electronic business registry. All veteran entrepreneurs, including Reservists and members of the National Guard who have been called to active duty of any duration, are encouraged to register their firms and capabilities in this database, which is called the VETBiz Vendor Information Pages (VIP). In addition to procurement assistance, CVE provides business coaching, networking, outreach, and other business assistance to veterans.

Contact CVE toll free at 866-584-2344 or access them on the web at http://www.vetbiz.gov.

SCORE

SCORE is a 501(c)(3) nonprofit organization headquartered in Washington, D.C., that provides a public service to America by offering small business advice and training. SCORE was formed in 1964 to help small businesses flourish, and it now has more than ten thousand volunteers who can assist business owners with more than six hundred business skills. Volunteers are working or retired business owners, executives, and corporate leaders who share their wisdom and lessons learned in business. As a result, SCORE "Counselors to America's Small Business" is America's premier source of free and confidential small business advice for entrepreneurs. To date, SCORE has helped more than 7.5 million small businesses through face-to-face small business counseling, low-cost workshops nationwide, and online support and business guidance.

Contact SCORE toll free at 800-634-0245 or access them on the web at http://www.score.org.

Association of Small Business Development Centers (ASBDC)

The mission of the Association of Small Business Development Centers is to represent the collective interest of their members by promoting, informing, supporting, and continuously improving the SBDC network, which delivers nationwide educational assistance to strengthen small/medium business management, thereby contributing to the growth of local, state, and national economies.

The Association of Small Business Development Centers (ASBDC) is a partnership program uniting private enterprise, government, higher education, and local nonprofit economic development organizations. ASBDC is dedicated to the sound development of small business throughout America. Founded in 1979, the ASBDC provides a vehicle for continuous improvement of the Small Business Development Center program; exchange of information among members regarding objectives, methods, and results in business management; and technical assistance and advocacy of America's small business community. Over 500,000 businesses are assisted by ASBDC member programs on an annual basis. A sizeable number of them are in the dynamic start-up mode, while most are existing businesses searching for stability or planning for growth. The mission of ASBDC is to continuously improve the SBDC network, which delivers nationwide educational assistance to strengthen small/medium business management, thereby contributing to the growth of local, state, and national economies.

Contact ASBDC by phone at 703-764-9850 or access them on the web at http://www.asbdc-us.org.

International Franchise Association (IFA)

The International Franchise Association, founded in 1960, is a membership organization of franchisors, franchisees, and suppliers. IFA's website is dedicated to providing members and guests with a one-stop shopping experience for franchise information. For more than forty years, the International Franchise Association has protected, enhanced, and promoted franchising worldwide. IFA is the official "Spokesperson for Responsible Franchising." Franchisors join for the legislative, educational, and networking benefits available as an IFA member. IFA's government and public relations programs are designed to educate and influence public policy makers and to reduce or eliminate regulations that threaten responsible franchise development. IFA provides information necessary to stay abreast of the changes facing the global franchise community through their educational programs, annual convention, legal symposium, and regional and local meetings. For veterans, IFA's Veterans Transition Franchise Initiative program is comprised of more than one hundred franchise companies that offer veterans financial incentives to buy and operate their franchises.

Contact IFA by phone at 202-628-8000 or on the web at http://www.franchise.org.

Boots2Business

Boots2Business, http://www.boots2business.com/, is a comprehensive online resource, providing education and workplace training that is uniquely tailored to meet the needs of America's military personnel, including those in theater in Iraq and Afghanistan, as well as veterans, members of the National Guard and Reserve, service-disabled veterans, and their families. Boots-2Business combines elements from successful programs used independently in thousands of vocational schools, job-training centers, community colleges, detention and correctional facilities, Job Corps centers, and adult education programs nationally. TVC has integrated these elements into a cohesive and interactive online program that provides support to the basic, transitional, workforce, family, and entrepreneurial needs of Guard and Reserve veterans, service-disabled veterans, and their families.

This program has five key areas:

- Basic Skills, Catching up/Stepping up
- Transition Skills, Job and Career Preparation
- Workforce Success Skills, Getting a Job and Keeping It
- Entrepreneurial Skills, Start and Grow a Small Business
- Family Resource Center, Life and Family Support

Within these five sections are thirty-one clusters with one thousand course lessons and many tutorials to guide the student through their specific needs. Access to this site is in the form of a scholarship to the veteran and his or her family. Each scholarship is for one year and is provided by granting organizations or by TVC directly. The cost for each scholarship is $100. Were a veteran to purchase access to all the elements of Boots2Business without TVC, the cost would exceed $132,000 per year. TVC currently has three hundred scholarships for veterans and service-disabled veterans in New Jersey that are provided by the Henry H. Kessler Foundation. TVC is directly sponsoring a block of six hundred scholarships divided equally between its three hubs. Each hub will coordinate a statewide outreach giving Boots2Business a four-state network. An additional two hundred scholarships have been made possible through a grant from the NEC Foundation of America for national outreach. TVC is currently working with a number of corporations and foundations to extend this valuable scholarship program to all veterans and their families.

Access to Surety Bonding

TVC provides veteran contractors with access to surety bonding through an exclusive partnership with the Surety and Fidelity Association of America. Unlike other bonding programs available, this program is designed solely for veterans, including members of the National Guard and Reserve. It is a fully mentored program with no cap on the amount of the bond you can receive. Last year, the value of construction put into place, excluding single-family residential construction, was about $550 billion. For veteran contractors to secure some of that work, especially in the public sector, they must be surety bonded.

Surety bonds provide financial security and construction assurance to project owners by verifying that contractors are capable of performing the work and will be subcontractors, laborers, and material suppliers. There are three basic types of contract surety bonds:

- Bid bond
- Performance bond
- Payment bond

Surety bonds are extremely important for contractors and subcontractors. By the Miller Act of 1935, federal law mandates performance bonds for public works contracts over $100,000 and payment bonds for contracts over $25,000. In addition, most states require performance and payment bonds on all state and local public works projects.

TVC's partnership with SFAA provides both current and emerging veteran contractors and subcontractors with the education and training they need to do business with the government. TVC members can become experts in government contracting and surety bonding with four unique, two-hour training modules conducted by SFAA:

- Module A—Introduction to Surety Bonding: presents the basics of surety bonding, including how to obtain a bond, the costs of bonding, and how to develop a surety bond relationship.
- Module B—Construction Accounting and Financial Management: provides accounting fundamentals from job costing to financial reporting as well as construction-specific practices for contractors.
- Module C—Project Management: covers such topics as project planning methods, estimating bids, job costing, and scheduling.
- Module D—Why Contractors Fail: identifies the most common reasons why contractors fail, the ways to avoid common pitfalls, and the role surety bonding plays in ensuring contractor success. If you are interested in doing business with the government, you won't want to miss out on TVC's comprehensive, fully mentoring bonding program. They can help you fully prepare for your bond, identify a knowledgeable surety bond producer, and have your bond application submitted to a surety company for underwriting. Visit http://www.veteranscorp.org/Public/SuretyBonding .aspx to get started today.

ConnectVets *Business Forum*

ConnectVets Business Forum is a mentored, online meeting place for veteran entrepreneurs to interact with each other through a peer network. The

Forum is a place where veterans can post business questions, offer advice, and share business experiences. Monitored by volunteer veteran business owners and TVC staff, the Forum is designed specifically for the growing community of veteran entrepreneurs with topics covering everything from education to business plans to government contracting and more. To join the forum and get in touch with other veterans in business, visit http://www.connectvets.com/forum/.

Virtual Business Incubator

The Veterans Virtual Business Incubator (VBI) created for TVC by Knowledge Industries is a complete one-stop resource for veteran entrepreneurs starting or growing a small business. The VBI guides veterans through business ownership with customized support tools and the ability to search by state for local business resources. This is an excellent tool if you need to search for resources that are local to you. Visit the VBI at http://www.myvbi .org/?co=vetcorp.

Virtual Business Resource Center

TVC, in partnership with SCORE, created a veteran front-end portal to assist veteran entrepreneurs in getting the one-on-one support they need to become successful in their business ventures. Through this direct link on TVC's website, veterans are able to access SCORE's network of experienced and qualified mentors who can answer business questions, provide advice, and offer guidance. This program provides a key advantage for service men and women who are members of the National Guard and Reserve as they pursue their dreams for business ownership through entrepreneurship. Get connected to a SCORE mentor by visiting http://www.connectvets.com/score/.

EMPLOYMENT RESTRICTIONS AFTER LEAVING THE MILITARY

Postgovernment (Military) Service Employment Restriction Counseling should be completed during the transition process. You will be informed about this requirement when completing your DD Form 2648, Preseparation Counseling Checklist.

Postgovernment (military) employment restriction information will be provided by the military services as appropriate. Transition/Command Career Counselors shall refer separating and retiring servicemembers to an installation legal office (staff judge advocate or counselor's office) to ensure they receive a postgovernment (military) employment restrictions briefing, counseling, or appropriate information from an ethics official.

Additional information about employment restrictions after leaving the military is provided below.

Personal Lifetime Ban

SIMPLIFIED RULE: After you leave government service, you may not represent someone else to the government regarding **particular matters** that you worked on while in government service.

RULE: Former servicemembers may not knowingly make a communication or appearance on behalf of any other person, with the intent to influence, before any officer or employee of any federal agency or court in connection with a **particular matter** in which the officer or employee *personally and substantially* participated, which involved a *specific party* at the time of the participation and representation, and in which the United States is a party or has a direct and substantial interest. (18 U.S.C. 207[a] [1]) (This rule does not apply to former military enlisted personnel.)

Official Responsibility Two-year Ban

SIMPLIFIED RULE: For *two years* after leaving government service, you may not represent someone else to the government regarding *particular matters* that you did not work on yourself, but were **pending under your responsibility** during your last year of government service.

RULE: For a period of two years after termination of government service, former government officers and employees may not knowingly make a communication or appearance on behalf of any other person, with the intent to influence, before any officer or employee of any federal agency or court, in connection with a particular matter which the employee reasonably should have known was actually pending under his or her *official responsibility* within one year before the employee left government service, which involved a specific party at that time, and in which the United States is a party or has a direct and substantial interest. (18 U.S.C. 207[a] [2]) (This rule does not apply to former military enlisted personnel.)

Trade or Treaty One-year Ban

SIMPLIFIED RULE: For *one year* after leaving government service, you may not aid, advise, or represent someone else regarding trade or treaty negotiations that you worked on during your last year of government service.

RULE: For a period of one year after leaving government service, former employees or officers may not knowingly represent, aid, or advise someone else on the basis of *covered information*, concerning any ongoing *trade or treaty negotiation* in which the employee participated personally and substantially in his last year of government service. (18 U.S.C. 207[b]) (This rule does not apply to former military enlisted personnel.)

Compensation for Representation to the Government by Others

RULE: After you leave government service, you may not accept compensation for representational services, which were provided by anyone while you were a government employee, before a federal agency or court regarding particular matters in which the government was a party or had a substantial interest. This prohibition may affect personnel who leave the government and share in the proceeds of the partnership or business for representational services that occurred before the employee terminated federal service (Examples: Lobbying, consulting, and law firms). (18 U.S.C. 203) (This rule does not apply to former military enlisted personnel.)

Additional Restrictions for Retired Military Personnel and Reservists

SIMPLIFIED RULE: Foreign Employment—Unless you receive prior authorization from your Service Secretary and the Secretary of State, you may forfeit your military pay during the time you perform services for a foreign government.

RULE: The U.S. Constitution prohibits retired military personnel and Reservists from receiving pay from *foreign governments* without congressional authorization. This can extend to receipt of pay from a U.S. contractor or subcontractor for providing services to a foreign government. In 37 U.S.C. 908, Congress authorizes the Secretary of State and secretary of the appropriate military department to approve such receipt of pay. Each military service has implementing directives. Retired personnel and Reservists who violate this constitutional proscription may forfeit pay equal in amount to their foreign pay.

Employment By DoD: To avoid the appearance of favoritism, 5 U.S.C. 3326 prohibits the appointment of retired military personnel to civil service positions (including a nonappropriated fund activity) in any DoD component for six months after retirement. (**This restriction has been temporarily waived during the current national emergency following the attacks of 9/11.**)

The Secretary concerned may waive this prohibition. However, DoD Directive 1402.1 requires the Secretary concerned to conduct intensive external recruitment before granting the waiver.

Employment during Terminal Leave

Holding a civil office in state or local government: While on active duty (including terminal leave) military *officers* are prohibited by 10 U.S.C. 973(b) from holding a "civil office" with a state or local government.

Civilian position in the U.S. government: Military personnel on terminal leave are authorized to accept a civilian position in the U.S. government and receive the pay and allowances of that position as well as their military pay and allowances. (5 U.S.C. 5534a)

Note: Please remember that while on terminal leave, you are still an active duty servicemember, and the restrictions that apply to you while on active duty still apply. For example: restrictions on political activities.

Outside employment: If you are currently required to obtain permission prior to engaging in outside employment, that requirement will most likely carry over to you during terminal leave. Check with your supervisor.

Restriction on representing others to the federal government: You may not represent anybody outside the government to the government on any particular matter involving the government. Military officers working on terminal leave (like all federal employees) are prohibited by 18 USC 205 and 18 USC 203 from representing their new employer to the government. In almost every case, this precludes a member from interacting or appearing in the federal workplace as a contractor. Being present in government offices on behalf of a contractor inherently is a representation. Of course, military officers on terminal leave may begin work with the contractor, but only "behind the scenes" at a contractor office or otherwise away from the government workplace. **Enlisted members are not subject to 18 USC 203 or 205.**

Prohibition on working for a foreign principal: Over and above the restriction of receiving compensation from a foreign government, there is also a specific prohibition of a public official from being or acting as an agent of a foreign principal required to register under the Foreign Agents Registration Act of 1938 (expanding the restriction beyond foreign governments to include persons, partnerships, and corporations) (18 U.S.C. 219).

Spouse Employment

Finding a job is difficult at the best of times with the current state of the economy, and it poses even more problems if as a spouse you have to relocate because of transitioning. If you work for a national or multinational company with lots of offices, you may be able to continue working with them at your new location. While some jobs are almost recession-proof—teaching, nursing, and so on—getting hired for other jobs can be a challenge.

However, if you want to find work, a lot of resources are at your disposal. Ask family and friends to keep an ear out for any likely openings, contact the local labor office, and scan the local newspapers—their websites often post jobs before they appear in print—and send your resume around to prospective employers. One way to test the water is to register with a temporary placement agency. Lots of temp jobs lead to permanent employment; it gives you an opportunity to decide whether you like working for the company, and it gives them the chance to test your competencies.

Depending on your skill sets, there are lots of work-from-home jobs provided you have a computer and Internet connection. Opportunities in this area include translation and transcription services, bookkeeping, data entry, call center services, and so on. Be careful, though, as there are many scams involving working from home; check your prospective employer out carefully.

Consider going back to school or taking training courses to qualify for more jobs. There are many online and offline training and further-education opportunities.

If you are relocating, start the job search before you move. Make sure your resume and references are up-to-date. Don't wait until you have moved to do this—that is the time you need to be settling into your new home and available to respond to any job opportunities that arise. For that reason, it is a good idea to carry your resumes with you when you move rather than packing them.

If you hold a license or certificate to practice in a particular state, see what is needed to get that transferred to the state you are moving to.

5

Finding a Home

MOVING

Planning your final move is a critical part of your transition from the military. In this chapter you will be given a great deal of information and counseling to assist you with this planning. Knowing about the basic procedures and your rights is essential to helping you make informed decisions and ensures your last move will be a smooth one.

CHOOSING WHERE TO LIVE

Think about where you'd like to live and then consider the realities. For example, if you were a ship navigator during your military career, you could have a difficult time finding a similar job in Idaho. On the other hand, if you were an Army nurse, you may find several excellent opportunities in Idaho's many fine hospitals.

Most career placement specialists recommend that job applicants choose the type of job they want first, *then* go where the jobs are. In making a decision to relocate, you might prioritize communities as follows:

1. **Job potential:** Which community is most likely to offer job opportunities that match your skills, experience, and career goals?
2. **Affordability:** Consider the not-so-obvious expenses in addition to the cost of living. Compare local, state income, property, and sales taxes. Does the state tax your military retirement pay? Does the location have income and career potential?

3. **Community:** Do you have family or friends there? Can you count on them to help make your transition easier? Do you need to be close to your aging parents for economic or medical reasons? Are you seeking upward mobility with the potential to move, or are you looking for a community to settle for the long term?
4. **Environment:** Would you be happiest living in a city, the suburbs, a small town, or a rural area? Does the climate suit you?

MOVING OUT OF THE AREA

Before moving, consult your nearest Family Center, the best source of relocation information and planning assistance. Other useful resources include local chambers of commerce, libraries, bookstores, and the Internet. Use them to find out what you need in order to make informed moving decisions.

Family Centers

Family Centers can refer you to offices, programs, and services that may be of assistance as you prepare to leave the military. Examples include the Relocation Assistance Program (RAP), the Personal Financial Management Program, Information and Referral, Spouse Employment Assistance Program, and the Exceptional Family Member Program (EFMP).

The term *Family Centers* is used here to refer to the following service-specific entities:

- Army: Army Community Service Center
- Air Force: Airman and Family Readiness Center
- Navy: Fleet and Family Support Center
- Marine Corps: Marine and Family Services

PLANNING

Start making lists—lists of bills to be paid, utilities and services to be cancelled or transferred, people to be informed, important telephone numbers, and so on.

Gather together documents that you may need, such as medical records, birth certificates, marriage certificates, power of attorney, living will, and insurances.

Create a countdown calendar and enter everything that needs doing three months ahead of time (if you have that luxury of planning time), everything that needs doing one month out, one week out, and on the day. Keep referring to this calendar and add to it as you think of new things that have to be done.

Stay in touch with family and friends—they will be a great support group during the move.

BUYING YOUR FIRST HOME

If you have lived on base during your military career, you will have to find a new home and decide whether you want to buy or rent.

Buying your own home is always a sound investment, but it is also a major investment and one that many young couples have to think seriously about. With the present housing market there has never been a better time to buy, and as a former military couple you are eligible for special mortgage rates.

There are a lot of things that have to be considered. Buying a home is not only a big investment, it is also an ongoing one, with upkeep and maintenance, property taxes, and other fees and services that have to be paid. There is no doubt, however, that if you can afford to buy a house now it will steadily appreciate in value and be a valuable nest egg in years to come.

Some of the advantages of buying your own home are that you save on your income tax because your mortgage interest payments are deductible every year, and you own the place, so you are not paying rent every month with nothing back in return. If you own your home you can customize it to your liking—something most landlords don't encourage. Why would you spend money on upgrading a property you do not own? Another major advantage is that your house will appreciate in value and as it does so, your equity in the property increases. In a few years, if you need extra cash you can take out a loan against that equity.

There are downsides as well. Buying a home is an expensive initial investment, although buyers can exert a lot of leverage at the moment, such as getting the seller to pay all or some of your closing costs. If the seller is anxious to sell, this might be acceptable to them in order to close the deal. There are other costs such as legal fees, surveys, deposits, and so on. Then there are the ongoing payouts for mortgage, taxes, and homeowners insurance.

If you buy you will become responsible for upkeep and maintenance—if something goes wrong, you have to fix it. There may be housing association fees that have to be paid. To buy or not to buy has to be a decision taken together after much thought. Do you both want to be tied down with home ownership and everything that goes with it? Can you afford to buy a property—do you earn enough to pay the mortgage every month and not get into arrears? Rushed decisions are seldom the right ones.

FREQUENTLY ASKED QUESTIONS

Why Should I Buy, Instead of Rent?

A home is an investment. When you rent, you write your monthly check and that money is gone forever. But when you own your home, you can deduct the cost of your mortgage loan interest from your federal income taxes, and usually from your state taxes. This will save you a lot each year because the interest you pay will make up most of your monthly payment for most of the years of your mortgage. You can also deduct the property taxes you pay as a homeowner. In addition, the value of your home may go up over the years. Finally, you'll enjoy having something that's all yours—a home where your own personal style will tell the world who you are.

What Are "HUD Homes," and Are They a Good Deal?

HUD homes can be a very good deal. When someone with a HUD-insured mortgage can't meet the payments, the lender forecloses on the home; HUD pays the lender what is owed; and HUD takes ownership of the home. Then HUD sells it at market value as quickly as possible. Read all about buying a HUD home. Check listings of HUD homes and homes being sold by other federal agencies.

Can I Become a Homebuyer Even if I Have Bad Credit and Don't Have Much for a Down Payment?

You may be a good candidate for one of the federal mortgage programs. Start by contacting one of the HUD-funded housing counseling agencies that can help you sort through your options. Also, contact your local government to see if there are any local home buying programs that might work for you. Look in the blue pages of your phone directory for your local office of housing and community development or, if you can't find it, contact your mayor's office or your county executive's office.

Should I Use a Real Estate Broker? How Do I Find One?

Using a real estate broker is a very good idea. All the details involved in home buying, particularly the financial ones, can be mind-boggling. A good real estate professional can guide you through the entire process and make the experience much easier. A real estate broker will be well acquainted with all the important things you'll want to know about a neighborhood you may be considering . . . the quality of schools, the number of children in the area, the safety of the neighborhood, traffic volume, and more. He or she will help you figure the price range you can afford and search the classified ads and multiple listing services for homes you'll want to see. With immediate access to homes as soon as they're put on the market, the broker can save you hours of wasted driving-around time. When it's time to make an offer on a home, the broker can point out ways to structure your deal to save you money. He or she will explain the advantages and disadvantages of different types of mortgages, guide you through the paperwork, and be there to hold your hand and answer last-minute questions when you sign the final papers at closing. And you don't have to pay the broker anything! The payment comes from the home seller—not from the buyer.

By the way, if you want to buy a HUD home, you will be required to use a real estate broker to submit your bid. To find a broker who sells HUD homes, check your local yellow pages or the classified section of your local newspaper.

How Much Money Will I Have to Come up with to Buy a Home?

Well, that depends on a number of factors, including the cost of the house and the type of mortgage you get. In general, you need to come up with enough money to cover three costs: *earnest money*, the deposit you make on the home when you submit your offer to prove to the seller that you are serious about wanting to buy the house; the *down payment*, a percentage of the cost of the home that you must pay when you go to settlement; and *closing costs*, the costs associated with processing the paperwork to buy a house.

When you make an offer on a home, your real estate broker will put your earnest money into an escrow account. If the offer is accepted, your earnest money will be applied to the down payment or closing costs. If your offer is not accepted, your money will be returned to you. The amount of your earnest money varies. If you buy a HUD home, for example, your deposit generally will range from $500 to $2,000.

The more money you can put into your down payment, the lower your mortgage payments will be. Some types of loans require 10 to 20 percent of the purchase price. That's why many first-time homebuyers turn to HUD's FHA for help. FHA loans require only 3 percent down—and sometimes less.

Closing costs—which you will pay at settlement—average 3 to 4 percent of the price of your home. These costs cover various fees your lender charges and other processing expenses. When you apply for your loan, your lender will give you an estimate of the closing costs, so you won't be caught by surprise. If you buy a HUD home, HUD may pay many of your closing costs.

How Do I Know if I Can Get a Loan?

Use one of the many simple online mortgage calculators to see how much mortgage you could pay—that's a good start. If the amount you can afford is significantly less than the cost of homes that interest you, then you might want to wait a while longer. But before you give up, why don't you contact a real estate broker or a HUD-funded housing counseling agency? They will help you evaluate your loan potential. A broker will know what kinds of mortgages the lenders are offering and can help you choose a lender with a program that might be right for you. Another good idea is to get prequalified for a loan. That means you go to a lender and apply for a mortgage before you actually start looking for a home. Then you'll know exactly how much you can afford to spend, and it will speed the process once you do find the home of your dreams.

How Do I Find a Lender?

You can finance a home with a loan from a bank, a savings and loan, a credit union, a private mortgage company, or various state government lenders. Shopping for a loan is like shopping for any other large purchase: you can save money if you take some time to look around for the best prices. Different lenders can offer quite different interest rates and loan fees; and as you know, a lower interest rate can make a big difference in how much home you can afford. Talk with several lenders before you decide. Most lenders need three to six weeks for the whole loan approval process. Your real estate broker will be familiar with lenders in the area and what they're offering. Or you can look in your local newspaper's real estate section—most papers list interest rates being offered by local lenders. You can find FHA-approved lenders in the yellow pages of your phone book. HUD does not make loans directly—you must use a HUD-approved lender if you're interested in an FHA loan.

In Addition to the Mortgage Payment, What Other Costs Do I Need to Consider?

Well, of course you'll have your monthly utilities. If your utilities have been covered in your rent, this may be new for you. Your real estate broker will be able to help you get information from the seller on how much utilities normally cost. In addition, you might have homeowner association or condo association dues. You'll definitely have property taxes, and you also may have city or county taxes. Taxes normally are rolled into your mortgage payment. Again, your broker will be able to help you anticipate these costs.

So What Will My Mortgage Cover?

Most loans have four parts: *principal*, the repayment of the amount you actually borrowed; *interest*, payment to the lender for the money you've borrowed; *homeowners insurance*, a monthly amount to insure the property against loss from fire, smoke, theft, and other hazards required by most lenders; and *property taxes*, the annual city/county taxes assessed on your property, divided by the number of mortgage payments you make in a year. Most loans are for thirty years, although fifteen-year loans are available, too. During the life of the loan, you'll pay far more in interest than you will in principal—sometimes two or three times more! Because of the way loans are structured, in the first years you'll be paying mostly interest in your monthly payments. In the final years, you'll be paying mostly principal.

What Do I Need to Take with Me When I Apply for a Mortgage?

Good question! If you have everything with you when you visit your lender, you'll save a good deal of time. You should have: 1) social security numbers for both you and your spouse, if both of you are applying for the loan; 2) copies of your checking and savings account statements for the past six months; 3) evidence of any other assets like bonds or stocks; 4) a recent paycheck stub detailing your earnings; 5) a list of all credit card accounts and the approximate monthly amounts owed on each; 6) a list of account numbers and balances due on outstanding loans, such as car loans; 7) copies of your last two years' income tax statements; and 8) the name and address of someone who can verify your employment. Depending on your lender, you may be asked for other information.

I Know There Are Lots of Types of Mortgages—How Do I Know Which One Is Best for Me?

You're right—there are many types of mortgages, and the more you know about them before you start, the better. Most people use a fixed-rate mortgage. In a fixed-rate mortgage, your interest rate stays the same for the term of the mortgage, which normally is thirty years. The advantage of a fixed-rate mortgage is that you always know exactly how much your mortgage payment will be and you can plan for it. Another kind of mortgage is an Adjustable Rate Mortgage (ARM). With this kind of mortgage, your interest rate and monthly payments usually start lower than a fixed-rate mortgage. But your rate and payment can change either up or down, as often as once or twice a year. The adjustment is tied to a financial index, such as the U.S. Treasury Securities index. The advantage of an ARM is that you may be able to afford a more expensive home because your initial interest rate will be lower. There are several government mortgage programs, including the Veterans Administration's programs. Most people have heard of FHA mortgages. FHA doesn't actually make loans. Instead, it insures loans so that if buyers default for some reason, the lenders will get their money. This encourages lenders to give mortgages to people who might not otherwise qualify for a loan. Talk to your real estate broker about the various kinds of loans before you begin shopping for a mortgage.

When I Find the Home I Want, How Much Should I Offer?

Again, your real estate broker can help you here. But there are several things you should consider: 1) Is the asking price in line with prices of similar homes in the area? 2) Is the home in good condition, or will you have to spend a substantial amount of money making it the way you want it? You probably want to get a professional home inspection before you make your offer. Your real estate broker can help you arrange one. 3) How long has the home been on the market? If it's been for sale for a while, the seller may be more eager to accept a lower offer. 4) How much mortgage will be required? Make sure you really can afford whatever offer you make. 5) How much do you really want the home? The closer you are to the asking price, the more likely your offer will be accepted. In some cases, you may even want to offer more than the asking price if you know you are competing with others for the house.

What If My Offer Is Rejected?

They often are! But don't let that stop you. Now you begin negotiating. Your broker will help you. You may have to offer more money, but you may ask the seller to cover some or all of your closing costs or to make repairs that wouldn't normally be expected. Often, negotiations on a price go back and forth several times before a deal is made. Just remember—don't get so caught up in negotiations that you lose sight of what you really want and can afford!

So What Will Happen at Closing?

Basically, you'll sit at a table with your broker, the broker for the seller, probably the seller, and a closing agent. The closing agent will have a stack of papers for you and the seller to sign. While he or she will give you a basic explanation of each paper, you may want to take the time to read each one and/or consult with your agent to make sure you know exactly what you're signing. After all, this is a large amount of money you're committing to pay for a lot of years! Before you go to closing, your lender is required to give you a booklet explaining the closing costs, a "good faith estimate" of how much cash you'll have to supply at closing, and a list of documents you'll need at closing. If you don't get those items, be sure to call your lender BEFORE you go to closing. Don't hesitate to ask questions.

CHAMBERS OF COMMERCE

Many communities across America have chambers of commerce. Each chamber of commerce promotes its community and is a good source of information about the surrounding area: the local job market, housing costs, local realtors, cost of living, local taxes, climate, schools, and availability of recreation or child care. Ask for the chamber's booklet—much like the relocation packet you received about a new installation when you changed stations.

You can find any chamber of commerce office in the nation at http://www.chamberofcommerce.com.

LIBRARIES AND BOOKSTORES

Each of the Service Library Programs provides electronic content through their respective portals (http://www.nko.mil; http://www.army.mil/ako; http://www.my.af.mil). The electronic content provides information on relocating, career opportunities, and educational opportunities.

The reference section of your nearest installation library, public library, or bookstore may offer atlases, maps, and geographical information that provide useful information. Tour books and guides in the travel section may provide insights into the community you may someday call home. Military libraries and public libraries also have many other free resources. Libraries also let customers use their computers, which can help you keep up-to-date on the latest news in your new community, let you apply for a job, check your e-mail, or just chat with friends.

Here are some helpful websites on useful topics:

Relocation:
http://www.relo.usa.com
http://www.militaryonesource.com

Education:
http://www.voled.doded.mil
http://www.collegeboard.com
http://education.military.com

Jobs:
http://www.ajb.dni.us
http://www.acinet.org/acinet
http://www.careersingovernment.com
http://www.khake.com
http://www.military.com/spouse

Make full use of the library databases that are behind Army Knowledge Online (AKO)—Army personnel only. Go to the "My Library" site under self-service on the first page of AKO. It is easy navigation from there to the library reference databases that will help you find business information on companies (Newsbank), college information (Peterson's), resume preparation (Peterson's), and help in making financial decisions (Morningstar).

RELOCATION ASSISTANCE

Your upcoming relocation is not a normal move; it is your final move out of military life. Specialists within the Relocation Assistance Program want to make sure that you are fully prepared for this unique transition.
RAP services include:

- Needs assessment and planning for individuals and families tailored to their personal circumstances and requirements.
- Extensive automated information on military and civilian communities worldwide can be obtained through the Military Installations and Plan My Move features of MilitaryHOMEFRONT (http://www.military-homefront.dod.mil). These features provide research and information, housing directories and services, employment, education, health and wellness, and family issues available near military installations.
- Help in developing a relocation plan—providing information specifically related to your unique situation, linking you with special programs, and referring you to other offices that can provide assistance.
- Workshops and individual sessions on managing relocation stress for all family members; planning a moving budget; how to buy, sell, and rent smart; settling into a new community; and a variety of other programs tailored to adults and children.
- Special reentry services and programs if transitioning from an overseas installation.

A visit to your RAP specialist will help you identify exactly what you need so that you can ask the right questions as you navigate through the rest of the relocation process.

AS SOON AS YOU KNOW YOUR DEPARTURE DATE . . .

Visit the Relocation Assistance Program office at your Family Center. RAP staff will make you a "smart consumer." They will tell you the questions you need to ask so you can get the most out of your move.

Authorized Leave/Permissive Temporary Duty (PTDY) and Travel for Job Hunters

Under regulations prescribed by the Secretary of Defense, the Secretary of the Military Department concerned may authorize administrative absence for any of the purposes outlined below for servicemembers:

- Participation in preseparation job search and house-hunting activities that facilitate relocation of members.
- The permissive temporary duty (PTDY) authority to facilitate transition into civilian life for house and job hunting for military members being involuntarily separated under honorable conditions or retiring from active duty is extended indefinitely.

The Secretary concerned shall grant members being discharged or released from active service as involuntary separatees under honorable conditions as defined in section 1141 of Title 10 of the United States Code as such excess leave for a period not in excess of thirty days, or such transition PTDY not to exceed ten days, as members require to facilitate relocation, unless to do so would interfere with military missions; and may authorize for members described above and for those being retired:

- an additional twenty days up to a total of thirty days transition PTDY for those members stationed outside the Continental United States (CONUS).
- an additional ten days up to a total of twenty days transition PTDY for those members stationed in the CONUS.
- an additional twenty days up to a total of thirty days transition PTDY for those members who were domiciliaries before entering active duty and continue to be domiciliaries of states, possessions, or territories of the United States located outside the continental United States (CONUS), including domiciliaries of foreign countries, and are stationed at a location other than the state, possession, territory, or country of their domicile.

Members may be authorized up to a total of thirty days transition PTDY only for house hunting and job hunting to the state, territory, possession, or country of their domicile.

Regulations permit you to use excess leave or permissive temporary duty (PTDY) in accordance with the following guidance:

- **If you are an eligible involuntary separatee or a retiree:** Your spouse may take one round trip on the military aircraft for house and job hunting, on a space-available basis and unaccompanied by a military spouse.
- **If you are attending a Department of Defense–approved transition assistance seminar:** If you are using excess leave, PTDY, or temporary additional duty to attend the seminar, you are authorized to use military air transportation, if available.
- Servicemembers separating at the end of a normal term of service (ETS—Expiration Term of Service or EAOS—End of Active Duty Obligated Service) are not eligible for PTDY.
- If you are traveling from overseas to CONUS to attend such a seminar, your spouse can accompany you on military air transportation on a space-available basis. Your spouse is *not* authorized to travel within CONUS.

Unless a servicemember falls into one of the above categories, he/she is not eligible.

Transportation to Your New Home

Once you have chosen your new hometown, you should arrange for transportation counseling.

Schedule an appointment with your installation's transportation office as soon as you have your orders. This is extremely important, because the availability of movers is limited. The reimbursement amount is determined by the regulations pertaining to your particular entitlement.

Entitlements vary with individual situations. Your exact entitlement and the time limits for its use will be explained to you during your appointment. For example, if you are overseas, you may be authorized to ship an automobile to the United States. Motorcycles may be shipped as part of your personal property.

Note: Airline tickets must be purchased from the Commercial Travel Office (CTO) under contract to your respective organization. For more information, please go to: https://secureapp2.hqda.pentagon.mil.perdiem/.

Housing

The following is important guidance about making the transition from your old housing to your new.

If you live in government quarters: You must arrange a time for a member of the housing staff to come to your home to perform a preinspection and explain the requirements for cleaning and vacating quarters, as well as options available for you to accomplish them.

If you live in government housing, you must make an appointment with the Housing Office as soon as your departure date is established.

If you are moving from a rental property: Notify your landlord as soon as possible. The Housing Office can assist you with any landlord problems you may have in conjunction with your separation—for example, breaking a lease or early termination of a lease.

Shipment and Storage of Household Goods

The following guidance applies to the shipment and storage of household goods:

- **Eligibility Involuntary Separatees and Retirees:** You are authorized storage and shipment of household goods for up to one full year. Your items may be shipped to:
  ○ any destination within the United States.
  ○ your home of record outside the United States. Your home of record is the place you lived when you entered the military.
  ○ the place from which you were initially called to active duty.
- **All Others:** You are authorized storage and shipment of household goods up to six months.

Your items may be shipped to whichever of the following points for which you collected separation travel pay:

- Your home of record. Your home of record is the place you lived when you entered the military.
- The place from which you were initially called to active duty.

Special-Needs Family Members

Families with special needs members can find information on the services available in your new hometown through the Family Center, the United Way/

Community Chest, the community social services office listed in the local telephone directory, or the closest veterans' hospital. Information is also available through the Special Needs website at http://www.militaryhome front.dod.mil/.

"It's Your Move"

Be sure to download the latest version of the "It's Your Move" pamphlet (http://www.apd.army.mil/). It will give you the basic information you need to get started planning your household goods shipment.

Sharing Responsibilities

Sharing household chores is one of the most important factors in a happy marriage—and far more significant than having children, a study has found.

The findings, from an American survey of more than two thousand people, show the extent to which couples no longer see parenthood as central to their relationship, instead favoring "personal satisfaction," said researchers. Having a good sex life, a nice house, and shared tastes and interests were also put ahead of raising a family in the study of couples' priorities by the Pew Research Center in Washington. Overall, having children came eighth out of a list of nine factors seen as contributing to a successful marriage—a drop of five places on the same survey in 1990.

The top was "faithfulness," followed by "a happy sexual relationship," with "sharing household chores" in third. However, fighting over domestic duties and chores around the house is second only to conflict over money in a marriage. Most men do not pull their weight when it comes to chores around the house, and this can lead to resentment, especially if the wife has a job outside the home as well. Resentment then turns to anger, and you are on a slippery, downhill slope. Even if the wife is at home with the children all day, there is no reason why the husband should not help out. After all, marriage is a partnership.

One way to resolve issues is to sit down together and write down everything that needs to be done and then agree who will do what. One advantage of the list is that it may well come as a surprise just how much needs to be done. You could agree to alternate cooking the nightly meal or take it in turns to do the weekly wash. Some chores you could agree to do together, like the weekly grocery shopping or tidying up the yard.

Once you have decided who is doing what, that person must be allowed to get on with it their way. Nothing is likely to cause friction more than you popping your head around the door and telling your spouse how you would do it.

If you have children and they are old enough, they should help in the chores as well. Starting with little things like helping to set the table and putting toys away will all help. As they become older and more responsible, they can take on more chores and earn their allowance.

Children

Moving is particularly hard on children, especially if they are at school, have made lots of friends, and have favorite teachers. It is important to talk to them as soon as you know you are moving so that you address any fears they may have and get them used to the idea. They may well resent having to move, but spend time with them on the computer exploring your new home area—looking at the schools, attractions, sports facilities, and so on. If possible, try to make a quick visit so that you and they will have a clear idea of where they are moving to. Get them involved in the planning, but try to carry out your family routine as normal so that there is as little disruption as possible. These will help reassure them, because sudden changes to their routine will make them anxious.

Younger children are more able to take a move in their stride because their lives are constantly changing, but teenagers will need to be handled carefully. As teens they are already going through all sorts of emotional and developmental issues and this is the last thing they want, especially if they have started dating or just won a place on one of the school's sports teams. Get them involved from day one and keep them involved throughout the process.

If you have a special needs child, you should talk to your advisor or coordinator so that things are in place on your arrival at your new home—such as the right school, medical specialists, support groups, and so on.

6

Going Back to School

EDUCATION/TRAINING

Servicemembers leaving the military sometimes find a gap between the civilian careers they want and the specific education or training they need to achieve them. The following section will help you identify the resources to assist you in getting the training and education needed to help close that gap.

Your Education Benefits: Montgomery GI Bill, Post-9/11 GI Bill, VEAP, and More

Several programs administered by the Department of Veterans Affairs (VA) provide financial assistance to veterans for education programs. This includes enrollment in degree programs, technical and vocational programs, correspondence courses, flight training courses, and on-the-job training and apprenticeship programs. To be eligible programs must be approved, usually by a state approving agency, before VA education program benefits are paid.

Two of these programs are the Post-Vietnam-era Veterans' Educational Assistance Program (VEAP) and the Montgomery GI Bill (MGIB). Both programs are intended to help you develop skills that will enhance your opportunities for employment. As a rule, the benefits under either of these programs must be used within ten years of separation from active duty.

Post-Vietnam-Era Veterans' Education Assistance Program (VEAP) Eligibility

With the exception of some people who signed delayed entry contracts before January 1, 1977, VEAP is for people who first entered active duty during the period January 1, 1977, through June 30, 1985, and who made a contribution to a VEAP account before April 1, 1987. If you participated in VEAP and withdrew your contribution, you may start a new allotment or make a lump-sum contribution at any time while you are on active duty.

Montgomery GI Bill (MGIB) Eligibility

MGIB eligibility is straightforward for most veterans, but it can be complex for others. If you have questions about MGIB eligibility, check with your education center or call the VA toll-free education number, 1-888-GI Bill-1 (1-888-442-4551). You may also get information at the VA Education Service website at http://www.gibill.va.gov/.

With the exception of some officers who received a commission, after December 31, 1976, as a result of graduating from a service academy or after completing a Reserve Officer Training Corps (ROTC) scholarship program, the MGIB is for people who first came on active duty on July 1, 1985, or later, and who did not decline—in writing—to participate in the MGIB program.

To be eligible for the full thirty-six months of MGIB benefits, veterans must normally meet the character of service and minimum length of service requirements. Some veterans who are separated from active duty early for the convenience of the government may also receive the full thirty-six months of MGIB benefits. Depending on the reason for separation, other veterans who are separated from active duty early may be eligible for prorated—reduced— MGIB benefits; one month of benefits for each full month of active duty.

Some veterans who were eligible for the Vietnam Era GI Bill (VRA) have increased MGIB eligibility. They must have had some remaining VRA entitlement on December 31, 1989, when all benefits under the VRA expired. With some exceptions, they must have served on active duty from July 1, 1985, through June 30, 1988. For these veterans, the ten-year period of time in which they must use MGIB benefits is reduced by any time, from January 1, 1977, through June 30, 1985, that they were not on active duty.

Individuals who are involuntarily separated from the military and who were not originally eligible for the MGIB may have a second opportunity to receive MGIB benefits. This includes officers not normally eligible for the MGIB because they were commissioned after December 31, 1976, as a result of graduating from a service academy or after completing an ROTC scholarship, and people who declined to participate in the MGIB. Contact your education center or VA for details.

$600 Buy-up Program: You can get up to $150 per month added to your standard MGIB "payment rate." This could increase your total GI Bill benefit by up to $5,400. To take advantage you must be on active duty and elect to contribute up to $600 (in $20 increments) before you leave the service. Each $300 contributed earns an additional $75 a month in benefits. You can use DD Form 2366-1, Increased Benefit Contribution Program, to process your request through your local payroll or personnel office (http://www.dtic.mil/whs/directives/infomgt/forms/eforms/dd2366-1.pdf).

GI Bill Apprenticeship and OJT Programs: The Department of Veterans Affairs On-the-Job Training (OJT) and Apprenticeship Program offer you an alternative way to use your Montgomery GI Bill education and training benefits.

When you are trained for a new job, you can receive monthly training benefits from the Department of Veterans Affairs (VA) in addition to your regular salary. This means that you can receive up to $990.75 a month (or $237.75 for Guard/Reserve) tax free on top of your regular salary! The VA pays veteran Montgomery GI Bill participants $990.75 a month for the first six months of training, $726.55 for the second six months of training, and $462.35 for remaining training. If you are qualified for the Montgomery GI Bill or the Montgomery GI Bill for Selected Reserve and you have or are planning to start a new job or apprenticeship program, you should apply for this little-known MGIB benefit. In some cases, the VA will even pay retroactively for OJT from the past twelve months.

Call 1-888-GIBILL-1 to speak to a VA representative about your eligibility for this valuable program.

Note: You may not receive GI Bill OJT benefits at the same time you receive other GI Bill education benefits.

NEW Post-9/11 GI Bill—Chapter 33

The Post-9/11 GI Bill is a new education benefit program that will provide servicemembers with college tuition and stipends for housing and books. This program went into effect on August 1, 2009. To qualify for this benefit you must serve a minimum of ninety days on active duty after September 10, 2001. This includes active duty service as a member of the Armed Forces or as a result of a call or order to active duty from a Reserve component (National Guard and Reserve) under certain sections of Title 10. The new Post-9/11 GI Bill will pay up to 100 percent for tuition, a monthly housing stipend based on the DoD Basic Allowance for Housing at the E-5 with dependents payment rate, and up to $1,000 a year for books and supplies.

Your benefits under the Post-9/11 GI Bill will vary depending on your state of residence, number of education units taken, and amount of post-September 11, 2001, active duty service. Here is a quick reference showing the percentage of total combined benefit eligibility based on the following periods of post-9/11 service:

- 100 percent—thirty-six or more cumulative months
- 100 percent—thirty or more consecutive days with disability-related discharge
- 90 percent—thirty or more cumulative months
- 80 percent—twenty-four or more cumulative months
- 70 percent—eighteen or more cumulative months
- 60 percent—twelve or more cumulative months
- 50 percent—six or more cumulative months
- 40 percent—ninety or more days

However, some periods of active duty service are excluded. Periods of service under the following do not count toward qualification for the Post-9/11 GI Bill:

- NOAA, PHS, or Active Guard Reserve;
- ROTC under 10 U.S.C. 2107(b);
- Service academy contract period;
- Service terminated due to defective enlistment agreement;
- Service used for loan repayment; *AND*
- Selected Reserve service used to establish eligibility under the Montgomery GI Bill (MGIB Chapter 30), MGIB for Selected Reserve (MGIB-SR Chapter 1606), or the Reserve Education Assistance Program (REAP Chapter 1607).

Learn more about the Post-9/11 GI Bill by downloading the Department of Veterans Affairs Post-9/11 GI Bill Pamphlet (PDF) at http://www.gibill .va.gov/pamphlets/CH33/CH33_Pamphlet.pdf.

For More Information

The VA can provide you with educational counseling after you leave the service. Contact the VA GI Bill Regional Processing Office by dialing toll free 1-888-GI Bill-1 (1-888-442-4551) or go to the MGIB website at http://www.gibill.va.gov.

To contact the VA Regional Office closest to you, go to http://www1.va.gov/ directory/guide/home.asp and click on "Type of Facility." Then, click on your state to locate the regional office nearest you. In addition, information on MGIB and other veterans' educational benefit programs is available from your installation's education center or from the admissions office and/or veterans' coordinator at most colleges and universities.

Did You Know? You qualify for Federal Financial Student Aid such as Pell Grants and the Stafford Loan Program even if you are still on active duty. Visit http://www.fafsa.ed.gov/ to learn how to apply.

ADDITIONAL EDUCATIONAL OR TRAINING OPTIONS

The transition from military to civilian life is an excellent time to take a serious look at your options for future success. Now is the best time to evaluate your educational options.

Guidance Counseling

Before you leave the military, go to your local education center, Navy college office, or Marine Corps Lifelong Learning Center. The counselors can provide assistance in determining the goals that are right for you. If you feel you need additional education or training, the Education Counselor will guide you to the appropriate curriculum and institution and help you with the paperwork necessary to enroll in an academic or vocational program.

Career Assessment

If you are not sure what you want to do upon leaving the military, then you should talk to a counselor at your local education center, Navy college office, Marine Corps Lifelong Learning Center, or transition office. The counselor can recommend aptitude tests or vocational interest inventories to help clarify your career goals. These tests can help you pinpoint job skills in which you might excel and then relate them to specific occupations and careers in the civilian world.

Your installation's education center, Navy college office, or Marine Corps Lifelong Learning Center may offer the Strong Interest Inventory, Self-Directed Search, or Career Assessment Inventory as well as computerized counseling systems like Discover. These can help you select jobs and careers that more closely match your personality, background, and career goals.

Academic Planning

Once you have identified your career goal, you may find you need a formal education to achieve it. Your education counselor can explore the possibilities with you. Counselors can also advise you on nontraditional educational opportunities that can make it easier for you to get a diploma, vocational certificate, or college degree. These nontraditional opportunities include the following:

- **Take "challenge exams," such as a college-level equivalency exam:** You can convert knowledge learned outside the classroom into credits toward a college program. This can save you time and money.
- **Go to school part time while continuing to hold down a full-time job:** This approach might make adult education more practical.
- **See the veterans' coordinator at the college, university, or vocational school of your choice:** The coordinator can help you understand your VA educational benefits and might lead you to special programs offered to former servicemembers.
- **Determine if your military learning experiences can translate to course credit:** Check with your service education center, Navy college office, or Marine Corps Lifelong Learning Center well in advance of your separation date to request copies of your transcripts.
- **Take advantage of distance learning opportunities:** With today's technological advances, you can enroll in an educational program in which courses are offered by accredited educational institutions in a variety of formats, i.e., CD-ROM, the Internet, satellite TV, cable TV, and video tapes.

Vocational Services

The education center, Navy college office, or Marine Corps Lifelong Learning Center can tell you about vocational and technical school programs designed to give you the skills needed to work in occupations that do not require a four-year college degree. The counselors at these centers can also show you how to get course credits for nontraditional learning experience (such as military certifications and on-the-job training). The counselors can help you explore these options. The counselors may also help you find out about certification and licensing requirements—for example, how to get a journeyman card for a particular trade. The counselors can give you information on vocational and apprenticeship programs.

   Note: Local trade unions may also offer vocational training in fields that interest you.

Licensing and Certification

Your military occupational specialty may require a license or certification in the civilian workforce. There are several resources available to assist you in finding civilian requirements for licensing and certification; see the Department of Labor website at http://www.acinet.org. Go to the "Career Tools" section to look up licenses by state, requirements for the license, and point-of-contact information for the state licensing board.

- DANTES website has information on certification programs: http://www.dantes.doded.mil/dantes_web/danteshome.asp.
- Find civilian credentials related to your military occupational specialty, learn what it takes to obtain the credentials, and see if there are available programs that will help pay credentialing fees: https://www.cool.army.mil/.
- Find civilian credentials related to your Navy rating, learn what it takes to obtain the credentials, and see if there are available programs that will help pay credentialing fees: https://www.cool.navy.mil/.

Testing Available through Your Education Center

Testing can be an important first step in your career development. Some colleges and universities may require you to provide test results as part of your application. Prior to your departure from military service, you are encouraged to take advantage of the testing services offered by the education center, Navy college office, and Marine Corps Lifelong Learning Center. These services include the following:

Vocational interest inventories: Most education centers, Navy college offices, and Marine Corps Lifelong Learning Centers offer free vocation interest inventories that can help you identify the careers most likely to interest you.

Academic entry exams: Before applying for college or other academic programs, you may want to take a college admission test, such as the Scholastic Aptitude Test (SAT), ACT, or the Graduate Record Examination (GRE). Some schools may require that you do so. Information on these tests is available from your education center, Navy college office, or Marine Corps Lifelong Learning Center. You must start early. These exams are offered only a few times each year.

Credit by examination: Your education center, Navy college office, and Marine Corps Lifelong Learning Center offers a variety of "challenge" exams that can lead to college credit. If you score high enough, you may be exempt from taking a certain class or course requirements—resulting in a big savings of time and money as you earn your degree. The College Level Examination Program (CLEP) and the DANTES Subject Standardized Tests (DSST) are also free to servicemembers on active duty.

Certification examinations: As a servicemember working in an important occupational field, you have received extensive training (service schools, correspondence courses, OJT) that has proved valuable in developing your professional skills. Your local education center, Navy college office, or Marine Corps Lifelong Learning Center can provide you information on certification examinations that "translate" military training into civilian terms. Examinations are available in many skill areas, and upon successful completion the documentation you receive is readily understood and received in the professional occupational civilian community.

Save time and money: You can get up to thirty college credits by taking the five CLEP general exams. If you are currently serving in the Armed Forces, you can take these exams for free.

Contact your installation education center, Navy college office, or Marine Corps Lifelong Learning Center to ensure that they have the capability to offer examinations you need in paper and pencil or computer-base-testing (CBT) format.

DOD VOLUNTARY EDUCATION PROGRAM WEBSITE

For separating servicemembers, the Department of Defense Voluntary Education Program website, http://apps.mhf.dod.mil/pls/psgprod/f?p=VOLED:HOME:0, offers a wide variety of educational information of interest and use. The website was originally established to provide support for military education center staffs worldwide. As the website developed, it took on the mission of providing direct support to Active and Reserve components' servicemembers and their families. This support includes information on all programs provided by the Defense Activity for Nontraditional Educational Support (DANTES), including the Distance Learning Program, Examination Program, Certification Program, Counselor Support Program, Troops to Teachers, and a wide variety of educational catalogs and directories.

Links are provided to each of the services' education programs and to a wide variety of education-related resources. There is also a directory of education centers on the website, which contains information on all of the services' education centers worldwide, to include addresses, phone numbers, and e-mail addresses.

The primary goal of the website is to provide on site, or through links, all information for servicemembers to select, plan, and complete their program of study, either while on active duty or upon separation.

SERVICE UNIQUE TRANSCRIPTS

Army: For everything you want to know about the free AARTS transcript (Army/American Council on Education Registry Transcript System), go to http://aarts.army.mil. This free transcript includes your military training, your Military Occupational Specialty (MOS), and college-level examination scores with the college credit recommended for those experiences. It is a valuable asset that you should provide to your college or your employer, and it is available for Active Army, National Guard, and Reserve soldiers. You can view and print your own transcript at this website.

Save time and money: Unless you know for sure that you need to take a particular course, wait until the school gets *all* your transcripts before you sign up for classes. Otherwise you may end up taking courses you don't need.

Navy and Marine Corps: Information on how to obtain the Sailor/Marine American Council on Education Registry Transcript (SMART) is available at https://www.navycollege.navy.mil/transcript.html. SMART is now available to document the American Council on Education (ACE) recommended college credit for military training and occupational experience. SMART is an academically accepted record that is validated by ACE. The primary purpose of SMART is to assist servicemembers in obtaining college credit for their military experience. Additional information on SMART can also be obtained from your nearest Navy college office or Marine Corps education center, or contact the Navy college center.

Air Force: The Community College of the Air Force (CCAF) automatically captures your training, experience, and standardized test scores. Transcript information may be viewed at the CCAF website, http://www.au.af.mil/au/ccaf/.

Coast Guard: The Coast Guard Institute (CGI) requires each servicemember to submit documentation of all training (except correspondence course records), along with an enrollment form, to receive a transcript. Transcript information can be found at the Coast Guard Institute website: http://www.uscg.mil/hq/cgi/.

U.S. DEPARTMENT OF EDUCATION FINANCIAL AID PROGRAMS

Federal Student Aid, an office of the U.S. Department of Education, offers over $80 billion in financial aid that helps millions of students manage the cost of education each year. There are three categories of federal student aid: grants, work-study, and loans. Even if you are still on active duty, you can apply for aid such as Pell Grants or Federal Stafford Loans. Find out more by visiting http://www.federalstudentaid.ed.gov/.

158

Chapter 6

How do I get this aid? By completing the Free Application for Federal Student Aid (FAFSA). You can apply online or on paper, but filing online is faster and easier. Get further instructions on the application process at http://www.fafsa.ed.gov/. You should also apply for a Federal Student Aid PIN (if you haven't done so already). The PIN allows you to sign your application electronically, which speeds up the application process even more. Apply for a PIN at http://www.pin.ed.gov/.

Whose information do I include on my FAFSA? There is a series of eight questions on the application that ask about your dependency status. If you are a veteran, or are currently serving on active duty in the U.S. Armed Forces for purposes other than training, you are considered an independent student and would only include your information (and that of your spouse, if married). For more detailed information go to http://www.fafsa.ed.gov/.

What determines my eligibility for federal student aid? Eligibility for federal student aid is based on financial need and on several other factors. The financial aid administrator at the college or career school you plan to attend will determine your eligibility. To receive aid from the programs, you must

- demonstrate financial need (except for certain loans—your school can explain which loans are not need based).
- have a high school diploma or a General Education Development (GED) certificate, pass a test approved by the U.S. Department of Education, meet other standards your state establishes that the Department approves, or complete a high school education in a home school setting that is treated as such under state law.
- be working toward a degree or certificate in an eligible program.
- be a U.S. citizen or eligible noncitizen.
- have a valid Social Security Number (unless you're from the Republic of the Marshall Islands, the Federated States of Micronesia, or the Republic of Palau).
- register with the Selective Service if required. You can use the paper or electronic FAFSA to register, you can register at http://www.sss.gov/, or you can call 1-847-688-6888. (TTY users can call 1-847-688-2567.)
- maintain satisfactory academic progress once in school.
- certify that you are not in default on a federal student loan and do not owe money on a federal student grant.
- certify that you will use federal student aid only for educational purposes.

Can I use my Montgomery GI Bill and still get Federal Student Aid at the same time? Yes. When you complete your FAFSA, you will be asked what you will be receiving in veterans' educational benefits, which the Montgomery GI Bill falls under. Your school will take into consideration the amount you list on the application, along with any other financial assistance you are eligible to receive, in preparing your financial aid package.

Can you tell me a little about the Veterans Upward Bound Program? The Veterans Upward Bound Program is a free U.S. Department of Education program designed to help eligible U.S. military veterans refresh their academic skills so that they can successfully complete the postsecondary school of their choosing.

The VUB program services include:

- Basic skills development, which is designed to help veterans successfully complete a high school equivalency program and gain admission to college education programs.
- Short-term remedial or refresher classes for high school graduates that have put off pursuing a college education.
- Assistance with applications to the college or university of choice.
- Assistance with applying for financial aid.
- Personalized counseling.
- Academic advice and assistance.
- Career counseling.
- Assistance in getting veterans services from other available resources.
- Exposure to cultural events, academic programs, and other educational activities not usually available to disadvantaged people.

The VUB program can help you improve your skills in:

- Mathematics
- Foreign Language
- Composition
- Laboratory Science
- Reading
- Literature
- Computer Basics
- Any other subjects you may need for success in education beyond high school
- Tutorial and Study Skills Assistance

To be eligible for VUB you must:

- be a U.S. military veteran with 181 or more days active duty service and discharged on/after January 31, 1955, under conditions other than dishonorable; *AND*

- meet the criteria for low income according to guidelines published annually by the U.S. Department of Education, AND/OR a first-generation
  potential college graduate; *AND*
- demonstrate academic need for Veterans Upward Bound; *AND*
- meet other local eligibility criteria as noted in the local VUB project's
  Approved Grant Proposal, such as county of residence, and so on.

For more information, as well as a link to individual program locations,
visit http://navub.org/.

What if I have children who will be getting ready for college soon? Will they
qualify for aid? Federal Student Aid has a new tool called FAFSA4caster, designed to help students and their families plan for college. The FAFSA4caster
provides students with an early estimate of their eligibility for federal student
financial assistance. Military dependents who are enrolled in college and are
eligible to receive Pell Grants should check out the two newest programs:
Academic Competitiveness Grants and National Science and Mathematics
Access to Retain Talent Grants (National SMART Grants). Visit their website at http://www.FederalStudentAid.ed.gov for more information.

7

Health and Insurance

Many servicemembers are caught by surprise when they realize the actual cost of providing health care insurance for themselves and their families. Before you leave military service, you need to arrange for health insurance to protect you and your family. This section will help you learn about your options and plan for your health care insurance needs.

PLANNING IS CRITICAL

Most people leaving the military get civilian jobs that provide health care insurance. The result is continuous coverage. Sometimes, however, there is a gap between the time your service-provided coverage ends and your new employer's coverage begins. During this time, you alone are responsible for paying all the medical bills that you and your family might acquire. This could be devastating. A one-day stay in the hospital could cost thousands of dollars!

Fortunately, several resources are available to ensure continuous, comprehensive, quality health care for you and your family. Your options will be explained to you during your appointment at your transition office. For specific health insurance questions, call the Health Benefits Advisor at your military medical treatment facility.

Expecting a Baby?

If you and your spouse are expecting a baby, make sure your insurance covers the infant from the date of birth, as opposed to twelve or thirteen days after birth. Medical expenses within these first two critical weeks can be costly and should be covered.

Expecting parents should meet with their local health benefits advisor early in the transition process to get additional information regarding health care and health insurance for the period following the servicemember's separation. Separating active duty servicemembers who separate from the military prior to delivery may be eligible to deliver the child in a military treatment facility after separation. Again, check with the commander at your military treatment facility and your health benefits advisor before you separate to see if you are eligible.

"Check Up" on Your Health before You Leave

While you are in the service, you and your family have health care coverage. The range of health care services is vast, yet your out-of-pocket expense is minimal. Use this time wisely and make an appointment early. Remember:

- **Get a physical:** If military treatment facilities, personnel resources, and local policy permit, you and your family members should arrange for your separation physicals as early as possible. Any problems can be treated while your medical expenses are still fully covered by the service. Take care of as much as you can prior to separation.
- **Get your records:** Even if you are in good health, get a copy (certified, if possible) of your medical records from your medical treatment facility. These records will provide useful background information to the health care professionals who will assist you in your upcoming civilian life. Your military health records will be transferred (with your consent) to the VA regional office nearest your separation address.

Post-traumatic Stress Disorder

Post-traumatic stress disorder can occur following a life-threatening event like military combat, natural disasters, terrorist incidents, serious accidents, or violent personal assaults like rape. Most survivors of trauma return to normal given a little time. However, some people have stress reactions that don't go away on their own or may even get worse over time. These individuals may develop PTSD.

People who suffer from PTSD often suffer from nightmares, flashbacks, difficulty sleeping, and feeling emotionally numb. These symptoms can significantly impair your daily life. In addition, PTSD is marked by clear physical and psychological symptoms. It often has symptoms like depression, substance abuse, problems of memory and cognition, and other physical and mental health problems. The disorder is also associated with difficulties in social or family life, including occupational instability, marital problems, family discord, and difficulties in parenting. If you think you may be suffering from PTSD, the following list of resources and information will help you find help in dealing with PTSD and related conditions.

Online PTSD Resources

DoD Mental Health Self-Assessment Program is a mental health and alcohol screening and referral program provided for military families and servicemembers affected by deployment and mobilization. This voluntary and anonymous program is offered online, by phone, and through special events held at installations and reserve units. Anonymous self-assessments are available for depression, bipolar disorder, alcohol use, post-traumatic stress disorder, and generalized anxiety disorder.

Individualized results and military health resources, including TRICARE, Vet Centers, and Military OneSource are provided at the end of every assessment.

National Center for Post-Traumatic Stress Disorder (PTSD)

A special center within the Department of Veterans Affairs was created to advance the clinical care and social welfare of America's veterans through research, education, and training in the science, diagnosis, and treatment of PTSD and stress-related disorders. Consult the website for more information: http://www.ncptsd.va.gov/index.html.

Ameriforce Deployment Guide

For fact sheets and information for servicemembers and their families on postdeployment, including home, finances, career, and more, see http://www .ameriforce.net/deployment/.

COURAGE TO CARE

A site created by Uniformed Services University for the Health Sciences, which belongs to the Center for Traumatic Studies and includes a wealth of additional information, "Courage to Care" is an electronic health campaign for military and civilian professionals serving the military community, and for

military men, women, and families. See http://www.usuhs.mil/psy/courage
.html.

MILITARY ONESOURCE

This free, twenty-four-hour service, provided by the Department of Defense,
is available to all active duty, Guard, and Reserve members and their families.
Consultants provide information and make referrals on a wide range of issues. You can reach the program by telephone at 1-800-342-9647 or through
the website at http://www.militaryonesource.com/.

TRANSITIONAL HEALTH CARE FOR YOU AND YOUR FAMILY

The Transitional Assistance Management Program (TAMP) offers transitional
TRICARE coverage to certain separating active duty members and their eligible family members. Care is available for a limited time. TRICARE eligibility
under the TAMP has been permanently extended to 180 days.

There are four categories of eligibility for TAMP:

- Members involuntarily separated from active duty and their eligible family members;
- National Guard and Reserve members, collectively known as the Reserve Component (RC), separated from active duty after being called up
  or ordered in support of a contingency operation for an active duty period
  of more than thirty days, and their family members;
- Members separated from active duty after being involuntarily retained
  in support of a contingency operation, and their family members; *AND*
- Members separated from active duty following a voluntary agreement
  to stay on active duty for less than one year in support of a contingency
  mission, and their family members.

Active duty sponsors and family members enrolled in TRICARE Prime
who desire to continue their enrollment upon the sponsor's separation from
active duty status are required to reenroll. To reenroll, the sponsor or family
member must complete and submit a TRICARE Prime enrollment application. Contact your servicing personnel center prior to separating to see if
you are TAMP eligible. Under TAMP, former active duty sponsors, former
activated reservists, and family members of both are not eligible to enroll
or reenroll in TRICARE Prime Remote or in TRICARE Prime Remote for

Active Duty Family Members because both programs require the sponsor to be on active duty. Under the TAMP, the sponsor is no longer on active duty and is treated as an active duty family member for benefits and cost-sharing purposes.

Note: Transitional health care does not apply to retirees.

Once your initial transitional health care ends: After this 180-day period, you and your family are no longer eligible to use military treatment facilities or TRICARE. However, you may purchase health care coverage, known as the Continued Health Care Benefit Program (CHCBP). You have sixty days after your initial transitional health care ends to enroll in CHCBP. You and your family members will be issued overstamped identification cards that will allow you to use military treatment facilities after your separation. The cards will be marked with the dates you are eligible for transitional health care.

You can learn more about TRICARE at http://www.tricare.mil/.

All Others

If you separate voluntarily, you and your family are not eligible to use military treatment facilities or TRICARE. However, you may purchase extended transitional health care coverage (CHCBP) for up to eighteen months of coverage. You have sixty days after separation to enroll in CHCBP. Your coverage will start the day after your separation.

CHCBP: YOUR OPTION TO PURCHASE TEMPORARY MEDICAL COVERAGE

Following the loss of eligibility to military medical benefits, you or a family member may apply for temporary, transitional medical coverage under CHCBP. CHCBP is a premium-based health care program providing medical coverage to a select group of former military beneficiaries. CHCBP is similar to, but not part of, TRICARE. The CHCBP program extends health care coverage to the following individuals when they lose military benefits:

- the servicemember (who can also enroll his or her family members)
- certain former spouses who have not remarried
- certain children who lose military coverage

DoD contracted with Humana Military Healthcare Services, Inc., to administer CHCBP. You may contact them in writing or by phone for information regarding CHCBP. This includes your eligibility for enrolling in the program, to request a copy of the CHCBP enrollment application, to obtain information regarding the health care benefits that are available to CHCBP enrollees, and to obtain information regarding the premiums and out-of-pocket costs once you are enrolled.

Humana Military Healthcare Services, Inc.
Attn: CHCBP
P.O. Box 740072
Louisville, KY 40201
1-800-444-5445

A copy of the CHCBP enrollment application can also be found on the web at http://www.humanamilitary.com/chcbp/pdf/dd2837.pdf.

CHCBP Basics

Continuous coverage: CHCBP is a health care program intended to provide you with continuous health care coverage on a temporary basis following your loss of military benefits. It acts as a "bridge" between your military health benefits and your new job's medical benefits, so you and your family will receive continuous medical coverage.

Preexisting condition coverage: If you purchase this conversion health care plan, CHCBP may entitle you to coverage for preexisting conditions often not covered by a new employer's benefit plan.

Benefits: The CHCBP benefits are comparable to the TRICARE Standard benefits.

Enrollment and Coverage

Eligible beneficiaries must enroll in CHCBP within sixty days following the loss of entitlement to the military health system. To enroll, you will be required to submit:

- a completed DD Form 2837, Continued Health Care Benefit Program (CHCBP) Application.
- documentation as requested on the enrollment form, e.g., DD Form 214, Certificate of Release or Discharge from Active Duty; final divorce decree; DD Form 1173, Uniformed Services Identification and Privilege Card. Additional information and documentation may be required to confirm an applicant's eligibility for CHCBP.
- a premium payment for the first ninety days of health coverage.

The premium rates are approximately $930 per quarter for individuals and $2,000 per quarter for families.

Humana Military Healthcare Services, Inc., will bill you for subsequent quarterly premiums through your period of eligibility once you are enrolled. The program uses existing TRICARE providers and follows most of the rules and procedures of the TRICARE Standard program.

Depending on your beneficiary category, CHCBP coverage is limited to either eighteen or thirty-six months as follows:

- eighteen months for separating servicemembers and their families
- thirty-six months for others who are eligible (in some cases, former spouses who have not remarried may continue coverage beyond thirty-six months if they meet certain criteria)

You may not select the effective date of coverage under CHCBP. For all enrollees, CHCBP coverage must be effective on the day after you lose military benefits.

Coverage for All Others

If you separate voluntarily, you and your family are not eligible to use military treatment facilities or TRICARE. However, you may purchase extended transitional health care coverage (CHCBP) for up to eighteen months. You have sixty days after separation to enroll in CHCBP. Your coverage will start the day after your separation.

For more information about CHCBP, visit their website at http://www .humanamilitary.com/south/bene/TRICAREPrograms/chcbp.asp or call their toll-free line at 1-800-444-5445.

MEDICAL CARE OVERVIEW FOR RETIREES

TRICARE offers retiree beneficiaries three options in obtaining medical care.

1. TRICARE Prime: This is a health maintenance organization-type managed care program for which retirees are required to pay an annual enrollment fee. Enrollees are assigned a primary care manager, who determines the most appropriate, available source of care—either a military treatment facility or a civilian network provider. Enrollees pay little or no copayment and usually are not required to file claims for their care.

2. TRICARE Extra: This is a preferred provider organization-type program; no enrollment is required, however, care has to be provided by a
   TRICARE network provider. You will be responsible for paying the annual deductible and cost shares at a reduced rate. The network provider
   will file your claim.
3. TRICARE Standard: This is a fee for service option that requires an annual
   deductible and cost shares after the deductible has been reached. Under
   TRICARE Standard you are responsible for filing your claim. Beneficiaries should contact their Health Benefits Advisors/Beneficiary Counselor
   and Assistance Coordinators (BCAC) at military treatment facilities or
   stop in at your TRICARE Service Center for more assistance. You can
   locate the BCAC for your state at http://www.tricare.mil/bcacdcao/.

TRICARE for Life

If a member or family member becomes entitled to Medicare Part A, whether
due to a disability or when they turn sixty-five, they are eligible for TRICARE
For Life (TFL). There are no TFL enrollment fees, but you are required to pay
Medicare Part B premiums (unless the sponsor is on active duty). When using
TFL, TRICARE is the second payer after Medicare in most cases. For more
information about TFL, visit http://wwww.tricare.mil/tfl or search online for
"TRICARE for Life"; you may also call Wisconsin Physicians Service–TFL
at 1-866-773-0404 (1-866-773-0405 TTY/TDD for the hearing impaired).

Survivors

Family members are entitled to TRICARE benefits as transitional survivors
or survivors if their active duty service sponsor died while serving on active duty for a period of more than thirty days. TRICARE pays transitional
survivor claims at the active duty family member payment rate and pays survivor claims at the retiree payment rate for surviving spouses while eligible
children claims process at the active duty family member rate. Transitional
survivors pay no enrollment fees or copayments when they use TRICARE
Prime. They will, however, pay cost shares and deductibles at the active duty
family member rate to use TRICARE Standard or TRICARE Extra. Contact
your regional contractor or visit http://www.tricare.mil/.

DEPARTMENT OF VETERANS AFFAIRS (VA) MEDICAL CARE

Recent legislation has changed the eligibility requirements for VA medical
care. In some cases, veterans and their families may still be eligible to receive

medical benefits through VA. However, VA's medical care system is set up to provide quality medical care to those who need it most and can afford it least.

This means that the least fortunate veterans may receive unlimited medical care at no cost. On the other hand, most veterans will find their VA medical benefits are limited. Therefore, these "typical" veterans should *not* rely on the VA as their sole source of medical services.

If you served in the Gulf War, the Office of the Special Assistant for Gulf War Illnesses has established a website at http://www.gulflink.osd.mil/ to provide information to you. In addition to the website, you may also call the Gulf War/Agent Orange Hotline at 1-800-749-8387 for additional information.

VA Health Care Eligibility

Eligibility for VA health care is dependent upon a number of variables, which may influence the final determination of the services for which you qualify. These factors include the nature of your discharge from military service (e.g., honorable, other than honorable, dishonorable), length of service, and the VA determination on any service-connected disability claims, income level, and the available VA resources. Generally, you must be enrolled in the VA health care system to receive benefits offered in the medical benefits package. To apply for VA health care benefits, including enrollment, you must fill out an application. Enrollment forms and instructions can be found at https://www.1010ez.med.va.gov/sec/vha/1010ez/.

The application process is used to determine:

1. Whether you have qualifying service as a veteran
2. What your veteran status is so that you can be placed into one of the eight priority groups

Eligibility for health care through VA is a two-step process:

1. VA must determine your eligibility status as a veteran by reviewing your:
   • character of discharge from active military service
   • length of active military service
2. VA must determine whether you qualify for one of eight enrollment priority groups.

Go to http://www.va.gov/healtheligibility/ for more information, or call your VA regional office toll free at 1-800-827-1000.

DISABLED VETERANS

The VA makes an important distinction among veterans with disabilities. Veterans whose disability is service connected fall under the mandatory classification of VA medical care. Veterans whose disability is nonservice connected fall under the discretionary classification.

Family Members and Survivors

The VA may provide medical care for the children and spouse of a veteran with a service-connected disability, even after the veteran's death.

LOWER-INCOME VETERANS

Lower-income veterans receive benefits similar to those in the mandatory classification. To contact the VA for details call 1-800-827-1000 or visit http://www.va.gov/ to find the nearest VA facility.

DENTAL CARE

Dental care is distinct from medical care. As a result, the types and amounts of coverage are different, as noted below.

- **Before you separate:** Early in your transition process, you and your family should have routine dental checkups. You should also ensure that your family members obtain necessary treatment under the TRICARE Family Member Dental Plan prior to your expiration of eligibility for the program. If problems are found early enough, work can be completed prior to separation, at little or no cost to you.
- Emergencies will also be taken care of until your separation.

TRICARE Dental Program

Shortly after you separate, the VA provides one-time dental care for veterans if you apply within ninety days after separation. However, you will not receive dental care if the military provided a dental examination and treatment within ninety days prior to your separation.

The TRICARE Dental Program (TDP) is offered by the Department of Defense (DoD) through the TRICARE Management Activity (TMA). United Concordia Companies, Inc., administers and underwrites the TDP for the TMA. The TDP is a high-quality, cost-effective dental care benefit for eligible family members of all active duty uniformed servicemembers as well as members of the Selected Reserve and Individual Ready Reserve (IRR) and their eligible family members.

TRICARE Retiree Dental Program

The TRICARE Retiree Dental Program (TRDP) is offered by the Department of Defense (DoD) through the TRICARE Management Activity (TMA). The Federal Services division of Delta Dental Plan of California, located in Sacramento, California, administers and underwrites the TRDP for the TMA. The TRDP offers comprehensive, cost-effective dental coverage for uniformed services retirees and their eligible family members.

The TRDP will also make available a premium-based dental insurance program for military retirees, members of the Retired Reserve receiving retired pay, unremarried surviving spouses, and dependents. Eligible beneficiaries will pay the full cost of the dental insurance coverage. TRDP will feature a basic dental care and treatment to include diagnostic services, preventative services, basic restoration services, endodontics, surgical services, and emergency services. Retiring members should explore this program, depending on their future employer's health benefits package. Retirees should check with their local military dental facility regarding dental services. Following separation, you will need to obtain dental insurance from your new employer or through a private insurer.

LIFE INSURANCE

Your current Servicemembers' Group Life Insurance (SGLI) will only continue to cover you for the first 120 days after your separation. The following section will give you information on how to meet your life insurance needs after you leave the military.

Servicemembers' Group Life Insurance (SGLI)

Servicemembers' Group Life Insurance is low-cost term insurance protection for members of the uniformed services. All servicemembers on active duty,

ready reservists, members of the Commissioned Corps of the National Oceanic and Atmospheric Administration and the Public Health Service, cadets
and midshipmen of the four service academies, and members of the Reserve
Officer Training Corps are eligible for SGLI.

SGLI will continue to cover you for the first 120 days after your separation, just as if you were still in uniform. If you are totally disabled at the time
of your separation, your SGLI coverage can continue, free of charge, for up
to two years from the date of your separation. Following expiration of your
coverage extension under your SGLI, you must make your own arrangements
for life insurance. One option is the Veterans' Group Life Insurance (VGLI),
offered by the VA, which is discussed in the next section.

Traumatic Injury Protection Program (TSGLI) is a disability rider to
the SGLI program that provides automatic traumatic injury coverage to all
servicemembers covered under the SGLI program who suffer losses due to
traumatic injuries. TSGLI payments range from $25,000 to a maximum of
$100,000 depending on the type and severity of injury.

Family SGLI (FSGLI) coverage is available for the spouses and dependent
children of active duty servicemembers and members of the Ready Reserve
insured under Servicemembers' Group Life Insurance program.

The servicemember's spouse may obtain coverage up to $100,000 or an
amount equal to the servicemembers' coverage, whichever is less. Age-based
premiums are charged for spouses. Each dependent child of the servicemember is automatically insured for $10,000 free of charge. A member can
decline or elect lesser spousal coverage in increments of $10,000 but may not
decline coverage for a dependent child.

For more information call toll free 1-800-419-1473 or visit http://www
.insurance.va.gov.

Traumatic Injury Protection (TSGLI)

Traumatic Injury Protection Insurance, known as TSGLI, is a Servicemembers' Group Life Insurance (SGLI) program designed to provide financial
assistance to servicemembers during their recovery period from serious traumatic injury.

All servicemembers eligible for SGLI are insured for traumatic injury
protection of up to $100,000 unless they decline SGLI coverage. A flat
monthly premium of $1.00 will be added to the monthly SGLI deduction,
regardless of the amount of SGLI coverage that the servicemember has
elected.

TSGLI is not disability compensation and has no effect on entitlement for
compensation and pension benefits provided by the Department of Veterans

Affairs or disability benefits provided by the Department of Defense. It is an insurance product similar to commercial dismemberment policies. For more information, servicemembers should contact their individual service. Points of contact for servicemembers are:

Army, Army Reserve
Phone: (800) 237-1336
E-mail: tsgli@conus.army.mil
Website: http://www.tsgli.army.mil

Army National Guard
Phone: (703) 607-5851
E-mail: raymond.holdeman@ng.army.mil
Website: www.tsgli.army.mil

Navy, Navy Reserve
Phone: (800) 368-3202 / 901-874-2501
E-mail: MILL_TSGLI@navy.mil
Website: http://www.npc.navy.mil/CommandSupport/CasualtyAssistance/TSGLI/

Air Force, Air Force Reserve
Active Duty Phone: (800) 433-0048
Air Reserve Phone: (800) 525-0102
Air National Guard Phone: (703) 607-0901
E-mail: afpc.casualty@randolph.af.mil
Website: ask.afpc.randolph.af.mil

Marine Corps
Phone: (877) 216-0825 or (703) 432-9277
E-mail: t-sgli@usmc.mil
Website: https://www.manpower.usmc.mil/pls/portal/url/page/m_ra_home/wwr/wwr_a_command_element/wwr_d_regimental_staff/3_s3/wwr_tsgli

Coast Guard, Coast Guard Reserve
Phone: (202) 475-5391
E-mail: compensation@comdt.uscg.mil
Website: www.uscg.mil/hq/g-w/g-wp/g-wpm/g-wpm-2/sgli.htm

U.S. Public Health Service (USPHS)
Phone: (301) 594-2963

National Oceanic and Atmospheric Administration (NOAA)
Phone: (301) 713-3444
E-mail: director.cpc@noaa.gov

The Department of Veterans Affairs TSGLI website offers more detailed information on how and where to submit claims at http://www.insurance.va.gov/sgliSite/TSGLI/TSGLI.htm.

Veterans' Group Life Insurance (VGLI)

Once your SGLI coverage extension ends, you must make your own arrangements for life insurance. One option is Veterans' Group Life Insurance, offered by the VA. Veterans' Group Life Insurance (VGLI) provides for the conversion of Servicemembers' Group Life Insurance (SGLI) to a renewable term life insurance policy. This policy is renewable every five years, regardless of health, and can be retained for life.

You are eligible to apply for VGLI if you are insured under SGLI *AND*:

- you are being released from active duty or the Reserves or were released within the last year and 120 days.
- you are a member of the Individual Ready Reserve (IRR) or Inactive National Guard (ING).
- you are a Reservist who suffered an injury or disability during active duty or inactive duty for training for a period of less than thirty-one days and became uninsurable at standard premium rates.

Remember: You can apply for VGLI within the first 120 days without evidence of good health. After the initial 120 days you have an additional year to apply, but good health requirements must be met. VGLI provides for the amount of SGLI coverage a member had in force at the time of separation from active duty or reserves. VGLI is issued in multiples of $10,000 up to a maximum $400,000. VGLI can be converted at any time to an individual permanent (i.e., whole life or endowment) plan with any of the participating commercial insurance companies.

Applying for Veterans' Group Life Insurance

Since SGLI coverage continues at no cost for 120 days after discharge, VGLI will not take effect until the 121st day. VGLI applications are mailed to eligible members on three occasions:

- generally within sixty days after separation.
- within 120 days after separation when the SGLI free coverage period ends.
- before the end of the sixteen-month application period.

Note: VGLI applications VA Form SGLV 8714 Application for Veterans' Group Life Insurance (http://www.insurance.va.gov/sgliSite/forms/8714

.htm) should be mailed to the address shown on your DD Form 214 or equivalent separation orders. It is your responsibility to apply within the time limits even if you do not receive an application in the mail.

Applications for VGLI coverage should be mailed to:
The Office of Servicemembers' Group Life Insurance
P.O. Box 5000
Millville, New Jersey 08332-9928

For more information call toll free 1-800-419-1473 or visit http://www .insurance.va.gov.

Service-Disabled Veterans Insurance (S-DVI)

Service-Disabled Veterans Insurance is life insurance for veterans who receive a service-connected disability rating by the Department of Veterans Affairs. The basic S-DVI program, commonly referred to as RH Insurance, insures eligible veterans for up to $10,000 of coverage. Veterans who have the basic S-DVI coverage and are totally disabled are eligible to have their premiums waived. If waiver is granted, totally disabled veterans may apply for additional coverage of up to $20,000 under the Supplemental SDVI program. Premiums for Supplemental S-DVI coverage, however, cannot be waived.

Veterans' Mortgage Life Insurance (VMLI)

Veterans' Mortgage Life Insurance (VMLI) is an insurance program that provides insurance coverage on the home mortgages of veterans with severe service-connected disabilities who:

- receive a Specially-Adapted Housing Grant from VA for assistance in building, remodeling, or purchasing an adapted home; *AND*
- Have title to the home; *AND*
- Have a mortgage on the home.

What to Look for in a Life Insurance Policy

Explore the various life insurance options, including those offered by VGLI. By checking each, you will be able to pick what is best for you. When shopping for life insurance, the program you choose should pay:

- Funeral expenses and related bills
- Debts or loans owed by the insured person at the time of death
- Lost earnings

Lost earnings are what the person would have made over the rest of his or her working life had he or she not died. There are a variety of ways to calculate lost earnings. For example: The sole wage earner for a family of four dies at age forty-five. He made $30,000 a year at the time of his death. Because the household has been reduced from four to three, three-fourths (75 percent) of his income needs to be replaced for twenty years (when he would have turned age sixty-five). This method shows lost earnings that need to be recovered through insurance as $450,000: 75% x ($30,000 x 20 years) = $450,000.

8

Transition Benefits

JOINT TRANSITION ASSISTANCE

The Departments of Veterans Affairs, Defense, and Labor launched a new and improved website for wounded warriors—the National Resource Directory (NRD). This directory (www.nationalresourcedirectory.gov) provides access to thousands of services and resources at the national, state, and local levels to support recovery, rehabilitation, and community reintegration. The NRD is a comprehensive online tool available nationwide for wounded, ill, and injured servicemembers, veterans, and their families.

The NRD includes extensive information for veterans seeking resources on VA benefits, including disability benefits, pensions for veterans and their families, VA health care insurance, and the GI Bill. The NRD's design and interface is simple, easy to navigate, and intended to answer the needs of a broad audience of users within the military, veteran, and caregiver communities.

Transition from Military to VA

VA has stationed personnel at major military hospitals to help seriously injured servicemembers returning from Operations Enduring Freedom and Iraqi Freedom (OEF/OIF) as they transition from military to civilian life. OEF/OIF servicemembers who have questions about VA benefits or need assistance in filing a VA claim or accessing services can contact the nearest VA office or call 1-800-827-1000.

Transition Assistance Program: The Transition Assistance Program (TAP) consists of comprehensive three-day workshops at military installations designed to help servicemembers as they transition from military to civilian life. The program includes job search, employment, and training information, as well as VA benefits information, for servicemembers who are within twelve months of separation or twenty-four months of retirement. A companion workshop, the Disabled Transition Assistance Program, provides information on VA's Vocational Rehabilitation and Employment Program, as well as other programs for the disabled. Additional information about these programs is available at www.dol.gov/vets/programs/tap/tap_fs.htm.

Predischarge Program: The Predischarge Program is a joint VA and DoD program that affords servicemembers the opportunity to file claims for disability compensation and other benefits up to 180 days prior to separation or retirement.

The two primary components of the Predischarge Program, Benefits Delivery at Discharge (BDD) and Quick Start, may be used by all separating CONUS servicemembers on active duty, including members of the Coast Guard and members of the National Guard and Reserves (activated under Titles 10 or 32).

BDD is offered to accelerate receipt of VA disability benefits with a goal of providing benefits within sixty days after release or discharge from active duty.

To participate in the BDD program, servicemembers must:

1. have at least 60 days, but not more than 180 days, remaining on active duty.
2. have a known date of separation or retirement.
3. provide the VA with service treatment records, originals or photocopies.
4. be available to complete all necessary examinations prior to leaving the point of separation.

Quick Start is offered to servicemembers who have less than sixty days remaining on active duty or are unable to complete the necessary examinations prior to leaving the point of separation.

To participate in the Quick Start Program, servicemembers must:

1. have at least one day remaining on active duty.
2. have a known date of separation or retirement.
3. provide the VA with service treatment records, originals or photocopies.

Servicemembers should contact the local transition assistance office or Army Career Alumni Program Center to schedule appointments to attend VA benefits briefings and learn how to initiate a predischarge claim. Servicemembers can obtain more information by calling VA toll free at 1-800-827-1000 or by visiting www.vba.va.gov/predischarge.

Federal Recovery Coordination Program

The Federal Recovery Coordination Program, a joint program of DOD and VA, helps coordinate and access federal, state, and local programs for benefits and services for seriously wounded, ill, and injured servicemembers and their families through recovery, rehabilitation, and reintegration into the community.

Federal Recovery Coordinators (FRCs) have the delegated authority for oversight and coordination of the clinical and nonclinical care identified in each client's Federal Individual Recovery Plan (FIRP). Working with a variety of case managers, FRCs assist their clients in reaching their FIRP goals. FRCs remain with their clients as long as they are needed regardless of the client's location, duty, or health status. In doing so, they often serve as the central point of contact and provide transition support for their clients.

Preseparation Counseling

Servicemembers may receive preseparation counseling twenty-four months prior to retirement or twelve months prior to separation from active duty. These sessions present information on education, training, employment assistance, National Guard and Reserve programs, medical benefits, and financial assistance.

Verification of Military Experience and Training

The Verification of Military Experience and Training (VMET) Document, DD Form 2586, helps servicemembers verify previous experience and training to potential employers, negotiate credits at schools, and obtain certificates or licenses. VMET documents are available only through Army, Navy, Air Force, and Marine Corps transition support offices and are intended for servicemembers who have at least six months of active service. Servicemembers should obtain VMET documents from their transition support office within twelve months of separation or twenty-four months of retirement.

Transition Bulletin Board

To find business opportunities, a calendar of transition seminars, job fairs, information on veterans associations, transition services, training and education opportunities, as well as other announcements, visit the TurboTAP website at www.turbotap.org.

DoD Transportal

To find locations and phone numbers of all transition assistance offices as well as minicourses on conducting successful job-search campaigns, writing resumes, using the Internet to find a job, and links to job search and recruiting websites, visit the DoD Transportal at www.veteranprograms.com/index .html.

EDUCATIONAL AND VOCATIONAL COUNSELING

The Vocational Rehabilitation and Employment (VR&E) Program provides educational and vocational counseling to servicemembers, veterans, and certain dependents (U.S.C. Title 38, Section 3697) at no charge. These counseling services are designed to help an individual choose a vocational direction, determine the course needed to achieve the chosen goal, and evaluate the career possibilities open to them.

Assistance may include interest and aptitude testing, occupational exploration, setting occupational goals, locating the right type of training program, and exploring educational or training facilities that can be used to achieve an occupational goal.

Counseling services include, but are not limited to, educational and vocational counseling and guidance; testing; analysis of and recommendations to improve job-marketing skills; identification of employment, training, and financial aid resources; and referrals to other agencies providing these services.

Eligibility: Educational and vocational counseling services are available during the period the individual is on active duty with the armed forces and is within 180 days of the estimated date of his or her discharge or release from active duty. The projected discharge must be under conditions other than dishonorable.

Servicemembers are eligible even if they are only considering whether or not they will continue as members of the armed forces. Veterans are eligible if not more than one year has elapsed since the date they were last discharged or released from active duty. Individuals who are eligible for VA education benefits may receive educational and vocational counseling at any time during their eligibility period. This service is based on having eligibility for a VA program such as Chapter 30 (Montgomery GI Bill); Chapter 31 (Vocational Rehabilitation and Employment); Chapter 32 (Veterans' Education Assistance Program—VEAP); Chapter 33 (Post-9/11 GI Bill); Chapter 35 (Dependents' Education Assistance Program) for certain spouses and dependent children; Chapter 18 (Spina Bifida Program) for certain dependent children; and Chapters 1606 and 1607 of Title 10.

Veterans and servicemembers may apply for counseling services using VA Form 28-8832, "Application for Counseling." Veterans and servicemembers may also write a letter expressing a desire for counseling services.

Upon receipt of either type of request for counseling from an eligible individual, an appointment for counseling will be scheduled. Counseling services are provided to eligible persons at no charge.

Veterans' Workforce Investment Program

Recently separated veterans and those with service-connected disabilities, significant barriers to employment, or who served on active duty during a period in which a campaign or expedition badge was authorized can contact the nearest state employment office for employment help through the Veterans' Workforce Investment Program. The program may be conducted through state or local public agencies, community organizations, or private, nonprofit organizations.

State Employment Services

Veterans can find employment information, education and training opportunities, job counseling, job search workshops, and resume preparation assistance at state Workforce Career or One-Stop Centers. These offices also have specialists to help disabled veterans find employment.

Unemployment Compensation

Veterans who do not begin civilian employment immediately after leaving military service may receive weekly unemployment compensation for a limited time. The amount and duration of payments are determined by individual states. Apply by contacting the nearest state employment office listed in your local telephone directory.

Veterans' Preference for Federal Jobs

Since the time of the Civil War, veterans of the U.S. armed forces have been given some degree of preference in appointments to federal jobs. Veterans' preference in its present form comes from the Veterans' Preference Act of 1944, as amended, and now codified in Title 5, United States Code. By law, veterans who are disabled or who served on active duty in the U.S. armed forces during certain specified time periods or in military campaigns are entitled to preference over others when hiring from a competitive list of eligible candidates and also in retention during a reduction in force (RIF).

To receive preference, a veteran must have been discharged or released from active duty in the U.S. armed forces under honorable conditions (honorable or general discharge). Preference is also provided for certain widows and widowers of deceased veterans who died in service; spouses of service-connected disabled veterans; and mothers of veterans who died under honorable conditions on active duty or have permanent and total service-connected disabilities. For each of these preferences, there are specific criteria that must be met in order to be eligible to receive the veterans' preference.

Recent changes in Title 5 clarify veterans' preference eligibility criteria for National Guard and Reserve members. Veterans eligible for preference include National Guard and Reserve members who served on active duty as defined by Title 38 at any time in the armed forces for a period of more than 180 consecutive days, any part of which occurred during the period beginning on September 11, 2001, and ending on the date prescribed by residential proclamation or by law as the last date of OEF/OIF. The National Guard and Reserve servicemembers must have been discharged or released from active duty in the armed forces under honorable conditions.

Another recent change involves veterans who earned the Global War on Terrorism Expeditionary Medal for service in OEF/OIF. Under Title 5, service on active duty in the armed forces during a war or in a campaign or expedition for which a campaign badge has been authorized also qualifies for veterans' preference. Any Armed Forces Expeditionary medal or campaign badge qualifies for preference. Medal holders must have served continuously for twenty-four months or the full period called or ordered to active duty.

As of December 2005, veterans who received the Global War on Terrorism Expeditionary Medal are entitled to veterans' preference if otherwise eligible. For additional information, visit the Office of Personnel Management (OPM) website at www.opm.gov/veterans/html/vetguide.asp#2.

Veterans' preference does not require an agency to use any particular appointment process. Agencies can pick candidates from a number of different special hiring authorities or through a variety of different sources. For example, the agency can reinstate a former federal employee, transfer someone from another agency, reassign someone from within the agency, make a selection under merit promotion procedures or through open, competitive exams, or appoint someone noncompetitively under special authority, such as a Veterans Readjustment Appointment or special authority for 30 percent or more disabled veterans. The decision on which hiring authority the agency desires to use rests solely with the agency.

When applying for federal jobs, eligible veterans should claim preference on their application or resume. Veterans should apply for a federal job by contacting the personnel office at the agency in which they wish to work.

For more information, visit www.usajobs.opm.gov/ for job openings or help creating a federal resume.

Veterans Employment Opportunities Act: When an agency accepts applications from outside its own workforce, the Veterans Employment Opportunities Act of 1998 allows preference-eligible candidates or veterans to compete for these vacancies under merit promotion procedures.

Veterans who are selected are given career or career-conditional appointments. Veterans are those who have been separated under honorable conditions from the U.S. armed forces with three or more years of continuous active service. For information, visit www.usajobs.opm.gov or www.fedshirevets.gov.

Veterans Recruitment Appointment: This agency allows federal agencies to appoint eligible veterans to jobs without competition. These appointments can be converted to career or career-conditional positions after two years of satisfactory work. Veterans should apply directly to the agency where they wish to work. For information, visit www.fedshirevets.gov/.

Small Businesses

VA's Center for Veterans Enterprise helps veterans interested in forming or expanding small businesses and helps VA contracting offices identify veteran-owned small businesses. For information, write the U.S. Department of Veterans Affairs (OOVE), 810 Vermont Avenue, N.W., Washington, DC 20420-0001, call toll free 1-866-584-2344, or visit www.vetbiz.gov/.

Small Business Contracts: Like other federal agencies, VA is required to place a portion of its contracts and purchases with small and disadvantaged businesses. VA has a special office to help small and disadvantaged businesses get information on VA acquisition opportunities. For information, write the U.S. Department of Veterans Affairs (OOSB), 810 Vermont Avenue, N.W., Washington, DC 20420-0001, call toll free 1-800-949-8387, or visit www.va.gov/osdbu/.

VETERANS BENEFITS

The Department of Veterans Affairs (VA) is responsible for ensuring that you, as a veteran, receive the care, support, and recognition that you have earned. The DVA, along with state and local agencies, are ready to assist you in your transition. The following section will give you an overview of the types of benefits you are eligible for and where you can find further information within the Preseparation Guide.

Department of Veterans Affairs–Provided Benefits

You may be eligible for the following federal veterans benefits:

Health Care

In October 1996, Congress passed the Veterans' Health Care Eligibility Reform Act, paving the way for the Medical Benefits Package plan, available to all enrolled veterans. The Medical Benefits Package emphasizes preventive and primary care, offering a full range of outpatient and inpatient services.

VA operates the nation's largest integrated health care system with more than 1,400 sites of care, including hospitals, community clinics, community living centers, domiciliary, readjustment counseling centers, and various other facilities. For additional information on VA health care, visit www.va.gov/health.

Basic Eligibility

A person who served in the active military, naval, or air service and who was discharged or released under conditions other than dishonorable may qualify for VA health care benefits. Reservists and National Guard members may also qualify for VA health care benefits if they were called to active duty (other than for training only) by a federal order and completed the full period for which they were called or ordered to active duty.

Minimum Duty Requirements: Veterans who enlisted after September 7, 1980, or who entered active duty after October 16, 1981, must have served twenty-four continuous months or the full period for which they were called to active duty in order to be eligible. This minimum duty requirement may not apply to veterans discharged for hardship, early out, or a disability incurred or aggravated in the line of duty.

Enrollment

For most veterans, entry into the VA health care system begins by applying for enrollment. To apply, complete VA Form 10-10EZ, Application for Health Benefits, which may be obtained from any VA health care facility or regional benefits office, online at www.1010ez.mvd.va.gov/sec/vha/1010ez/, or by calling 1-877-222-VETS (8387). Once enrolled, veterans can receive health care at VA health care facilities anywhere in the country.

Veterans enrolled in the VA health care system are afforded privacy rights under federal law. VA's Notice of Privacy Practices, which describes how VA may use and disclose veterans' medical information, is also available online at www.va.gov/vhapublications/viewpublication.asp?pub_ID=1089.

The following four categories of veterans are not required to enroll but are urged to do so to permit better planning of health resources:

1. Veterans with a service-connected disability of 50 percent or more.
2. Veterans seeking care for a disability the military determined was incurred or aggravated in the line of duty, but which VA has not yet rated, within twelve months of discharge.
3. Veterans seeking care for a service-connected disability only.
4. Veterans seeking registry examinations (Ionizing Radiation, Agent Orange, Gulf War/Operation Iraqi Freedom, and Depleted Uranium).

Priority Groups

During enrollment, each veteran is assigned to a priority group. VA uses priority groups to balance demand for VA health care enrollment with resources. Changes in available resources may reduce the number of priority groups VA can enroll. If this occurs, VA will publicize the changes and notify affected enrollees. A description of priority groups follows:

Group 1: Veterans with service-connected disabilities rated 50 percent or more and/or veterans determined by VA to be unemployable due to service-connected conditions.

Group 2: Veterans with service-connected disabilities rated 30 or 40 percent.

Group 3: Veterans with service-connected disabilities rated 10 and 20 percent; veterans who are former Prisoners of War (POW) or were awarded a Purple Heart medal; veterans awarded special eligibility for disabilities incurred in treatment or participation in a VA Vocational Rehabilitation program; and veterans whose discharge was for a disability incurred or aggravated in the line of duty.

Group 4: Veterans receiving aid and attendance or housebound benefits and/or veterans determined by VA to be catastrophically disabled.

Group 5: Veterans receiving VA pension benefits or eligible for Medicaid programs, and nonservice-connected veterans and noncompensable, zero percent service-connected veterans whose gross annual household income and/ or net worth are below the VA national income threshold and geographically adjusted income threshold for their resident area.

Group 6: Veterans of World War I; veterans seeking care solely for certain conditions associated with exposure to ionizing radiation during atmospheric testing or during the occupation of Hiroshima and Nagasaki; for any illness associated with participation in tests conducted by the Department of Defense (DoD) as part of Project 112/Project SHAD; veterans with zero percent service-connected disabilities who are receiving disability compensation benefits; and veterans who served in a theater of combat operations after November 11, 1998, as follows:

1. veterans discharged from active duty on or after January 28, 2003, who were enrolled as of January 28, 2008, and veterans who apply for enrollment after January 28, 2008, for five years postdischarge
2. veterans discharged from active duty before January 28, 2003, who apply for enrollment after January 28, 2008, until January 27, 2011

Group 7: Veterans with gross household income below the geographically adjusted income threshold (GMT) for their resident location and who agree to pay copays.

Group 8: Veterans with gross household income and/or net worth above the VA national income threshold and the geographic income threshold who agree to pay copays.

Note: Due to income relaxation rules implemented on June 15, 2009, veterans with household income above the VA national threshold or the GMT income threshold for their resident location by 10 percent or less, who agree to pay copays, are eligible for enrollment in Priority Group 8.

The GMT thresholds can be located at http://www.va.gov/healtheligibility/library/pubs/gmtincomethresholds.

Recently Discharged Combat Veterans

Veterans, including activated Reservists and members of the National Guard, are eligible for the enhanced Combat Veteran benefits if they served on active duty in a theater of combat operations after November 11, 1998, and have been discharged under other than dishonorable conditions.

Effective January 28, 2008, combat veterans discharged from active duty on or after January 28, 2003, are eligible for enhanced enrollment placement into Priority Group 6 (unless eligible for higher enrollment Priority Group placement) for five years postdischarge.

Veterans with combat service after November 11, 1998, who were discharged from active duty before January 28, 2003, and who apply for enrollment on or after January 28, 2008, are eligible for this enhanced enrollment benefit through January 27, 2011. During this period of enhanced enrollment benefits, these veterans receive VA care and medications at no cost for any condition that may be related to their combat service.

Veterans who enroll with VA under this Combat Veteran authority will retain enrollment eligibility even after their five-year postdischarge period ends. At the end of their postdischarge period, VA will reassess the veteran's information (including all applicable eligibility factors) and make a new enrollment decision. For additional information, call 1-877-222-VETS (8387).

Special Access to Care

Service-disabled veterans who are 50 percent or more disabled from service-connected conditions, unemployable due to service-connected conditions, or are receiving care for a service-connected disability receive priority in scheduling for hospital or outpatient medical appointments.

Women Veterans

Women veterans are eligible for the same VA benefits as male veterans. Comprehensive health services are available to women veterans, including primary care, specialty care, mental health care, and reproductive health care services.

VA provides management of acute and chronic illnesses, preventive care, contraceptive services, menopause management, and cancer screenings, including pap smear and mammograms, and gynecology. Maternity care is covered in the medical benefits package, and referrals are made to appropriate clinicians in the community for services that VA is unable to provide. Infertility evaluation and limited treatments are also available. For information, visit www.publichealth.va.gov/womenshealth.

Women Veterans Program Managers are available at all VA facilities. See the facility locator at www2.va.gov/directory/guide/home.asp?isFlash=1 to help veterans seeking treatment and benefits. For additional information, visit www.publichealth.va.gov/womenshealth/.

Financial Assessment

Most veterans not receiving VA disability compensation or pension payments must provide information on their gross annual household income and net worth to determine whether they are below the annually adjusted financial thresholds. Veterans who decline to disclose their information or have income above the thresholds must agree to pay copays in order to receive certain health benefits, effectively placing them in Priority Group 8. VA is currently not enrolling new applicants who decline to provide financial information unless they have a special eligibility factor.

This financial assessment includes all household income and net worth, including Social Security, retirement pay, unemployment insurance, interest and dividends, workers' compensation, black lung benefits, and any other income. Also considered are assets such as the market value of property that is not the primary residence, stocks, bonds, notes, individual retirement accounts, bank deposits, savings accounts, and cash.

VA also compares veterans' financial assessment with geographically based income thresholds. If the veteran's gross annual household income is above VA's national means test threshold and below VA's geographic means test threshold, or is below both the VA national threshold and the VA geographically based threshold, but their gross annual household income plus net worth exceeds VA's ceiling (currently $80,000), the veteran may be eligible for Priority Group 7 placement and qualify for an 80 percent reduction in inpatient copay rates.

VA Medical Services and Medication Copays

Some veterans are required to make copays to receive VA health care and/ or medications.

Inpatient Care: Priority Group 7 and certain other veterans are responsible for paying 20 percent of VA's inpatient copay or $213.60 for the first ninety days of inpatient hospital care during any 365-day period. For each additional ninety days, the charge is $106.80. In addition, there is a $2 per diem charge.

Priority Group 8 and certain other veterans are responsible for VA's inpatient copay of $1,100 for the first ninety days of care during any 365-day period. For each additional ninety days, the charge is $550. In addition, there is a $10 per diem charge.

Extended Care: For extended care services, veterans may be subject to a copay determined by information supplied by completing a VA Form 10-10EC. VA social workers can help veterans interpret their eligibility and copay requirements. The copay amount is based on each veteran's financial situation and is determined upon application for extended care services and will range from $0 to $97 a day.

Outpatient Care: A three-tiered copay system is used for all outpatient services. The copay is $15 for a primary care visit and $50 for some specialized care. Service-connected veterans 10 percent disability or greater are exempt from copay requirements for inpatient and outpatient medical care for service-connected and nonservice-connected treatment. Zero percent service-connected veterans may be required to complete a copay test to determine if copay requirements are advised.

Outpatient Visits Not Requiring Copays: Certain services are not charged a copay. Copays do not apply to publicly announced VA health fairs or outpatient visits solely for preventive screening and/or vaccinations, such as vaccinations for influenza and pneumococcal, or screening for hypertension, hepatitis C, tobacco, alcohol, hyperlipidemia, breast cancer, cervical cancer, colorectal cancer by fecal occult blood testing, education about the risks and benefits of prostate cancer screening, HIV testing and counseling, and weight reduction or smoking cessation counseling (individual and group). Laboratory, flat film radiology, electrocardiograms, and hospice care are also exempt from copays. While hepatitis C screening and HIV testing and counseling are exempt, medical care for HIV and hepatitis C are NOT exempt from copays.

Medication: Many nonservice-connected veterans are charged $8 for each thirty-day or less supply of medication provided by VA for treatment of nonservice-connected conditions. For veterans enrolled in Priority Groups 2 through 6, the maximum copay for medications that will be charged in calendar year 2009 is $960 to 40 percent service-connected veterans, who are responsible for paying a copay for nonservice-connected medications. The following groups of veterans are not charged medication copays: veterans with a service-connected disability of 50 percent or more; veterans receiving medication for service-connected conditions; veterans whose annual income does not exceed the maximum annual rate of the VA pension; veterans enrolled in Priority Group 6 who receive medication under their special authority; veterans receiving medication for conditions related to sexual trauma related to service on active duty; certain veterans receiving medication for treatment of cancer of the head or neck; veterans receiving medication for a VA-approved research project; and former POWs.

Note: Copays apply to prescription and over-the-counter medications, such as aspirin, cough syrup, or vitamins, dispensed by a VA pharmacy. However, veterans may prefer to purchase over-the-counter drugs, such as aspirin or vitamins, at a local pharmacy rather than making the copay. Copays are not charged for medications injected during the course of treatment or for medical supplies, such as syringes or alcohol wipes.

HSA/HRA: Health Savings Accounts (HSA) cannot be used to make VA copays. In addition, if the veteran receives any health benefits from the VA or one of its facilities, including prescription drugs, in the last three months, he/she will not be eligible for an HSA. Health Reimbursement Arrangements (HRA) are not considered health plans, and third-party payers cannot be billed.

Private Health Insurance Billing

VA is required to bill private health insurance providers for medical care, supplies, and prescriptions provided for treatment of veterans' non-service-connected conditions. Generally, VA cannot bill Medicare but can bill Medicare supplemental health insurance for covered services. VA is not authorized to bill a High Deductible Health Plan (which is usually linked to a Health Savings Account).

All veterans applying for VA medical care are required to provide information on their health insurance coverage, including coverage provided under policies of their spouses. Veterans are not responsible for paying any remaining balance of VA's insurance claim not paid or covered by their health insurance, and any payment received by VA may be used to offset "dollar for dollar" a veteran's VA copay responsibility.

Reimbursement of Travel Costs

Certain veterans may be provided special mode travel (e.g., wheelchair van, ambulance) or reimbursed for travel costs when traveling for approved VA medical care. Reimbursement is paid at 41.5 cents per mile and is subject to a deductible of $3 for each one-way trip and $6 for a round trip; with a maximum deductible of $18 or the amount after six one-way trips (whichever occurs first) per calendar month. Two exceptions to the deductible are travel in relation to a VA compensation or pension examination and travel requiring a special mode of transportation. The deductible may be waived when their imposition would cause a severe financial hardship.

Eligibility: The following are eligible for VA travel:

1. Veterans whose service-connected disabilities are rated 30 percent or more.
2. Veterans traveling for treatment of service-connected conditions.
3. Veterans who receive a VA pension.
4. Veterans traveling for scheduled compensation or pension examinations.
5. Veterans whose gross household income does not exceed the maximum annual VA pension rate.
6. Certain veterans in certain emergency situations.
7. Veterans whose medical condition requires a special mode of transportation, if they are unable to defray the costs and travel is preauthorized. Advance authorization is not required in an emergency if a delay would be hazardous to life or health.
8. Certain nonveterans when related to the care of a veteran (attendants and donors).

Beneficiary travel fraud can take money out of the pockets of deserving veterans. Inappropriate uses of beneficiary travel benefits include: incorrect addresses provided resulting in increased mileage; driving/riding together and making separate claims; and taking no cost transportation, such as DAV, and making claims. Veterans making false statements for beneficiary travel reimbursement may be prosecuted under applicable laws.

Reporting fraud: Help VA's Secretary ensure integrity by reporting suspected fraud, waste, or abuse in VA programs or operations.

VAOIG hotline: 1-800-488-8244
E-mail: vaoighotline@va.gov
Fax: (202) 565-7936
VA Inspector General Hotline
P.O. Box 50410
Washington, DC 20091-0410

VA Medical Programs

Veteran Health Registries: Certain veterans can participate in a VA health registry and receive free medical examinations, including laboratory and other diagnostic tests deemed necessary by an examining clinician. VA maintains health registries to provide special health examinations and health-related information. To participate, contact the Environmental Health (EH) Coordinator at the nearest VA health care facility or visit www.publichealth .va.gov/exposures, where a directory of EH coordinators is maintained.

Gulf War Registry: This registry is for veterans who served on active military duty in Southwest Asia during the Gulf War, which began in 1990 and continues to the present, including Operation Iraqi Freedom (OIF). The Gulf War examination registry was established after the first Gulf War to identify possible diseases resulting from U.S. military personnel service in certain areas of Southwest Asia. These diseases were endemic to the area or may have been due to hazardous exposures, including heavy metals. Furthermore, air pollutants such as carbon monoxide sulfur oxides, hydrocarbons, particulate matter, and nitrogen oxides, singly or in combination, could have caused chronic health problems.

Depleted Uranium Registries: Depleted uranium is natural uranium left over after most of the U-235 isotope has been removed, such as that used as fuel in nuclear power plants. DU possesses about 60 percent of the radioactivity of natural uranium; it is a radiation hazard primarily if internalized, such as in shrapnel, contaminated wounds, and inhalation. In addition to its radioactivity, DU has some chemical toxicity related to being a heavy metal (similar to lead).

Veterans who are identified by the Department of Defense (DoD) or have concerns about possible depleted uranium exposure are eligible for a

DU evaluation. VA maintains two registries for veterans possibly exposed to depleted uranium. The first is for veterans who served in the Gulf War, including Operation Iraqi Freedom. The second is for veterans who served elsewhere, including Bosnia and Afghanistan.

Agent Orange Registry: This registry is for veterans possibly exposed to dioxin or other toxic substances in herbicides used during the Vietnam War, between 1962 and 1975, regardless of length of service, or while serving in Korea in 1968 or 1969, or as a result of testing, transporting, or spraying herbicides for military purposes. DoD has provided a list of locations and dates where herbicides, including Agent Orange, were used. This DoD list is available at www.publichealth.va.gov/exposures. For those sites not listed, the Vietnam veteran should provide some proof of exposure to obtain a registry examination.

Ionizing Radiation Registry: This registry is for veterans possibly exposed to and who are concerned about possible adverse effects of their atomic exposure during the following activities: on-site participation in an atmospheric detonation of a nuclear device, whether or not the testing nation was the United States; occupation of Hiroshima or Nagasaki from August 6, 1945, through July 1, 1946; or internment as a POW in Japan during World War II, which the Secretary of Veterans Affairs determines resulted in an opportunity for exposure to ionizing radiation comparable to that of veterans involved in the occupation of Hiroshima or Nagasaki.

In addition, VA regulations provide that "radiation-risk activity" means service at Department of Energy gaseous diffusion plants at Paducah, Kentucky; Portsmouth, Ohio; or the K-25 area at Oak Ridge, Tennessee; for at least 250 days before February 1, 1992, or if the veteran was monitored for each of the 250 days using dosimetry badges to monitor radiation to external body parts, or if the veteran served for at least 250 days in a position that had exposures comparable to a job that was monitored using dosimetry badges, such as Longshot, Milrow, or Cannikin underground nuclear tests at Amchitka Island, Alaska, before January 1, 1974, or veterans who received nasopharyngeal (NP)—nose and throat—radium irradiation treatments while in the active military, naval, or air service.

Readjustment Counseling Services

VA provides outreach and readjustment counseling services through 232 community-based Vet Centers located in all fifty states, the District of Columbia, Guam, Puerto Rico, American Samoa, and the U.S. Virgin Islands.

Eligibility: Veterans are eligible if they served on active duty in a combat theater during World War II, the Korean War, the Vietnam War, the Gulf

War, or the campaigns in Lebanon, Grenada, Panama, Somalia, Bosnia, Kosovo, Afghanistan, Iraq, and the Global War on Terror. Veterans, who served in the active military during the Vietnam era but not in the Republic of Vietnam, must have requested services at a Vet Center before January 1, 2004. Vet Centers do not require enrollment in the VHA Health Care System.

Services Offered: Vet Center counselors provide individual, group, and family readjustment counseling to combat veterans to assist them in making a successful transition from military to civilian life; counseling services treatment for post-traumatic stress disorder (PTSD); and help with any other military-related problems that affect functioning within the family, work, school, or other areas of everyday life. Other psychosocial services include outreach, education, medical referral, homeless veteran services, employment, VA benefit referral, and the brokering of non-VA services. The Vet Centers also provide military sexual trauma counseling to veterans of both genders and of any era of military service.

Bereavement Counseling Related to Servicemembers: Bereavement counseling is available through Department of Veterans Affairs (VA) Vet Centers to all immediate family members (including spouses, children, parents, and siblings) of servicemembers who die in the line of duty while on active service. This includes federally activated members of the National Guard and Reserve components. Vet Center bereavement services for surviving family members of servicemembers may be accessed by calling (202) 461-6530.

For additional information, contact the nearest Vet Center, listed in the back of this book, or visit www.vetcenter.va.gov/.

Prosthetic and Sensory Aids

Veterans receiving VA care for any condition may receive VA prosthetic appliances, equipment, and services, such as home respiratory therapy, artificial limbs, orthopedic braces and therapeutic shoes, wheelchairs, powered mobility, crutches, canes, walkers, and other durable medical equipment and supplies.

VA will provide hearing aids and eyeglasses to veterans who receive increased pension based on the need for regular aid and attendance or being permanently housebound; receive compensation for a service-connected disability; or are former POWs or a Purple Heart award recipient.

Otherwise, hearing aids and eyeglasses are provided only in special circumstances and not for normally occurring hearing or vision loss. For additional information, contact the Prosthetic Chief or Representative at the nearest VA health care facility or go to the website: prosthetics.va.gov.

Home Improvements and Structural Alterations

VA provides up to $4,100 lifetime benefit for service-connected veterans and up to $1,200 for non-service-connected veterans to make home improvements necessary for the continuation of treatment or for disability access to the home and essential lavatory and sanitary facilities.

Home Improvement and Structural Alterations grants provide for medically necessary improvements and/or structural changes to the veteran's residence for the following purposes:

1. Allowing entrance to, or exit from, the veteran's residence.
2. Use of essential lavatory and sanitary facilities.
3. Allowing accessibility to kitchen or bathroom sinks or counters.
4. Improving entrance paths or driveways in immediate areas of the home to facilitate access to the home by the veteran.
5. Improving plumbing or electrical systems made necessary due to installation of dialysis equipment in the home.

For application information, contact the prosthetic representative at the nearest VA health care facility.

Special Eligibility Programs

Special Eligibility for Children with Spina Bifida: VA provides needed health care benefits, including prosthetics, medical equipment, and supplies to certain children of Vietnam veterans, i.e., children who are suffering from spina bifida or a disability associated with such condition.

Special Eligibility for Veterans Participating in Vocational Rehabilitation: Veterans participating in VA's vocational rehabilitation program may receive VA health care benefits including prosthetics, medical equipment, and supplies.

Limitations on Benefits Available to Veterans outside the United States: Veterans outside the United States are eligible for prosthetics, medical equipment, and supplies only for a service-connected disability.

Services for Blind and Visually Impaired Veterans

Blind veterans may be eligible for services at a VA medical center or for admission to an inpatient or outpatient VA blind rehabilitation program. In addition, blind veterans enrolled in the VA health care system may receive:

1. A total health and benefits review as well as counseling on obtaining benefits that may be due to the veteran but have not been received.

2. Adjustment to blindness training and counseling.
3. Home improvements and structural alterations.
4. Specially adapted housing and adaptations.
5. Automobile grant.
6. Rehabilitation assessment and training to improve independence and quality of life.
7. Low-vision devices and training in their use.
8. Electronic and mechanical aids for the blind, including adaptive computers and computer-assisted devices such as reading machines and electronic travel aids.
9. Facilitation and recommendation for guide dogs and training in the use of guide dogs.
10. Costs for veterinary care and equipment for guide dogs.
11. Talking books, tapes, and Braille literature.
12. Family support.

Eligible visually impaired veterans (who are not blind) enrolled in the VA health care system may be eligible for services at a VA medical center or for admission to an outpatient VA blind rehabilitation program and may also receive:

1. A total health and benefits review.
2. Adjustment to vision loss counseling.
3. Rehabilitation assessment and training to improve independence and quality of life.
4. Low-vision devices and training in their use.
5. Electronic and mechanical aids for the visually impaired, including adaptive computers and computer-assisted devices, such as reading machines and electronic travel aids, and training in their use.
6. Family support.

Mental Health Care Treatment

Veterans eligible for VA medical care may apply for general mental health treatment, including specialty services. Mental health services are available in specialty clinics, primary care clinics, nursing homes, and residential care facilities where veterans receive health care.

Specialized programs, such as mental health intensive case management, day centers, work programs, and psychosocial rehabilitation are provided for those with serious mental health problems.

The list of services and programs that mental health supports include: inpatient care, residential care, outpatient mental health care, homeless programs,

programs for incarcerated veterans, specialized PTSD services, military sexual trauma, psychosocial rehabilitation and recovery services, substance use disorders, suicide programs, geriatrics, violence prevention, evidence-based psychotherapy programs, and mental health disaster response/postdeployment activities.

For more information on VA mental health services, visit http://www.mentalhealth.va.gov/VAMentalHealthGroup.asp.

Suicide Prevention Lifeline

Veterans experiencing an emotional distress/crisis or who need to talk to a trained mental health professional may call the National Suicide Prevention Lifeline toll-free number, 1-800-273-TALK (8255). The hotline is available twenty-four hours a day, seven days a week. Callers are immediately connected with a qualified and caring provider who can help.

On July 3, 2009, the VA launched a pilot online Chat Service, in partnership with Lifeline. The Veterans Chat Service is located at the VA National Suicide Prevention Hotline. Veterans Chat enables veterans, their families, and friends to go online where they can anonymously chat with a trained VA counselor. Veterans Chat can be accessed through the suicide prevention website www.suicidepreventionlifeline.org. by clicking on the Veterans Chat tab on the right side of the web page.

Mental Health Residential Rehabilitation Treatment Program

Mental Health Residential Rehabilitation Treatment Programs (MH RRTP) (including Domiciliary RRTPs) provide residential rehabilitative and clinical care to veterans who have a wide range of problems, illnesses, or rehabilitative care needs that can be medical, psychiatric, substance use, homelessness, vocational, educational, or social.

The MH RRTP provides a twenty-four-hour therapeutic setting using a milieu of peer and professional support. The programs provide a strong emphasis on psychosocial rehabilitation and recovery services that instill personal responsibility to achieve optimal levels of independence upon discharge to independent or supportive community living. MH RRTP also provides rehabilitative care for veterans who are homeless.

Eligibility: The VA may provide domiciliary care to veterans whose annual gross household income does not exceed the maximum annual rate of VA pension or to veterans the Secretary of Veterans Affairs determines have no adequate means of support.

The copays for extended care services apply to domiciliary care. Call your nearest benefits or health care facility to obtain the latest information.

Work Restoration Programs

VA provides vocational assistance and therapeutic work opportunities through several programs for veterans receiving VA health care. Each program offers treatment and rehabilitation services to help veterans live and work in their communities.

Participation in the following VA Work Restoration Programs cannot be used to deny or discontinue VA compensation or pension benefits. Payments received from Incentive Therapy and Compensated Work Therapy transitional work are not taxable.

Incentive Therapy (IT) provides a diversified work experience at VA medical centers for veterans who exhibit severe mental illness and/or physical impairments. IT services may consist of full- or part-time work with nominal remuneration limited to the maximum of one half of the federal minimum wage.

CWT/Sheltered Workshop (CWT) operates sheltered workshops at approximately thirty-five VA medical centers. CWT Sheltered Workshop is a preemployment vocational activity that provides an opportunity for work hardening and assessment in a simulated work environment. Participating veterans are paid on a piece rate basis.

CWT/Transitional Work (CWT/TW) is a vocational assessment program that operates in VA medical centers and/or local community businesses and industries. CWT/TW participants are matched to real-life work assignments for a time-limited basis. Veterans are supervised by personnel of the sponsoring site under the same job expectations experienced by non-CWT workers. CWT/TW participants are not considered employees and receive no traditional employee benefits.

Participants receive the greater of federal or state minimum wage, or more depending on the type of work. Over 40 percent of participants secure competitive employment at the time of discharge.

CWT/Supported Employment (CWT/SE) consists of full-time or part-time competitive employment with extensive clinical supports. The focus of CWT/SE is to assist veterans with psychosis and other serious mental illness to gain access to meaningful competitive employment. CWT/SE follow-along support services are generally phased out after the veteran is able to maintain employment independently.

Outpatient Dental Treatment

Veterans are eligible for outpatient dental treatment if they meet specific criteria. Please visit www.va.gov/healtheligibility/Library/pubs/Dental/Dental .pdf to review the details.

For more information about eligibility for VA medical and dental benefits, contact the Health Benefits Service Center at 1-877-222-8387.

Nursing Home Care

VA provides nursing home services to veterans through three national programs: VA owned and operated Community Living Centers (CLC), state veterans' homes owned and operated by the states, and the contract community nursing home program. Each program has admission and eligibility criteria specific to the program.

VA Community Living Centers: Community Living Centers (CLC) provide a dynamic array of short stay (less than ninety days) and long stay (ninety-one days or more) services. Short stay services include but are not limited to skilled nursing, respite care, rehabilitation, hospice, and maintenance care for veterans awaiting placement in the community. Short stay services are available for veterans who are enrolled in VA health care and require CLC services. Long stay services are available for enrolled veterans who need nursing home care for life or for an extended period of time for a service-connected disability, and those rated 60 percent service-connected and unemployable; or veterans who have a 70 percent or greater service-connected disability. All others are based on available resources.

State Veterans' Home Program: State veterans' homes are owned and operated by the states. The states petition VA for grant dollars for a portion of the construction costs followed by a request for recognition as a state home. Once recognized, VA pays a portion of the per diem if the state meets VA standards. States establish eligibility criteria and determine services offered for short- and long-term care. Specialized services offered are dependent upon the capability of the home to render them.

Contract Community Nursing Home Program: VA health care facilities establish contracts with community nursing homes. The purpose of this program is to meet the nursing home needs of veterans who require long-term nursing home care in their own community, close to their families, and meet the enrollment and eligibility requirements.

Admission Criteria: The general criteria for nursing home placement in each of the three programs requires that a resident must be medically stable, that is, not acutely ill, have sufficient functional deficits to require inpatient nursing home care, and is assessed by an appropriate medical provider to be in need of institutional nursing home care. Furthermore, the veteran must meet the specific eligibility criteria for community living center care or the contract nursing home program and the eligibility criteria for the specific state veterans home.

Noninstitutional Long-term Care Services: In addition to nursing home care, VA offers a variety of other long-term care services either directly or by contract with community-based agencies. Such services include adult day health care, respite care, geriatric evaluation and management, hospice and palliative care, home-based skilled nursing, and home-based primary care. Veterans receiving these services may be subject to a copay.

Emergency Medical Care in U.S. Non-VA Facilities

In the case of medical emergencies, VA may reimburse or pay for emergency non-VA medical care not previously authorized that is provided to certain eligible veterans when VA or other federal facilities are not feasibly available. This benefit may be dependent upon other conditions, such as notification to VA, the nature of treatment sought, the status of the veteran, the presence of other health care insurance, and third-party liability. Because there are different regulatory requirements that may affect VA payment and veteran liability for the cost of care, it is very important that the nearest VA medical facility to where emergency services are furnished be notified as soon as possible after emergency treatment is sought. If emergency inpatient services are required, VA will assist in transferring the veteran to a department facility, if available. Limitations on the time to file a claim apply. For additional information, contact the nearest VA medical facility. Please note that reimbursement criteria for veterans living or traveling outside the United States fall under VA's Foreign Medical Program (FMP) and differ from the criteria for payment of emergency treatment received in the United States. Please refer to the section below on VA's Foreign Medical Program.

Foreign Medical Program

VA will pay for medical services for service-connected disabilities or any disability associated with and found to be aggravating a service-connected disability for those veterans living or traveling outside the United States. This program will also reimburse for the treatment of foreign medical services needed as part of an approved VA vocational rehabilitation program. Veterans living in the Philippines should register with the U.S. Veterans Affairs office in Pasay City, telephone 011-632-838-4566, or by e-mail at manlopc .inqry@vba.va.gov. All other veterans living or planning to travel outside the United States should register with the Denver Foreign Medical Program office, P.O. Box 469061, Denver, CO 80246-9061, USA; telephone 303-331-7590. For information, visit www.va.gov/hac/forbeneficiaries/ fmp/fmp.asp.

Some veterans traveling or living overseas can telephone the Foreign Medical Program toll free from these countries: Germany 0800-1800-011; Australia 1800-354-965; Italy 800-782-655; United Kingdom (England and Scotland) 0800-032-7425; Mexico 001-877-345-8179; Japan 00531-13-0871; Costa Rica 0800-013-0759; and Spain 900-981-776. (Note: Veterans in Mexico or Costa Rica must first dial the U.S. country code.)

Online Health Services

My HealtheVet (www.myhealth.va.gov) is VA's award-winning online Personal Health Record. Access is easy and convenient anywhere the Internet is available. My HealtheVet is for veterans, active duty servicemembers, their dependents, and caregivers. With My HealtheVet users access trusted and secure VA health information to better manage their health care and facts about other VA benefits and services to which they may be entitled. My HealtheVet helps users to partner with their health care teams and provides them opportunities and tools to make informed decisions.

To register, simply go to www.myhealth.va.gov and follow the directions. Users can then record and track health information and history for their family and themselves; enter past and present military service events; keep activity and food journals; record, track, and graph vital signs; and maintain other health measures.

Veterans enrolled at a VA health care facility can also access advanced features of My HealtheVet and can link their Personal Health Record with information from their VA electronic health record. To access the advanced features, veterans must complete a one-time process called In-Person Authentication or IPA. This includes making a visit to their VA facility to verify their identity in person. After completing the IPA, VA patients can use My HealtheVet to:

- Refill their VA prescriptions by name, not just by the prescription number
- Record non-VA medications
- Receive VA Wellness Reminders
- Access new features as they become available

Expected in 2010, VA patients who complete the IPA also will see their VA appointments, VA lab test results, and VA list of allergies. They may also communicate with their health care teams through secure messaging, as this feature becomes available at their local VA facility.

Register for My HealtheVet today at www.myhealth.va.gov. If you are a VA patient and want to access advanced features, don't forget to complete the one-time IPA process, which takes only a few minutes. Start now and benefit from using My HealtheVet. It's quick, easy, and it's for you.

SERVICE-CONNECTED DISABILITIES

Disability Compensation: Disability compensation is a monetary benefit paid to veterans who are disabled by an injury or illness that was incurred or aggravated during active military service. These disabilities are considered to be service connected. Disability compensation varies with the degree of disability and the number of a veteran's dependents, and is paid monthly. Veterans with certain severe disabilities may be eligible for additional special monthly compensation. The benefits are not subject to federal or state income tax.

The payment of military retirement pay, disability severance pay, and separation incentive payments, known as SSB (Special Separation Benefits) and VSI (Voluntary Separation Incentives), affects the amount of VA compensation paid to disabled veterans. To be eligible, the service of the veteran must have been terminated through separation or discharge under conditions other than dishonorable. For additional details, visit the website at www.vba .va.gov/bln/21/.

Receiving Disability Benefit Payments: VA offers three disability benefit payment options. Most veterans receive their payments by direct deposit to a bank, savings and loan, or credit union account. In some areas, veterans who do not have a bank account can open a federally insured Electronic Transfer Account, which costs about $3 a month, provides a monthly statement, and allows for cash withdrawals. Other veterans may choose to receive benefits by check. To choose or change a payment method, call toll free 1-877-838-2778, Monday through Friday, 7:30 a.m. to 4:50 p.m., CST.

Presumptive Conditions for Disability Compensation: All veterans who develop Amyotrophic Lateral Sclerosis (ALS), also known as Lou Gehrig's disease, at any time after separation from service may be eligible for compensation for that disability. Certain veterans are eligible for disability compensation based on the presumption that their disability is service connected.

2010 VA Disability Compensation Rates for Veterans

Veteran's Disability Rating	Monthly Rate Paid to Veterans
10 percent	$123
20 percent	$243
30 percent*	$376
40 percent*	$541
50 percent*	$770
60 percent*	$974
70 percent*	$1,228
80 percent*	$1,427
90 percent*	$1,604
100 percent*	$2,673

*Veterans with disability ratings of at least 30 percent are eligible for additional allowances for dependents, including spouses, minor children, children between the ages of eighteen and twenty-three who are attending school, children who are permanently incapable of self-support because of a disability arising before age eighteen, and dependent parents. The additional amount depends on the disability rating and the number of dependents.

Prisoners of War: For former POWs who were imprisoned for any length of time, the following disabilities are presumed to be service connected if they are rated at least 10 percent disabling any time after military service: psychosis, any of the anxiety states, dysthymic disorder, organic residuals of frostbite, post-traumatic osteoarthritis, heart disease or hypertensive vascular disease and their complications, stroke, residuals of stroke, and, effective October 10, 2008, osteoporosis if the veteran has post-traumatic stress disorder (PTSD).

For former POWs who were imprisoned for at least thirty days, the following conditions are also presumed to be service connected: avitaminosis, beriberi, chronic dysentery, helminthiasis, malnutrition (including optic atrophy), pellagra and/or other nutritional deficiencies, irritable bowel syndrome, peptic ulcer disease, peripheral neuropathy, cirrhosis of the liver, and effective September 28, 2009, osteoporosis.

Veterans Exposed to Agent Orange and Other Herbicides: A veteran who served in the Republic of Vietnam between January 9, 1962, and May 7, 1975, is presumed to have been exposed to Agent Orange and other herbicides used in support of military operations.

Twelve illnesses are presumed by VA to be service connected for such veterans: chloracne or other acneform disease similar to chloracne, porphyria cutanea tarda, soft-tissue sarcoma (other than osteosarcoma, chondrosarcoma,

Kaposi's sarcoma, or mesothelioma), Hodgkin's disease, multiple myeloma, respiratory cancers (lung, bronchus, larynx, trachea), non-Hodgkin's lymphoma, prostate cancer, acute and subacute peripheral neuropathy, diabetes mellitus (Type 2), chronic lymphocytic leukemia, and AL amyloidosis.

Veterans Exposed to Radiation: For veterans who participated in "radiation risk activities" as defined in VA regulations while on active duty, active duty for training, or inactive duty training, the following conditions are presumed to be service connected: all forms of leukemia (except for chronic lymphocytic leukemia); cancer of the thyroid, breast, pharynx, esophagus, stomach, small intestine, pancreas, bile ducts, gall bladder, salivary gland, urinary tract (renal pelvis, ureter, urinary bladder, and urethra), brain, bone, lung, colon, and ovary; bronchiolo-alveolar carcinoma; multiple myeloma; lymphomas (other than Hodgkin's disease); and primary liver cancer (except if cirrhosis or hepatitis B is indicated).

To determine service connection for other conditions or exposures not eligible for presumptive service connection, VA considers factors such as the amount of radiation exposure, duration of exposure, elapsed time between exposure and onset of the disease, gender and family history, age at time of exposure, the extent to which a non-service-related exposure could contribute to disease, and the relative sensitivity of exposed tissue.

Gulf War Veterans with Chronic Disabilities: Veterans may receive disability compensation for chronic disabilities resulting from undiagnosed illnesses and/or medically unexplained chronic multisymptom illnesses defined by a cluster of signs or symptoms. A disability is considered chronic if it has existed for at least six months.

The undiagnosed illnesses must have appeared either during active service in the Southwest Asia theater of operations during the Gulf War period of August 2, 1990, to July 31, 1991, or to a degree of at least 10 percent at any time since then through December 31, 2011. This theater of operations includes Iraq, Kuwait, Saudi Arabia, the neutral zone between Iraq and Saudi Arabia, Bahrain, Qatar, the United Arab Emirates, Oman, the Gulf of Aden, the Gulf of Oman, the Persian Gulf, the Arabian Sea, the Red Sea, and the airspace above these locations.

The following are examples of symptoms of an undiagnosed illness: chronic fatigue syndrome, fibromyalgia, skin disorders, headache, muscle pain, joint pain, neurological symptoms, neuropsychological symptoms, symptoms involving the respiratory system, sleep disturbances, gastrointestinal symptoms, cardiovascular symptoms, abnormal weight loss, and menstrual disorders.

Concurrent Retirement and Disability Payments (CRDP) restores retired pay on a graduated ten-year schedule for retirees with a 50 to 90 percent

VA-rated disability. Concurrent retirement payments increase 10 percent per year through 2013. Veterans rated 100 percent disabled by VA are entitled to full CRDP without being phased in. Veterans receiving benefits at the 100 percent rate due to individual unemployability are entitled to full CRDP effective January 1, 2005.

Eligibility: To qualify, veterans must also meet all three of the following criteria:

1. Have twenty or more years of active duty, or full-time National Guard duty, or satisfactory service as a Reservist
2. Be in a retired status
3. Be receiving retired pay (must be offset by VA payments)

Retirees do not need to apply for this benefit. Payment is coordinated between VA and the Department of Defense (DoD).

Combat-Related Special Compensation (CRSC) provides tax-free monthly payments to eligible retired veterans with combat-related injuries. With CRSC, veterans can receive both their full military retirement pay and their VA disability compensation if the injury is combat related.

Eligibility: Retired veterans with combat-related injuries must meet all of the following criteria to apply for CRSC:

1. Active or Reserve component with twenty years of creditable service or medically retired
2. Receiving military retired pay
3. Have a 10 percent or greater VA-rated injury
4. Military retired pay is reduced by VA disability payments (VA waiver)

In addition, veterans must be able to provide documentary evidence that their injuries were a result of one of the following:

- Training that simulates war (e.g., exercises, field training)
- Hazardous duty (e.g., flight, diving, parachute duty)
- An instrumentality of war (e.g., combat vehicles, weapons, Agent Orange)
- Armed conflict (e.g., gunshot wounds, Purple Heart)

For information, visit www.defenselink.mil, or call the toll-free phone number for the veteran's branch of service: Army 1-866-281-3254; Air Force 1-800-616-3775; Navy 1-877-366-2772. The Army has its own website at https://www.hrc.army.mil/site/crsc/index.html and e-mail at crsc.info@ us.army.mil.

Programs for Service-Connected Disabilities

The **Vocational Rehabilitation and Employment (VR&E)** Program assists veterans who have service-connected disabilities obtain and maintain suitable employment. Independent living services are also available for severely disabled veterans who are not currently ready to seek employment. Additional information is available on VA's website at www.vetsuccess.gov.

Eligibility: A veteran must have a VA service-connected disability rated at least 20 percent with an employment handicap, or rated 10 percent with a serious employment handicap, and be discharged or released from military service under other than dishonorable conditions. Servicemembers pending medical separation from active duty may also apply if their disabilities are reasonably expected to be rated at least 20 percent following their discharge.

Entitlement: A VA counselor must decide if the individual has an employment handicap based upon the results of a comprehensive evaluation. After an entitlement decision is made, the individual and counselor will work together to develop a rehabilitation plan. The rehabilitation plan will specify the rehabilitation services to be provided.

Services: Rehabilitation services provided to participants in the VR&E Program are under one of five tracks. VA pays the cost of approved training that is included in an individual's rehabilitation plan. A subsistence allowance may also be provided. The five tracks are:

- **Reemployment with Previous Employer:** For individuals who are separating from active duty or in the National Guard or Reserves and are returning to work for their previous employer.
- **Rapid Access to Employment:** For individuals who either wish to obtain employment soon after separation or who already have the necessary skills to be competitive in the job market in an appropriate occupation.
- **Self-Employment:** For individuals who have limited access to traditional employment, need flexible work schedules, or who require more accommodation in the work environment due to their disabling conditions or other life circumstances.
- **Employment through Long-Term Services:** For individuals who need specialized training and/or education to obtain and maintain suitable employment.
- **Independent Living Services:** For veterans who are not currently able to work and need rehabilitation services to live more independently.

Period of a Rehabilitation Program: Generally, veterans must complete a program within twelve years from their separation from military service or within twelve years from the date VA notifies them that they have a compensable service-connected disability. Depending on the length of program needed, veterans may be provided up to forty-eight months of full-time services or their part-time equivalent. These limitations may be extended in certain circumstances.

Work-Study: Veterans training at the three-quarter or full-time rate may participate in VA's work-study program and provide VA outreach services, prepare/process VA paperwork, work at a VA medical facility, or perform other VA-approved activities. A portion of the work-study allowance equal to 40 percent of the total may be paid in advance.

Specially Adapted Housing Grants

Certain veterans and servicemembers with service-connected disabilities may be entitled to a Specially Adapted Housing (SAH) grant from VA to help build a new specially adapted house, to adapt a home they already own, or to buy a house and modify it to meet their disability-related requirements. Eligible veterans or servicemembers may now receive up to three grants, with the total dollar amount of the grants not to exceed the maximum allowable. Previous grant recipients who had received assistance of less than the current maximum allowable may be eligible for an additional SAH grant.

Eligibility for up to $63,780: VA may approve a grant of not more than 50 percent of the cost of building, buying, or adapting existing homes or paying to reduce indebtedness on a currently owned home that is being adapted, up to a maximum of $63,780. In certain instances, the full grant amount may be applied toward remodeling costs. Veterans and servicemembers must be determined eligible to receive compensation for a permanent and total service-connected disability due to one of the following:

1. Loss or loss of use of both lower extremities, such as to preclude locomotion without the aid of braces, crutches, canes, or a wheelchair.
2. Loss or loss of use of both upper extremities at or above the elbow.
3. Blindness in both eyes, having only light perception, plus loss or loss of use of one lower extremity.
4. Loss or loss of use of one lower extremity together with (a) residuals of organic disease or injury, or (b) the loss or loss of use of one upper extremity that so affects the functions of balance or propulsion as to preclude locomotion without the use of braces, canes, crutches, or a wheelchair.
5. Severe burn injuries.

Eligibility for up to $12,756: VA may approve a grant for the cost, up to a maximum of $12,756, for necessary adaptations to a veteran's or servicemember's residence or to help them acquire a residence already adapted with special features for their disability, to purchase and adapt a home, or for adaptations to a family member's home in which they will reside.

To be eligible for this grant, veterans and servicemembers must be entitled to compensation for permanent and total service-connected disability due to one of the following:

1. Blindness in both eyes with 5/200 visual acuity or less.
2. Anatomical loss or loss of use of both hands.
3. Severe burn injuries.

Eligible veterans and servicemembers who are temporarily residing in a home owned by a family member may also receive a Temporary Residence Adaptation (TRA) grant to help the veteran or servicemember adapt the family member's home to meet his or her special needs. Those eligible for a $63,780 grant would be permitted to use up to $14,000, and those eligible for a $12,756 grant would be permitted to use up to $2,000. Grant amounts will also be adjusted annually based on a cost-of-construction index.

The first adjustment occurred on October 1, 2009, with future adjustments each October 1 thereafter. These adjustments will increase the grant amounts or leave them unchanged; they will not decrease the grant amounts. The maximum amount for a TRA grant is not indexed and remains unchanged.

The property may be located outside the United States, in a country or political subdivision that allows individuals to have or acquire a beneficial property interest, and in which the Secretary of Veterans Affairs, in his or her discretion, has determined that it is reasonably practicable for the Secretary to provide assistance in acquiring specially adapted housing. For more information on the use of such grants, contact Brian Bixler, Specially Adapted Housing, at 202-461-9546 or via e-mail at brian.bixler@va.gov.

Supplemental Financing: Veterans and servicemembers with available loan guaranty entitlement may also obtain a guaranteed loan or a direct loan from VA to supplement the grant to acquire a specially adapted home. Amounts with a guaranteed loan from a private lender will vary, but the maximum direct loan from VA is $33,000. Additional information about the Specially Adapted Housing Program is available on VA's website at www.homeloans.va.gov/sah.htm.

Automobile Allowance

Veterans and servicemembers may be eligible for a one-time payment of not more than $11,000 toward the purchase of an automobile or other conveyance if they have service-connected loss or permanent loss of use of one or both hands or feet, permanent impairment of vision of both eyes to a certain degree, or ankylosis (immobility) of one or both knees or one or both hips.

They may also be eligible for adaptive equipment, and for repair, replacement, or reinstallation required because of disability or for the safe operation of a vehicle purchased with VA assistance. To apply, contact a VA regional office at 1-800-827-1000 or the nearest VA health care facility.

Clothing Allowance

Any veteran who is service connected for a disability for which he or she uses prosthetic or orthopedic appliances may receive an annual clothing allowance. This allowance is also available to any veteran whose service-connected skin condition requires prescribed medication that irreparably damages outer garments. To apply, contact the prosthetic representative at the nearest VA medical center.

Aid and Attendance for Housebound Veterans

A veteran who is determined by VA to be in need of the regular aid and attendance of another person, or a veteran who is permanently housebound, may be entitled to additional disability compensation or pension payments. A veteran evaluated at 30 percent or more disabled is entitled to receive an additional payment for a spouse who is in need of the aid and attendance of another person.

Vocational Rehabilitation and Employment Rates

In some cases, a veteran requires additional education or training to become employable. A subsistence allowance is paid each month during training and is based on the rate of attendance (full time or part time), the number of dependents, and the type of training. The charts below show the rates as of October 1, 2009.

Subsistence allowance is paid at the following monthly rates for training in an institution of higher learning.

Training Time	Veterans with No Dependents	Veterans with One Dependent	Veterans with Two Dependents	Additional Dependent
Full time	$547.54	$679.18	$800.36	$58.34
3/4 time	$411.41	$510.12	$598.38	$44.86
1/2 time	$275.28	$341.07	$400.92	$29.93

Subsistence allowance is paid at the following monthly rates for full-time training only in nonpay or nominal pay on-the-job training in a federal, state, local, or federally recognized Indian tribe agency; training in the home; and vocational training in a rehabilitation facility or sheltered workshop.

Training Time	Veterans with No Dependents	Veterans with One Dependent	Veterans with Two Dependents	Additional Dependent
Full time	$547.54	$679.18	$800.36	$58.34

Subsistence allowance is paid at the following monthly rates for full-time training only in farm cooperative, apprenticeship, and other on-the-job training. Payments are variable, based on the wages received. The maximum rates are:

Training Time	Veterans with No Dependents	Veterans with One Dependent	Veterans with Two Dependents	Additional Dependent
Full time	$478.73	$578.92	$667.21	$43.40

Subsistence allowance is paid at the following monthly rates for nonpay or nominal pay work experience in a federal, state, local, or federally recognized Indian tribe agency.

Training Time	Veterans with No Dependents	Veterans with One Dependent	Veterans with Two Dependents	Additional Dependent
Full time	$547.54	$679.18	$800.36	$58.34
3/4 time	$411.41	$510.12	$598.38	$44.86
1/2 time	$275.28	$341.07	$400.92	$29.93

Subsistence allowance is paid at the following monthly rates for training programs that include a combination of institutional and on-the-job training.

Greater Than Half-Time	Veterans with No Dependents	Veterans with One Dependent	Veterans with Two Dependents	Additional Dependent
Institutional	$547.54	$679.18	$800.36	$58.34
On the job	$478.73	$578.92	$667.21	$43.40

Subsistence allowance is paid at the following monthly rates for full-time training only for nonfarm cooperative institutional training and nonfarm cooperative on-the-job training.

Training Time	Veterans with No Dependents	Veterans with One Dependent	Veterans with Two Dependents	Additional Dependent
Institutional	$547.54	$679.18	$800.36	$58.34
On the job	$478.73	$578.92	$667.21	$43.40

Subsistence allowance is paid at the following monthly rates during the period of enrollment in a rehabilitation facility when a veteran is pursuing an approved independent-living program plan.

Training Time	Veterans with No Dependents	Veterans with One Dependent	Veterans with Two Dependents	Additional Dependent
Full time	$547.54	$679.18	$800.36	$58.34
3/4 time	$411.41	$510.12	$598.38	$44.86
1/2 time	$275.28	$341.07	$400.92	$29.93

Subsistence allowance is paid at the following monthly rates during the period of enrollment in a rehabilitation facility when a veteran requires this service for the purpose of extended evaluation.

Training Time	Veterans with No Dependents	Veterans with One Dependent	Veterans with Two Dependents	Additional Dependent
Full time	$547.54	$679.18	$800.36	$58.34
3/4 time	$411.41	$510.12	$598.38	$44.86
1/2 time	$275.28	$341.07	$400.92	$29.93
1/4 time	$137.62	$170.55	$200.45	$14.93

VA PENSIONS

Eligibility for Disability Pension: Veterans with low incomes who are either permanently and totally disabled, or age sixty-five and older, may be eligible for monetary support if they have ninety days or more of active military service, at least one day of which was during a period of war. (Veterans who entered active duty on or after September 8, 1980, or officers who entered active duty on or after October 16, 1981, may have to meet a longer minimum period of active duty.) The veteran's discharge must have been under conditions other than dishonorable, and the disability must be for reasons other than the veteran's own willful misconduct.

Payments are made to bring the veteran's total income, including other retirement or Social Security income, to a level set by Congress. Unreimbursed medical expenses may reduce countable income for VA purposes.

Protected Pension: Pension beneficiaries, who were receiving a VA pension on December 31, 1978, and do not wish to elect the Improved Pension, will continue to receive the pension rate received on that date. This rate generally continues as long as the beneficiary's income remains within established limits or net worth does not bar payment, and the beneficiary does not lose any dependents.

Beneficiaries must continue to meet basic eligibility factors, such as permanent and total disability for veterans. VA must adjust rates for other reasons, such as a veteran's hospitalization in a VA facility.

Medal of Honor Pension: VA administers pensions to recipients of the Medal of Honor. Congress set the monthly pension at $1,194.

Improved Disability Pension: Congress establishes the maximum annual improved disability pension rates. Payments are reduced by the amount of countable income of the veteran, spouse, and dependent children. When a veteran without a spouse or a child is furnished nursing home or domiciliary care by VA, the pension is reduced to an amount not to exceed $90 per month after three calendar months of care. The reduction may be delayed if nursing-home care is being continued to provide the veteran with rehabilitation services.

2010 VA Improved Disability Pension Rates*

Status of Veteran's Family Situation and Caretaking Needs	*Maximum Annual Rate*
Veteran without dependents	$11,830
Veteran with one dependent	$15,493
Veteran permanently housebound, no dependents	$14,457
Veteran permanently housebound, one dependent	$18,120
Veteran needing regular aid and attendance, no dependents	$19,736
Veteran needing regular aid and attendance, one dependent	$23,396
Two veterans married to one another	$15,493
Increase for each additional dependent child	$2,020

*Additional information can be found in the Compensation and Pension Benefits section of VA's Internet pages at www.vba.va.gov/bln/21/index.htm.

EDUCATION AND TRAINING: GI BILL

Up to thirty-six months of education benefits can be used for education, training, certification, apprenticeship, and on-the-job training programs. National Guard and Selected Reserve may be eligible under previous active-duty enlistment.

Post-9/11 GI Bill

Eligibility: The Post-9/11 GI Bill is a new education benefit program for servicemembers and veterans who served on active duty on or after September 11, 2001. Benefits are payable for training pursued on or after August 1, 2009. No payments can be made under this program for training pursued before that date.

To be eligible, the servicemember or veteran must serve at least ninety aggregate days on active duty after September 10, 2001, and remain on active duty or be honorably:

1. discharged from active duty status;
2. released from active duty and placed on the retired list or temporary disability retired list;
3. released from active duty and transferred to the Fleet Reserve or Fleet Marine Corps Reserve;
4. released from active duty for further service in a reserve component of the Armed Forces.

Veterans may also be eligible if they were honorably discharged from active duty for a service-connected disability after serving thirty continuous days after September 10, 2001. Generally, servicemembers or veterans may receive up to thirty-six months of entitlement under the Post-9/11 GI Bill.

Eligibility for benefits expires fifteen years from the last period of active duty of at least ninety consecutive days. If released for a service-connected disability after at least thirty days of continuous service, eligibility ends fifteen years from when the member is released for the service-connected disability.

If, on August 1, 2009, the servicemember or veteran is eligible for the Montgomery GI Bill; the Montgomery GI Bill—Selected Reserve; or the Reserve Educational Assistance Program; and qualifies for the Post-9/11 GI Bill, an irrevocable election must be made to receive benefits under the Post-9/11 GI Bill.

In most instances, once the election to receive benefits under the Post-9/11 GI Bill is made, the individual will no longer be eligible to receive benefits under the relinquished program.

Based on the length of active duty service, eligible participants are entitled to receive a percentage of the following:

1. Cost of tuition and fees, not to exceed the most expensive in-state undergraduate tuition at a public institution of higher education (paid directly to the school);
2. Monthly housing allowance equal to the basic allowance for housing payable to a military E-5 with dependents, in the same zip code as the primary school (paid directly to the servicemember or veteran);
3. Yearly books and supplies stipend of up to $1,000 per year (paid directly to the servicemember or veteran); and
4. A one-time payment of $500 paid to certain individuals relocating from highly rural areas.

Note: The housing allowance and books and supplies stipend are not payable to individuals on active duty. The housing allowance is not payable to those pursuing training at half time or less or to individuals enrolled solely in distance-learning programs.

Benefits may be used for any approved program offered by a school in the United States that is authorized to grant an associate (or higher) degree. Call 1-888-442-4551 or visit www.gibill.va.gov for information about attending school in a foreign country.

If entitlement to the Post-9/11 GI Bill was the result of transferring from the Montgomery GI Bill, the Montgomery GI Bill—Selected Reserve, or the Reserve Education Assistance Program, recipients may also receive Post-9/11 GI Bill benefits for flight training, apprenticeship or on-the-job training programs, and correspondence courses.

Individuals serving an aggregate period of active duty after September 10, 2001, can receive the following percentages based on length of service:

Active Duty Service	*Maximum Benefit*
At least thirty-six months	100%
At least thirty continuous days and discharged due to service-connected disability	100%
At least thirty months < thirty-six months	90%
At least twenty-four months < thirty months	80%
At least eighteen months < twenty-four months	70%
At least twelve months < eighteen months	60%
At least six months < twelve months	50%
At least ninety days < six months	40%

Transfer of Entitlement (TOE): DoD may offer members of the armed forces on or after August 1, 2009, the opportunity to transfer benefits to a spouse or dependent children. DoD and the military services must approve all requests for this benefit. Members of the armed forces approved for the TOE may only transfer any unused portion of their Post-9/11 GI Bill benefits while a member of the armed forces, subject to their period of eligibility.

The Yellow Ribbon GI Education Enhancement Program: This program was enacted to potentially assist eligible individuals with payment of their tuition and fees in instances where costs exceed the most expensive in-state undergraduate tuition at a public institution of higher education. To be eligible, the student must be a veteran receiving benefits at the 100 percent benefit rate payable, a transfer-of-entitlement-eligible dependent child, or a transfer-of-entitlement eligible spouse of a veteran. The school of attendance must have accepted VA's invitation to participate in the program, state how much student tuition will be waived (up to 50 percent), and how many participants will be accepted into the program during the current academic year. VA will match the school's percentage (up to 50 percent) to reduce or eliminate out-of-pocket costs for eligible participants.

Work-Study Program: Veterans and eligible transfer-of-entitlement recipients who train at the three-quarter rate of pursuit or higher may be eligible for a work-study program in which they work for VA and receive hourly wages. Students under the work-study program must be supervised by a VA employee, and all duties performed must relate to VA. The types of work allowed include:

1. VA paperwork processing at schools or other training facilities.
2. Assistance with patient care at VA hospitals or domiciliary care facilities.
3. Work at national or state veterans' cemeteries.
4. Various jobs within any VA regional office.
5. Other VA-approved activities.

Marine Gunnery Sergeant John David Fry Scholarship: This scholarship entitles children of those who die in the line of duty on or since September 11, 2001, to use Post-9/11 GI Bill benefits.

Eligible children:

- are entitled to thirty-six months of benefits at the 100 percent level
- have fifteen years to use the benefit beginning on their eighteenth birthday

- may use the benefit until their thirty-third birthday
- are not eligible for the Yellow Ribbon Program

Montgomery GI Bill

Eligibility: VA educational benefits may be used while the servicemember is on active duty or after the servicemember's separation from active duty with a fully honorable military discharge. Discharges "under honorable conditions" and "general" discharges do not establish eligibility. Eligibility generally expires ten years after the servicemember's discharge. However, there are exceptions for disability, reentering active duty, and upgraded discharges.

All participants must have a high school diploma, equivalency certificate, or have completed twelve hours toward a college degree before applying for benefits.

Previously, servicemembers had to meet the high school requirement before they completed their initial active duty obligation. Those who did not may now meet the requirement and reapply for benefits. If eligible, they must use their benefits either within ten years from the date of last discharge from active duty or by November 2, 2010, whichever is later.

Additionally, every veteran must establish eligibility under one of four categories.

Category 1: Service after June 30, 1985.

For veterans who entered active duty for the first time after June 30, 1985, did not decline MGIB in writing, and had their military pay reduced by $100 a month for twelve months. Servicemembers can apply after completing two continuous years of service. Veterans must have completed three continuous years of active duty, or two continuous years of active duty if they first signed up for less than three years or have an obligation to serve four years in the Selected Reserve (the 2 x 4 program) and enter the Selected Reserve within one year of discharge.

Servicemembers or veterans who received a commission as a result of graduation from a service academy or completion of an ROTC scholarship are not eligible under Category 1 unless they received their commission:

1. after becoming eligible for MGIB benefits (including completing the minimum service requirements for the initial period of active duty); or
2. after September 30, 1996, and received less than $3,400 during any one year under ROTC scholarship.

Servicemembers or veterans who declined MGIB because they received repayment from the military for education loans are also ineligible under

Category 1. If they did not decline MGIB and received loan repayments, the months served to repay the loans will be deducted from their entitlement.

Early Separation from Military Service: Servicemembers who did not complete the required period of military service may be eligible under Category 1 if discharged for one of the following:

1. Convenience of the government—with thirty continuous months of service for an obligation of three or more years, or twenty continuous months of service for an obligation of less than three years
2. Service-connected disability
3. Hardship
4. A medical condition diagnosed prior to joining the military
5. A condition that interfered with performance of duty and did not result from misconduct
6. A reduction in force (in most cases)
7. Sole Survivorship (if discharged after September 11, 2001)

Category 2: Vietnam-era GI Bill Conversion

This program is for veterans who had remaining entitlement under the Vietnam-era GI Bill on December 31, 1989, and served on active duty for any number of days during the period October 19, 1984, to June 30, 1985, for at least three continuous years beginning on July 1, 1985; or at least two continuous years of active duty beginning on July 1, 1985, followed by four years in the Selected Reserve beginning within one year of release from active duty.

Veterans not on active duty on October 19, 1984, may be eligible under Category 2 if they served three continuous years on active duty beginning on or after July 1, 1985, or two continuous years of active duty at any time followed by four continuous years in the Selected Reserve beginning within one year of release from active duty.

Veterans are barred from eligibility under Category 2 if they received a commission after December 31, 1976, as a result of graduation from a service academy or completion of an ROTC scholarship.

However, such a commission is not a disqualifier if they received the commission after becoming eligible for MGIB benefits or received the commission after September 30, 1996, and received less than $3,400 during any one year under ROTC scholarship.

Category 3: Involuntary Separation/Special Separation

For veterans who meet one of the following requirements:

1. elected MGIB before being involuntarily separated; or
2. were voluntarily separated under the Voluntary Separation Incentive or the Special Separation Benefit program, elected MGIB benefits before being separated, and had military pay reduced by $1,200 before discharge.

Category 4: Veterans Educational Assistance Program

For veterans who participated in the Veterans' Educational Assistance Program (VEAP) and:

1. served on active duty on October 9, 1996;
2. participated in VEAP and contributed money to an account;
3. elected MGIB by October 9, 1997, and paid $1,200.

Veterans who participated in VEAP on or before October 9, 1996, may also be eligible even if they did not deposit money in a VEAP account if they served on active duty from October 9, 1996, through April 1, 2000, elected MGIB by October 31, 2001, and contributed $2,700 to MGIB.

Certain National Guard servicemembers may also qualify under Category 4 if they:

1. served for the first time on full-time active duty in the National Guard between June 30, 1985, and November 29, 1989, and had no previous active duty service;
2. elected MGIB during the nine-month window ending on July 9, 1997; and
3. paid $1,200.

Payments: Effective October 1, 2009, the rate for full-time training in college, technical, or vocational school is $1,368 a month for those who served three years or more or two years plus four years in the Selected Reserve. For those who served less than three years, the monthly rate is $1,111.

Benefits are reduced for part-time training. Payments for other types of training follow different rules. VA will pay an additional amount, called a "kicker" or "college fund," if directed by DoD. Visit www.gibill.va.gov for more information.

The maximum number of months veterans can receive payments is thirty-six months at the full-time rate or the part-time equivalent.

The following groups qualify for the maximum: veterans who served the required length of active duty, veterans with an obligation of three years or more who were separated early for the convenience of the government and served thirty continuous months, and veterans with an obligation of less than three years who were separated early for the convenience of the government and served twenty continuous months.

Types of Training Available:

1. Courses at colleges and universities leading to associate, bachelor, or graduate degrees, including accredited independent study offered through distance education.

2. Courses leading to a certificate or diploma from business, technical, or vocational schools.
3. Apprenticeship or on-the-job training for those not on active duty, including self-employment training begun on or after June 16, 2004, for ownership or operation of a franchise.
4. Correspondence courses, under certain conditions.
5. Flight training, if the veteran holds a private pilot's license upon beginning the training and meets the medical requirements.
6. State-approved teacher certification programs.
7. Preparatory courses necessary for admission to a college or graduate school.
8. License and certification tests approved for veterans.
9. Entrepreneurship training courses to create or expand small businesses.
10. Tuition assistance using MGIB as "Top-Up" (active duty servicemembers).

Accelerated payments for certain high-cost programs are authorized.

Work-Study Program: Veterans who train at the three-quarter or full-time rate may be eligible for a work-study program in which they work for VA and receive hourly wages.

Students under the work-study program must be supervised by a VA employee, and all duties performed must relate to VA. The types of work allowed include:

1. VA paperwork processing at schools or other training facilities.
2. Assistance with patient care at VA hospitals or domiciliary care facilities.
3. Work at national or state veterans' cemeteries.
4. Various jobs within any VA regional office.
5. Other VA-approved activities.

Veterans' Educational Assistance Program

Eligibility: Active duty personnel could participate in the Veterans' Educational Assistance Program (VEAP) if they entered active duty for the first time after December 31, 1976, and before July 1, 1985, and made a contribution prior to April 1, 1987.

The maximum contribution is $2,700. Active duty participants may make a lump-sum contribution to their VEAP account. For more information, visit the website at www.gibill.va.gov.

Servicemembers who participated in VEAP are eligible to receive benefits while on active duty if:

1. at least three months of contributions are available, except for high school or elementary, in which only one month is needed;
2. and they enlisted for the first time after September 7, 1980, and completed twenty-four months of their first period of active duty.

Servicemembers must receive a discharge under conditions other than dishonorable for the qualifying period of service. Servicemembers who enlisted for the first time after September 7, 1980, or entered active duty as an officer or enlistee after October 16, 1981, must have completed twenty-four continuous months of active duty, unless they meet a qualifying exception.

Eligibility generally expires ten years from release from active duty but can be extended under special circumstances.

Payments: DoD will match contributions at the rate of $2 for every $1 put into the fund and may make additional contributions, or "kickers," as necessary. For training in college, vocational, or technical schools, the payment amount depends on the type and hours of training pursued. The maximum amount is $300 a month for full-time training.

Training, Work-Study, Counseling: VEAP participants may receive the same training, work-study benefits, and counseling as provided under the MGIB.

HOME LOAN GUARANTY

This program enables eligible veterans and servicemembers to purchase a home without making a down payment.

VA home loan guaranties are issued to help eligible servicemembers, veterans, reservists, and unmarried surviving spouses obtain homes, condominiums, residential cooperative housing units, and manufactured homes, and to refinance loans. For additional information or to obtain VA loan guaranty forms, visit www.homeloans.va.gov/.

Loan Uses: A VA guaranty helps protect lenders from loss if the borrower fails to repay the loan. It can be used to obtain a loan to:

1. buy or build a home
2. buy a residential condominium unit
3. buy a residential cooperative housing unit
4. repair, alter, or improve a residence owned by the veteran and occupied as a home

5. refinance an existing home loan
6. buy a manufactured home and/or lot
7. install a solar heating or cooling system or other energy-efficient improvements

Eligibility: In addition to the periods of eligibility and conditions of service requirements, applicants must have a good credit rating, sufficient income, a valid Certificate of Eligibility (COE), and agree to live in the property in order to be approved by a lender for a VA home loan.

To obtain a COE, complete VA Form 26-1880, Request for a Certificate of Eligibility, and mail to: VA Eligibility Center, P.O. Box 20729, Winston-Salem, NC 27120.

It is also possible to obtain a COE from your lender. Most lenders have access to VA's WebLGY system. This Internet-based application can establish eligibility and issue an online COE in seconds. Not all cases can be processed online—only those for which VA has sufficient data in its records. However, veterans are encouraged to ask their lenders about this method of obtaining a COE before sending an application to the Eligibility Center. For more information, visit www.homeloans.va.gov/eligibility.htm.

Periods of Eligibility: World War II: (1) active duty service after September 15, 1940, and prior to July 26, 1947; (2) discharge under other than dishonorable conditions; and (3) at least ninety days total service unless discharged early for a service-connected disability.

Post–World War II Period: (1) active duty service after July 25, 1947, and prior to June 27, 1950; (2) discharge under other than dishonorable conditions; and (3) 181 days continuous active duty service unless discharged early for a service-connected disability.

Korean War: (1) active duty after June 26, 1950, and prior to February 1, 1955; (2) discharge under other than dishonorable conditions; and (3) at least ninety days total service, unless discharged early for a service-connected disability.

Post–Korean War Period: (1) active duty after January 31, 1955, and prior to August 5, 1964; (2) discharge under other than dishonorable conditions; (3) 181 days continuous service, unless discharged early for a service-connected disability.

Vietnam War: (1) active duty after August 4, 1964, and prior to May 8, 1975; (2) discharge under other than dishonorable conditions; and (3) ninety days total service, unless discharged early for a service-connected disability. For veterans who served in the Republic of Vietnam, the beginning date is February 28, 1961.

Post–Vietnam Period: (1) active duty after May 7, 1975, and prior to August 2, 1990; (2) active duty for 181 continuous days, all of which occurred after May 7, 1975; and (3) discharge under conditions other than dishonorable or early discharge for service-connected disability.

Twenty-four-Month Rule: If service was between September 8, 1980 (October 16, 1981, for officers) and August 1, 1990, veterans must generally complete twenty-four months of continuous active duty service or the full period (at least 181 days) for which they were called or ordered to active duty and be discharged under conditions other than dishonorable.

Exceptions are allowed if the veteran completed at least 181 days of active duty service but was discharged earlier than twenty-four months for (1) hardship, (2) the convenience of the government, (3) reduction in force, (4) certain medical conditions, or (5) a service-connected disability.

Gulf War: Veterans of the Gulf War era—August 2, 1990, to a date to be determined—must generally complete twenty-four months of continuous active duty service or the full period (at least ninety days) for which they were called to active duty and be discharged under other than dishonorable conditions.

Exceptions are allowed if the veteran completed at least ninety days of active duty but was discharged earlier than twenty-four months for (1) hardship, (2) the convenience of the government, (3) reduction in force, (4) certain medical conditions, or (5) a service-connected disability. Reservists and National Guard members are eligible if they were activated after August 1, 1990, served at least ninety days, and received an honorable discharge.

Active Duty Personnel: Until the Gulf War era is ended, persons on active duty are eligible after serving ninety continuous days.

VA Guaranty amounts vary with the size of the loan and the location of the property. Because lenders are able to obtain this guaranty from VA, borrowers do not need to make a down payment, provided they have enough home loan entitlement.

VA will guarantee 25 percent of the principal loan amount, up to the maximum guaranty. The maximum guaranty varies depending upon the location of the property. For all locations in the United States other than Alaska, Guam, Hawaii, and the U.S. Virgin Islands, the maximum guaranty is the greater of 25 percent of (a) $417,000 or (b) 125 percent of the area median price for a single-family residence, but in no case will the guaranty exceed 175 percent of the Freddie Mac loan limit for a single-family residence in the county in which the property securing the loan is located. This translates to a maximum loan amount of $1,094,625 for 2010. In Alaska, Guam, Hawaii, and the U.S. Virgin Islands, the maximum guaranty is the greater of 25 percent of (a) $625,500 or (b) 125 percent of the area median price for a single-family residence, but in no case will the guaranty exceed 175 percent of the Freddie Mac loan limit for a single-family residence in the county in which the property securing the loan is located. This translates to a maximum loan amount of $1,641,937.50 for 2010.

A list of 2010 county loan limits can be found at the following website: www.homeloans.va.gov/loan_limits.htm.

The VA funding fee and up to $6,000 of energy-efficient improvements can be included in VA loans. Other closing costs must be paid by the veteran, except on refinancing loans where most costs can be included in the loan.

Loan Amount	Maximum Guaranty	Special Provisions
Up to $45,000	50% of loan amount	25% on Interest Rate Reduction Refinancing Loans
$45,001–$56,250	$22,500	Same as above
$56,251–$144,000	40% of the loan amount, with a maximum of $36,000	Same as above
$144,000 or more	Up to an amount equal to 25% of the county loan limit	Same as above

An eligible borrower can use a VA-guaranteed Interest Rate Reduction Refinancing Loan to refinance an existing VA loan to lower the interest rate and payment. Typically, no credit underwriting is required for this type of loan. The loan may include the entire outstanding balance of the prior loan, the costs of energy-efficient improvements, as well as closing costs, including up to two discount points.

An eligible borrower who wishes to obtain a VA-guaranteed loan to purchase a manufactured home or lot can borrow up to 95 percent of the home's purchase price. The amount VA will guarantee on a manufactured home loan is 40 percent of the loan amount or the veteran's available entitlement, up to a maximum amount of $20,000.

VA Appraisals: No loan can be guaranteed by VA without first being appraised by a VA-assigned fee appraiser. A lender can request a VA appraisal by accessing The Appraisal System (TAS), which is located in the VA Veteran Information Portal (VIP). TAS electronically assigns appraisals to VA fee appraisers on a rotational basis. The requester pays for the appraisal upon completion, according to a fee schedule approved by VA. This VA appraisal estimates the value of the property. It is not an inspection and does not guarantee the house is free of defects. VA guarantees the loan, not the condition of the property.

Closing Costs: For purchase home loans, payment in cash is required on all closing costs, including title search and recording fees, hazard insurance premiums, and prepaid taxes. For refinancing loans, all such costs may be included in the loan, as long as the total loan does not exceed the reasonable value of the property. Interest rate reduction loans may include closing costs, including a maximum of two discount points.

All veterans, except those receiving VA disability compensation, those who are rated by VA as eligible to receive compensation as a result of predischarge disability examination and rating, and unmarried surviving spouses of veterans who died in service or as a result of a service-connected disability, are charged a VA funding fee. For all types of loans, the loan amount may include this funding fee.

Required Occupancy: To qualify for a VA home loan, a veteran or the spouse of an active duty servicemember must certify that he or she intends to occupy the home. When refinancing a VA-guaranteed loan solely to reduce the interest rate, a veteran need only certify to prior occupancy.

Financing, Interest Rates, and Terms: Veterans obtain VA-guaranteed loans through the usual lending institutions, including banks, credit unions, and mortgage brokers. VA-guaranteed loans can have either a fixed interest rate or an adjustable rate, where the interest rate may adjust up to 1 percent annually and up to 5 percent over the life of the loan. VA does not set the interest rate. Interest rates are negotiable between the lender and borrower on all loan types.

Veterans may also choose a different type of adjustable rate mortgage called a hybrid ARM, where the initial interest rate remains fixed for three to ten years. If the rate remains fixed for less than five years, the rate adjustment cannot be more than 1 percent annually and 5 percent over the life of the loan. For a hybrid ARM with an initial fixed period of five years or more, the initial adjustment may be up to 2 percent. The Secretary has the authority to determine annual adjustments thereafter. Currently, annual adjustments may be up to two percentage points and 6 percent over the life of the loan.

If the lender charges discount points on the loan, the veteran may negotiate with the seller as to who will pay points or if they will be split between buyer and seller. Points paid by the veteran may not be included in the loan (with the exception that up to two points may be included in interest rate reduction refinancing loans). The term of the loan may be for as long as thirty years and thirty-two days.

Loan Assumption Requirements and Liability: VA loans made on or after March 1, 1988, are not assumable without the prior approval of VA or its authorized agent (usually the lender collecting the monthly payments). To approve the assumption, the lender must ensure that the borrower is a satisfactory credit risk and will assume all of the veteran's liabilities on the loan. If approved, the borrower will have to pay a funding fee that the lender sends to

VA, and the veteran will be released from liability to the federal government. A release of liability does not mean that a veteran's guaranty entitlement is restored. That occurs only if the borrower is an eligible veteran who agrees to substitute his or her entitlement for that of the seller. If a veteran allows assumption of a loan without prior approval, then the lender may demand immediate and full payment of the loan, and the veteran may be liable if the loan is foreclosed and VA has to pay a claim under the loan guaranty.

Loans made prior to March 1, 1988, are generally freely assumable, but veterans should still request VA's approval in order to be released of liability. Veterans whose loans were closed after December 31, 1989, usually have no liability to the government following a foreclosure, except in cases involving fraud, misrepresentation, or bad faith, such as allowing an unapproved assumption. However, for the entitlement to be restored, any loss suffered by VA must be paid in full.

2010 VA Funding Fees

A funding fee must be paid to VA unless the veteran is exempt from such a fee because he or she receives VA disability compensation. The fee may be paid in cash or included in the loan. Closing costs such as VA appraisal, credit report, loan processing fee, title search, title insurance, recording fees, transfer taxes, survey charges, or hazard insurance may not be included in the loan.

Loan Category	*Active Duty and Veterans*	*Reservists and National Guard*
Loans for purchase or construction with down payments of less than 5%, refinancing, and home improvement	2.15 percent	2.40 percent
Loans for purchase or construction with down payments of at least 5% but less than 10%	1.50 percent	1.75 percent
Loans for purchase or construction with down payments of 10% or more	1.25 percent	1.50 percent
Loans for manufactured homes	1 percent	1 percent
Interest rate reduction refinancing loans	.50 percent	.50 percent
Assumption of a VA-guaranteed loan	.50 percent	.50 percent
Second or subsequent use of entitlement with no down payment	3.3 percent	3.3 percent

VA Assistance to Veterans in Default: When a veteran's home loan becomes delinquent, the veteran should contact the lender as soon as possible to explain what caused the missed payments and discuss how they can be repaid.

Depending on a veteran's situation, the lender may offer any of the following options to avoid foreclosure:

- **Repayment Plan:** make a regular payment each month plus part of the late payments.
- **Forbearance:** lender temporarily suspends payments to allow the veteran time to accumulate funds to reinstate the loan or sell the property.
- **Loan Modification:** lender provides a fresh start by adding delinquency to the loan balance and establishing a new payment schedule.
- **Compromise Sale/Short Sale:** lender approves a sale of the home for less than what is needed to pay off the loan. The remainder is written off and/or paid by VA guaranty.
- **Deed in Lieu of Foreclosure:** lender accepts a deed to the property instead of going through a lengthy foreclosure process.

VA does not have funds to lend veterans to make delinquent payments but can offer financial counseling to veterans with VA-guaranteed, conventional, or subprime loans. For veterans with VA-guaranteed loans, VA may be able to intercede with the lender to help arrange an alternative option to foreclosure, but it does not have that authority on other loans. VA's toll-free number for the Home Loan Guaranty program is 1-877-827-3702.

Property Foreclosures: VA acquires properties as a result of foreclosures. A private contractor is currently marketing the properties through listing agents using local Multiple Listing Services. A listing of "VA Properties for Sale" may be found at va.reotrans.com. Contact a real estate agent for information on purchasing a VA-acquired property.

Loans for Native American Veterans: Eligible Native American veterans can obtain a loan from VA to purchase, construct, or improve a home on Federal Trust Land or to reduce the interest rate on such a VA loan. Native American Direct Loans are only available if a memorandum of understanding exists between the tribal organization and VA.

Veterans who are not Native American but who are married to Native American nonveterans may be eligible for a direct loan under this program. To be eligible for such a loan, the qualified non-Native American veteran and the Native American spouse must reside on Federal Trust Land, and both the veteran and spouse must have a meaningful interest in the dwelling or lot.

The following safeguards have been established to protect veterans:

1. VA may suspend from the loan program those who take unfair advantage of veterans or discriminate because of race, color, religion, sex, disability, family status, or national origin.

2. The builder of a new home (or manufactured) is required to give the purchasing veteran either a one-year warranty or a ten-year, insurance-backed protection plan.
3. The borrower obtaining a loan may only be charged closing costs allowed by VA.
4. The borrower can prepay without penalty the entire loan or any part not less than one installment or $100.
5. VA encourages holders to extend forbearance if a borrower becomes temporarily unable to meet the terms of the loan.

VETERANS' GROUP LIFE INSURANCE (VGLI)

VGLI is a life insurance program that allows servicemembers to convert their SGLI coverage to renewable term insurance.

If you are unable to visit a VA counselor at your installation, call the nearest VA regional office at the toll-free number listed below. A Veterans Service Representative will be happy to provide information about specific benefits and how to file a claim.

To get complete information concerning all the VA benefits to which you and your family members may be entitled, please visit the website at http://www.va.gov. You can also submit a specific question at the above website by sending an inquiry through the VA Inquiry Routing & Information System (IRIS). This application provides VA customers with secure communication of personal data, should they voluntarily choose to send it to VA.

For complete details on government life insurance, visit the VA Internet site at www.insurance.va.gov or call VA's Insurance Center toll free at 1-800-669-8477. Specialists are available between the hours of 8:30 a.m. and 6 p.m. Eastern Time to discuss premium payments, insurance dividends, address changes, policy loans, naming beneficiaries, and reporting the death of the insured.

If the insurance policy number is not known, send whatever information is available, such as the veteran's VA file number, date of birth, Social Security number, military serial number, or military service branch and dates of service to:

Department of Veterans Affairs
Regional Office and Insurance Center
Box 42954
Philadelphia, PA 19101

For information about Servicemembers' Group Life Insurance, Veterans' Group Life Insurance, Servicemembers' Group Life Insurance Traumatic Injury

Protection, or Servicemembers' Group Life Insurance Family Coverage, visit the website above or call the Office of Servicemembers' Group Life Insurance directly at 1-800-419-1473.

Servicemembers' Group Life Insurance: The following are automatically insured for $400,000 under Servicemembers' Group Life Insurance (SGLI):

1. Active-duty members of the Army, Navy, Air Force, Marines, and Coast Guard.
2. Commissioned members of the National Oceanic and Atmospheric Administration (NOAA) and the Public Health Service (PHS).
3. Cadets or midshipmen of the U.S. military academies.
4. Members, cadets, and midshipmen of the ROTC while engaged in authorized training and practice cruises.
5. Members of the Ready Reserves/National Guard who are scheduled to perform at least twelve periods of inactive training per year.
6. Members who volunteer for a mobilization category in the Individual Ready Reserve.

Individuals may elect in writing to be covered for a lesser amount or not at all. Part-time coverage may be provided to Reservists who do not qualify for full-time coverage. Premiums are automatically deducted from the servicemember's pay. At the time of separation from service, SGLI can be converted to either Veterans' Group Life Insurance (VGLI) or a commercial plan through participating companies. SGLI coverage continues for 120 days after separation at no charge.

Coverage of $10,000 is also automatically provided for dependent children of members insured under SGLI with no premium required.

SGLI Traumatic Injury Protection: Members of the armed services serve our nation heroically during times of great need, but what happens when they experience great needs of their own because they have sustained a traumatic injury? Servicemembers' Group Life Insurance Traumatic Injury Protection (TSGLI) helps severely injured servicemembers through their time of need with a one-time payment. The amount varies depending on the injury, but it could make a difference in the lives of servicemembers by allowing their families to be with them during their recovery. TSGLI helps them with unforeseen expenses or gives them a financial head start on life after recovery.

TSGLI is an insurance program that is bundled with Servicemembers' Group Life Insurance (SGLI). An additional $1.00 has been added to the servicemember's SGLI premium to cover TSGLI. After December 1, 2005, all servicemembers who are covered by SGLI are automatically also covered by TSGLI, regardless of where their qualifying traumatic injury occurred. However, TSGLI claims require approval.

In addition, there is retroactive TSGLI coverage for servicemembers who sustained a qualifying traumatic injury while in theater supporting Operation Enduring Freedom (OEF), Operation Iraqi Freedom (OIF), or while on orders in a Combat Zone Tax Exclusion (CZTE) area from October 7, 2001, through November 30, 2005. TSGLI coverage is available for these servicemembers regardless of whether SGLI coverage was in force.

For more information and branch of service contact information, visit the website at www.insurance.va.gov/sgliSite/TSGLI/TSGLI.htm, or call 1-800-237-1336 (Army); 1-800-368-3202 (Navy); 1-877-216-0825 (Marine Corps); 1-800-433-0048 (Active Duty Air Force); 1-800-525-0102 (Air Force Reserves); 1-703-607-0901 (Air National Guard); 1-202-475-5391 (U.S. Coast Guard); 1-301-594-2963 (PHS); or 1-301-713-3444 (NOAA).

Servicemembers' Group Life Insurance Family Coverage: Servicemembers' Group Life Insurance Family Coverage (FSGLI) provides up to $100,000 of life insurance coverage for spouses of servicemembers with full-time SGLI coverage, not to exceed the amount of SGLI the member has in force. FSGLI is a servicemembers' benefit; the member pays the premium and is the only person allowed to be the beneficiary of the coverage. FSGLI spousal coverage ends when: 1) the servicemember elects in writing to terminate coverage on the spouse; 2) the servicemember elects to terminate his or her own SGLI coverage; 3) the servicemember dies; 4) the servicemember separates from service; or 5) the servicemember divorces the spouse. The insured spouse may convert his or her FSGLI coverage to a policy offered by participating private insurers within 120 days of the date of any of the termination events noted above.

Veterans' Group Life Insurance: SGLI may be converted to Veterans' Group Life Insurance (VGLI), which provides renewable term coverage to:

1. Veterans who had full-time SGLI coverage upon release from active duty or the reserves.
2. Members of the Ready Reserves/National Guard with part-time SGLI coverage who incur a disability or aggravate a preexisting disability during a period of active duty or a period of inactive duty for less than thirty-one days that renders them uninsurable at standard premium rates.
3. Members of the Individual Ready Reserve and Inactive National Guard.

SGLI can be converted to VGLI up to the amount of coverage the servicemember had when separated from service. Veterans who submit an application and the initial premium within 120 days of leaving the service will be covered regardless of their health. Veterans who don't apply within this period can still convert to VGLI if they submit an application, pay the initial premium, and show evidence of insurability within one year after the end of the 120-day period.

SGLI Disability Extension: Servicemembers who are totally disabled at the time of separation are eligible for free SGLI Disability Extension of up to two years. They must apply to the Office of Servicemembers' Group Life Insurance (OSGLI) at 80 Livingston Ave., Roseland, New Jersey 07068-1733.

Those covered under the SGLI Disability Extension are automatically converted to VGLI at the end of their extension period. VGLI is convertible at any time to a permanent plan policy with any participating commercial insurance company.

Accelerated Death Benefits: SGLI, FSGLI, and VGLI policyholders who are terminally ill (prognosis of nine months or less to live) have a one-time option of requesting up to 50 percent of their coverage amount paid in advance.

Service-Disabled Veterans' Insurance: A veteran who was discharged under other than dishonorable conditions and who has a service-connected disability but is otherwise in good health may apply to VA for up to $10,000 in life insurance coverage under the Service-Disabled Veterans' Insurance (S-DVI) program. Applications must be submitted within two years from the date of being notified of the approval of a new service-connected disability by VA. This insurance is limited to veterans who left service on or after April 25, 1951.

Veterans who are totally disabled may apply for a waiver of premiums and additional supplemental insurance coverage of up to $20,000. However, premiums cannot be waived on the additional supplemental insurance. To be eligible for this type of supplemental insurance, veterans must meet all of the following three requirements:

1. be under age sixty-five
2. be eligible for a waiver of premiums due to total disability
3. apply for additional insurance within one year from the date of notification of waiver approval on the S-DVI policy

Veterans' Mortgage Life Insurance

Veterans' Mortgage Life Insurance (VMLI) is mortgage protection insurance available to severely disabled veterans who have been approved by VA for a Specially Adapted Housing Grant (SAH). Maximum coverage is the amount of the existing mortgage up to $90,000 and is payable only to the mortgage company. Protection is issued automatically following SAH approval, provided the veteran submits information required to establish a premium and does not decline coverage. Coverage automatically terminates when the mortgage is paid off. If a mortgage is disposed of through sale of the property, VMLI may be obtained on the mortgage of another home.

Other Insurance Information

The following information applies to policies issued to World War I, World War II, Korean, and Vietnam-era veterans and any Service-Disabled Veterans Insurance policies. Policies in this group are prefixed by the letters K, V, RS, W, J, JR, JS, or RH.

Insurance Dividends Issued Annually: World War I, World War II, and Korean-era veterans with active policies beginning with the letters V, RS, W, J, JR, JS, or K are issued tax-free dividends annually on the policy anniversary date. (Policies prefixed by RH do not earn dividends.) Policyholders do not need to apply for dividends but may select from among the following dividend options:

1. Cash: The dividend is paid directly to the insured either by a mailed check or by direct deposit to a bank account.
2. Paid-up Additional Insurance: The dividend is used to purchase additional insurance coverage.
3. Credit or Deposit: The dividend is held in an account for the policyholder with interest. Withdrawals from the account can be made at any time. The interest rate may be adjusted.
4. Net Premium Billing Options: These options use the dividend to pay the annual policy premium. If the dividend exceeds the premium, the policyholder has options to choose how the remainder is used. If the dividend is not enough to pay an annual premium, the policyholder is billed the balance.
5. Other Dividend Options: Dividends can also be used to repay a loan or pay premiums in advance.

Reinstating Lapsed Insurance: Lapsed term policies may be reinstated within five years from the date of lapse. A five-year term policy that is not lapsed at the end of the term is automatically renewed for an additional five years. Lapsed permanent plans may be reinstated within certain time limits and with certain health requirements. Reinstated permanent plan policies require repayment of all back premiums, plus interest.

Converting Term Policies: Term policies are renewed automatically every five years, with premiums increasing at each renewal. Premiums do not increase after age seventy. Term policies may be converted to permanent plans, which have fixed premiums for life and earn cash and loan values.

Paid-up Insurance Available on Term Policies: Effective September 2000, VA provides paid-up insurance on term policies whose premiums have been capped. Veterans with National Service Life Insurance (NSLI) term insurance that has been renewed at age seventy-one or older and who stop paying premiums on their policies will be given a termination dividend. This dividend will be used to purchase a reduced amount of paid-up insurance, which insures the veteran for life with no premium payments required. The amount of insurance remains level. This does not apply to S-DVI (RH) policies.

Borrowing on Policies: Policyholders with permanent plan policies may borrow up to 94 percent of the cash surrender value of their insurance after the insurance is in force for one year or more. Interest is compounded annually. The loan interest rate is variable and may be obtained by calling toll free 1-800-669-8477.

BURIAL AND MEMORIAL BENEFITS

Eligibility

Veterans discharged from active duty under conditions other than dishonorable and servicemembers who die while on active duty, active duty for training, or inactive duty training, as well as spouses and dependent children of veterans and active duty servicemembers, may be eligible for VA burial and memorial benefits. The veteran does not have to die before a spouse or dependent child for them to be eligible.

With certain exceptions, active duty service beginning after September 7, 1980, as an enlisted person, and after October 16, 1981, as an officer, must be for a minimum of twenty-four consecutive months or the full period of active duty (as in the case of Reservists or National Guard members called to active duty for a limited duration). Active duty for training, by itself, while serving in the Reserves or National Guard, is not sufficient to confer eligibility. Reservists and National Guard members, as well as their spouses and dependent children, are eligible if they were entitled to retired pay at the time of death, or would have been upon reaching requisite age.

VA's National Cemetery Scheduling Office or local national cemetery directors verify eligibility for burial. A copy of the veteran's discharge document that specifies the period(s) of active duty and character of discharge is usually sufficient to determine eligibility. In some instances, a copy of the deceased's death certificate and proof of relationship to the veteran (for eligible family members) may be required.

Under Section 2411 of Title 38 of the United States Code, certain otherwise eligible individuals found to have committed federal or state capital crimes are barred from burial or memorialization in a VA national cemetery and from receipt of government-furnished headstones, markers, burial flags, and Presidential Memorial Certificates.

Veterans and other claimants for VA burial benefits have the right to appeal decisions made by VA regarding eligibility for national cemetery burial or other memorial benefits.

This chapter contains information on the full range of VA burial and memorial benefits. Readers with questions may contact the nearest national cemetery, listed by state in the VA Facilities section of this book, call 1-800-827-1000, or visit the website at www.cem.va.gov/.

Burial in VA National Cemeteries

Burial in a VA national cemetery is available for eligible veterans, their spouses, and dependents at no cost to the family and includes the gravesite, grave liner, opening and closing of the grave, a headstone or marker, and perpetual care as part of a national shrine. For veterans, benefits also include a burial flag (with case for active duty) and military funeral honors. Family members and other loved ones of deceased veterans may request Presidential Memorial Certificates.

VA operates 131 national cemeteries, of which seventy-one are open for new casketed interments and nineteen are open to accept only cremated remains. Burial options are limited to those available at a specific cemetery but may include in-ground casket, or interment of cremated remains in a columbarium, in ground or in a scatter garden. Contact the national cemetery directly or visit the website at www.cem.va.gov/ to determine if a particular cemetery is open for new burials and which other options are available.

The funeral director or the next of kin makes interment arrangements by contacting the National Cemetery Scheduling Office or national cemetery in which burial is desired. VA normally does not conduct burials on weekends. Gravesites cannot be reserved; however, VA will honor reservations made under previous programs.

Surviving spouses of veterans who died on or after January 1, 2000, do not lose eligibility for burial in a national cemetery if they remarry. Burial of dependent children is limited to unmarried children under twenty-one years of age, or under twenty-three years of age if a full-time student at an approved educational institution. Unmarried adult children who become physically or mentally disabled and incapable of self-support before age twenty-one, or age twenty-three if a full-time student, also are eligible for burial.

Headstones and Markers: Veterans, active duty servicemembers, and retired Reservists and National Guard servicemembers are eligible for an inscribed headstone or marker for their grave at any cemetery—national, state veterans, or private. VA will deliver a headstone or marker at no cost, anywhere in the world. For eligible veterans whose deaths occurred on or after November 1, 1990, VA may provide a government headstone or marker even if the grave is already marked with a private one. Spouses and dependent children are eligible for a government headstone or marker only if they are buried in a national or state veterans cemetery.

Flat markers are available in bronze, granite, or marble. Upright head-stones come in granite or marble. In national cemeteries, the style chosen will be consistent with existing monuments at the place of burial. Niche markers are available to mark columbaria used for inurnment of cremated remains.

Headstones and markers previously provided by the government may be replaced at the government's expense if badly deteriorated, illegible, vandalized, or stolen. To check the status of a claim for a headstone or marker for a national or state veterans cemetery, call the cemetery. To check the status of one being placed in a private cemetery, call 1-800-697-6947.

Inscription: Headstones and markers must be inscribed with the name of the deceased, branch of service, and year of birth and death. They also may be inscribed with other optional information, including an authorized emblem of belief and, space permitting, additional text including military rank; war service such as "World War II"; complete dates of birth and death; military awards; military organizations; civilian or veteran affiliations; and personalized words of endearment.

Private Cemeteries: To submit a claim for a headstone or marker for a private cemetery, mail a completed VA Form 40-1330 (available at www .va.gov/vaforms/va/pdf/VA40-1330.pdf), Application for Standard Government Headstone or Marker, and a copy of the veteran's military discharge document to Memorial Programs Service (41A1), Department of Veterans Affairs, 5109 Russell Rd., Quantico, VA 22134-3903. The form and supporting documents may also be faxed toll free to 1-800-455-7143.

Before ordering, check with the cemetery to ensure that the government-furnished headstone or marker will be accepted. All installation fees are the responsibility of the applicant.

"In Memory Of" Markers: VA provides memorial headstones and markers with "In Memory Of" as the first line of inscription, to memorialize those whose remains have not been recovered or identified, were buried at sea, donated to science, or cremated and scattered. Eligibility is the same as for regular headstones and markers. There is no fee when the "In Memory Of" marker is placed in a national cemetery. All installation fees are the responsibility of the applicant.

Medallions in Lieu of Government Headstone/Marker: Public Law 110-157, enacted December 26, 2007, expanded VA authority to provide a medallion instead of a headstone or marker for veterans' graves in private cemeteries when the grave is already marked with a privately purchased headstone or marker. Claimants will have the option to apply for either a traditional headstone or marker to place on the grave or a medallion to affix to a privately purchased headstone or marker. VA anticipates the medallion will be available during 2010. Current information regarding medallion availability is located at www.cem.va.gov.

Presidential Memorial Certificates are issued upon request to recognize the U.S. military service of honorably discharged deceased veterans. Next of kin, relatives, and other loved ones may apply for a certificate by mailing, e-mailing, or faxing a completed and signed VA Form 40-0247 along with a copy of the veteran's military discharge documents or proof of honorable military service. The form and eligibility requirements can be found at www.cem.va.gov. All requests must be sent with supporting military documents or proof of honorable military service.

Completed and signed documents along with supporting military documents can be submitted as follows:

- by U.S. mail to the Department of Veterans Affairs, Presidential Memorial Certificates Program (41A1C), 5109 Russell Road, Quantico VA 22134.
- faxed to the toll-free fax service at 1-800-455-7143.
- scanned and attached to an e-mail addressed to pmc@va.gov. E-mail requests must have forms and documents attached.

For all PMC requests for deceased active duty servicemembers, we encourage you to send documents to the Washington, D.C., fax line at 1-202-565-8054. Please be sure to provide a copy of the servicemember's DD Form 1300 (Report of Casualty) with each request.

Burial Flags: VA will furnish a U.S. burial flag to memorialize:

1. Veterans who served during wartime or after January 31, 1955.
2. Veterans who were entitled to retired pay for service in the Reserve or National Guard, or would have been entitled if over age sixty.
3. Members or former members of the Selected Reserve who served their initial obligation, or were discharged for a disability incurred or aggravated in the line of duty, or died while a member of the Selected Reserve.

Reimbursement of Burial Expenses: VA will pay a burial allowance up to $2,000 if the veteran's death is service connected. In such cases, the person who bore the veteran's burial expenses may claim reimbursement from VA.

In some cases, VA will pay the cost of transporting the remains of a veteran whose death was service connected to the nearest national cemetery with available gravesites. There is no time limit for filing reimbursement claims in service-connected death cases.

Burial Allowance: VA will pay a $300 burial and funeral allowance for veterans who, at time of death, were entitled to receive pension or compensation or would have been entitled if they were not receiving military retirement pay. Eligibility also may be established when death occurs in a VA facility, a VA-contracted nursing home, or a state veterans nursing home. In cases in which the veterans's death was not service connected, claims must be filed within two years after burial or cremation.

Plot Allowance: VA will pay a $300 plot allowance when a veteran is buried in a cemetery not under U.S. government jurisdiction if the veteran was discharged from active duty because of a disability incurred or aggravated in the line of duty; the veteran was receiving compensation or pension or would have been if the veteran was not receiving military retired pay; or the veteran died in a VA facility.

The $300 plot allowance may be paid to the state for the cost of a plot or interment in a state-owned cemetery reserved solely for veteran burials if the veteran is buried without charge. Burial expenses paid by the deceased's employer or a state agency will not be reimbursed.

Military Funeral Honors: Upon request, DoD will provide military funeral honors consisting of the folding and presentation of the U.S. flag and the playing of "Taps." A funeral honors detail consists of two or more uniformed members of the armed forces, with at least one member from the deceased's branch of service.

Family members should inform their funeral director if they want military funeral honors. DoD maintains a toll-free number (1-877-MIL-HONR) for use by funeral directors only to request honors. VA can help arrange honors for burials at VA national cemeteries. Veterans service organizations or volunteer groups may help provide honors. For more information, visit www.militaryfuneralhonors.osd.mil/.

Veterans Cemeteries Administered by Other Agencies

Arlington National Cemetery: Administered by the Department of the Army. Eligibility is more restrictive than at VA national cemeteries. For information, call (703) 607-8000, write to the Superintendent, Arlington National Cemetery, Arlington, VA 22211, or visit www.arlingtoncemetery.org/.

Department of the Interior: Administers two active national cemeteries— Andersonville National Cemetery in Georgia and Andrew Johnson National Cemetery in Tennessee. Eligibility is similar to VA national cemeteries.

State Veterans Cemeteries: Seventy-four state veterans cemeteries offer burial options for veterans and their families. These cemeteries have similar eligibility requirements, but many require state residency. Some services, particularly for family members, may require a fee. Contact the state cemetery or state veterans affairs office for information. To locate a state veterans cemetery, visit www.cem.va.gov/cem/scg/lsvc.asp.

RESERVE AND NATIONAL GUARD

Eligibility for VA Benefits

Reservists who serve on active duty establish veteran status and may be eligible for the full range of VA benefits, depending on the length of active military service and a discharge or release from active duty under conditions other than dishonorable. In addition, Reservists not activated may qualify for some VA benefits.

National Guard members can establish eligibility for VA benefits if activated for federal service during a period of war or domestic emergency. Activation for other than federal service does not qualify Guard members for all VA benefits. Claims for VA benefits based on federal service filed by members of the National Guard should include a copy of the military orders, presidential proclamation, or executive order that clearly demonstrates the federal nature of the service.

Qualifying for VA Health Care

Effective January 28, 2008, veterans discharged from active duty on or after January 28, 2003, are eligible for enhanced enrollment placement into Priority Group 6 (unless eligible for higher Priority Group placement) for five years postdischarge. Veterans with combat service after November 11, 1998, who were discharged from active duty before January 28, 2003, and who apply for enrollment on or after January 28, 2008, are eligible for this enhanced enrollment benefit through January 27, 2011.

Activated Reservists and members of the National Guard are eligible if they served on active duty in a theater of combat operations after November 11, 1998, and have been discharged under other than dishonorable conditions.

Veterans who enroll with VA under this Combat Veteran authority will retain enrollment eligibility even after their five-year postdischarge period ends. At the end of their postdischarge period, VA will reassess the veteran's information (including all applicable eligibility factors) and make a new enrollment decision. For additional information, call 1-877-222-VETS.

Disability Benefits

VA pays monthly compensation benefits for disabilities incurred or aggravated during active duty and active duty for training as a result of injury or disease and for disabilities due to injury, heart attack, or stroke that occurred during inactive duty training. For additional information see chapter 2, "Veterans with Service-Connected Disabilities."

Montgomery GI Bill—Selected Reserve

Members of reserve elements of the Army, Navy, Air Force, Marine Corps, and Coast Guard, and members of the Army National Guard and the Air National Guard, may be entitled to up to thirty-six months of educational benefits under the Montgomery GI Bill (MGIB)—Selected Reserve. To be eligible, the participant must:

1. have a six-year obligation in the Selected Reserve or National Guard signed after June 30, 1985, or, if an officer, agree to serve six years in addition to the original obligation.
2. complete initial active duty for training.
3. have a high school diploma or equivalency certificate before applying for benefits.
4. remain in good standing in a Selected Reserve or National Guard unit.

Reserve components determine eligibility for benefits. VA does not make decisions about eligibility and cannot make payments until the reserve component has determined eligibility and notified VA.

Period of Eligibility: Benefits generally end the day a Reservist or National Guard member separates from the military. Additionally, if in the Selected Reserve and called to active duty, VA can generally extend the eligibility period by the length of time on active duty plus four months for each period of active duty. Once this extension is granted, it will not be taken away if you leave the Selected Reserve.

Eligible members separated because of unit deactivation, a disability that was not caused by misconduct, or otherwise involuntarily separated during October 1, 1991, through December 31, 2001, have fourteen years after their eligibility date to use benefits. Similarly, members involuntarily separated from the Selected Reserve due to a deactivation of their unit between October 1, 2007, and September 30, 2014, may receive a fouteen-year period of eligibility.

Payments: The rate for full-time training effective October 1, 2009, is $333 a month for thirty-six months. Part-time benefits are reduced proportionately.

For complete current rates, visit www.gibill.va.gov/. DoD may make additional contributions.

Training: Participants may pursue training at a college or university or take technical training at any approved facility. Training includes undergraduate, graduate, or postgraduate courses; state licensure and certification; courses for a certificate or diploma from business, technical, or vocational schools; cooperative training; apprenticeship or on-the-job training; correspondence courses; independent study programs; flight training; entrepreneurship training; or remedial, deficiency, or refresher courses needed to complete a program of study. Accelerated payments for certain high-cost programs are authorized effective January 28, 2008.

Work-Study: Participants who train at the three-quarter or full-time rate may be eligible for a work-study program in which they work for VA and receive hourly wages. Students under the work-study program must be supervised by a VA employee, and all duties performed must relate to VA. The types of work allowed include:

1. VA paperwork processing at schools or other training facilities.
2. assistance with patient care at VA hospitals or domiciliary care facilities.
3. work at national or state veterans cemeteries.
4. various jobs within any VA regional office.
5. other VA-approved activities.

Note: MGIB–Selected Reserve work-study students may also assist with an activity relating to the administration of this education benefit at DoD, Coast Guard, or National Guard facilities.

Reserve Educational Assistance Program (REAP)

This program provides educational assistance to members of National Guard and Reserve components—Selected Reserve and Individual Ready Reserve (IRR)—who are called or ordered to active duty service in response to a war or national emergency as declared by the president or Congress. Visit www .gibill.va.gov/ for more information.

Eligibility: Eligibility is determined by DoD or the Department of Homeland Security. Generally, a servicemember who serves on active duty on or after September 11, 2001, for at least ninety consecutive days or accumulates a total of three or more years of service is eligible.

Payments: Reserve or National Guard members whose eligibility is based upon continuous service receive a payment rate based upon their number of continuous days on active duty. Members who qualify after the accumulation of three or more years aggregate active duty service receive the full payment allowable.

Reserve Educational Assistance Rates

Active Duty, Reserves, and National Guard Members	Monthly Payment Rate for Full-Time Students*
Ninety days but less than one year	$547.20
One year but less than two years	$820.80
Two or more continuous years	$1,094.40

*Effective October 1, 2009.

Training: Participants may pursue training at a college or university or take technical training at any approved facility. Training includes undergraduate, graduate, or postgraduate courses; state licensure and certification courses; courses for a certificate or diploma from business, technical, or vocational schools; cooperative training; apprenticeship or on-the-job training; correspondence courses; independent study programs; flight training; entrepreneurship training; or remedial, deficiency, or refresher courses needed to complete a program of study. Accelerated payments for certain high-cost programs are authorized.

Period of Eligibility: Prior to January 28, 2008, members of the Selected Reserve called to active duty were eligible as long as they continued to serve in the Selected Reserve. They lost eligibility if they went into the Inactive Ready Reserve (IRR). Members of the IRR called to active duty were eligible as long as they stayed in the IRR or Selected Reserve.

Effective January 28, 2008, members who are called up from the Selected Reserve, complete their REAP-qualifying period of active duty service, and then return to the Selected Reserve for the remainder of their service contract have ten years to use their benefits after separation.

In addition, members who are called up from the IRR or Inactive National Guard (ING), complete their REAP-qualifying period of active duty service, and then enter the Selected Reserve to complete their service contract have ten years to use their benefits after separation.

Work-Study Program: Reserve Education Assistance Program students in the work-study program may also assist with an activity relating to the administration of this education benefit at DoD, Coast Guard, or National Guard facilities.

Home Loan Guaranty

National Guard members and Reservists are eligible for a VA home loan if they have completed at least six years of honorable service, are mobilized for active duty service for a period of at least ninety days, or are discharged because of a service-connected disability.

Reservists who do not qualify for VA housing loan benefits may be eligible for loans on favorable terms insured by the Federal Housing Administration (FHA), part of HUD.

Life Insurance

National Guard members and Reservists are eligible to receive Service-members' Group Life Insurance (SGLI), Veterans' Group Life Insurance (VGLI), and Family Servicemembers' Group Life Insurance (FSGLI). They may also be eligible for SGLI Traumatic Injury Protection if severely injured and suffering a qualifying loss, Service-Disabled Veterans Insurance if they receive a service-connected disability rating from VA, and Veterans' Mortgage Life Insurance if approved for a Specially Adapted Housing Grant.

Burial and Memorial Benefits

VA provides a burial flag to memorialize members or former members of the Selected Reserve who served their initial obligation or were discharged for a disability incurred or aggravated in the line of duty or died while a member of the Selected Reserve.

Reemployment Rights

A person who left a civilian job to enter active duty in the armed forces is entitled to return to the job after discharge or release from active duty if they:

1. gave advance notice of military service to the employer.
2. did not exceed five years cumulative absence from the civilian job (with some exceptions).
3. submitted a timely application for reemployment.
4. did not receive a dishonorable or other punitive discharge.

The law calls for a returning veteran to be placed in the job as if he/she had never left, including benefits based on seniority such as pensions, pay increases, and promotions. The law also prohibits discrimination in hiring, promotion, or other advantages of employment on the basis of military service. Veterans seeking reemployment should apply, verbally or in writing, to the company's hiring official and keep a record of their application. If problems arise, contact the Department of Labor's Veterans' Employment and Training Service (VETS) in the state of the employer.

Federal employees not properly reemployed may appeal directly to the Merit Systems Protection Board. Nonfederal employees may file complaints in U.S. District Court. For information, visit www.dol.gov/vets/programs/userra/main.htm.

Army Reserve Warrior and Family Assistance Center

The Army Reserve Warrior and Family Assistance Center (AR-WFAC) provides Army Reserve soldiers, veterans, families, and units with a single source to resolve situations related to medical issues and education on programs available to Army Reserve soldiers. The center was established in 2007 to ensure that Reservists receive appropriate support under the Army Medical Action Plan. The center provides a sponsor to each Army Reserve soldier and family currently assigned to a Warrior Transition Unit, Community-Based Health Care Organization, or VA PolyTrauma Center. The AR-WFAC also assists Army Reserve commands at all echelons with the resolution of medical and other issues and provides education on programs and benefits available to Army Reserve soldiers. For information, call 1-866-436-6290 or visit www.arfp.org/wfac.

Transition Assistance Advisors

The Transition Assistance Advisor (TAA) program places a National Guard/VA-trained expert at each National Guard State Joint Forces Headquarters to act as an advocate for Guard members and their families within the state. They also serve as advisors on veterans affairs issues for the Family Programs and Joint Forces Headquarters staffs. TAAs receive annual training by VA experts in health care and benefits for both Department of Defense and Department of Veterans Affairs and help Guard members and their families access care at VA and TRICARE facilities in their state or network.

The TAA works with the State Director of Veterans Affairs and other state coalition partners to integrate the delivery of VA and community services to Guard and Reserve veterans. You can reach your Transition Assistance Advisor (TAA) through your state National Guard Joint Forces Headquarters.

APPEALS OF VA CLAIMS DECISIONS

Veterans and other claimants for VA benefits have the right to appeal decisions made by a VA regional office, medical center, or National Cemetery Administration (NCA) office. Typical issues appealed are disability compensation, pension, education benefits, recovery of overpayments, reimbursement for unauthorized medical services, and denial of burial and memorial benefits.

A claimant has one year from the date of the notification of a VA decision to file an appeal. The first step in the appeal process is for a claimant to file a written notice of disagreement with the VA regional office, medical center, or NCA office that made the decision.

Following receipt of the written notice, VA will furnish the claimant a "Statement of the Case" describing what facts, laws, and regulations were used in deciding the case. To complete the request for appeal, the claimant must file a Substantive Appeal within sixty days of the mailing of the Statement of the Case, or within one year from the date VA mailed its decision, whichever period ends later.

Board of Veterans' Appeals: The Board of Veterans' Appeals makes decisions on appeals on behalf of the Secretary of Veterans Affairs. Although it is not required, a veterans service organization, an agent, or an attorney may represent a claimant. Appellants may present their cases in person to a member of the Board at a hearing in Washington, D.C., at a VA regional office, or by video conference.

Decisions made by the Board can be found on the website at www.va.gov/vbs/bva/. The pamphlet, "Understanding the Appeal Process," is available on the website or may be requested by writing: Hearings and Transcription Unit (014HRG), Board of Veterans' Appeals, 811 Vermont Avenue, NW, Washington, DC 20420.

U.S. Court of Appeals for Veterans Claims

A final Board of Veterans' Appeals decision that does not grant a claimant the benefits desired may be appealed to the U.S. Court of Appeals for Veterans Claims—an independent court, not part of the Department of Veterans Affairs.

Notice of an appeal must be received by the court with a postmark that is within 120 days after the Board of Veterans' Appeals mailed its decision. The court reviews the record considered by the Board of Veterans' Appeals. It does not hold trials or receive new evidence.

Appellants may represent themselves before the court or have lawyers or approved agents as representatives. Oral argument is held only at the direction of the court. Either party may appeal a decision of the court to the U.S. Court of Appeals for the Federal Circuit and may seek review in the Supreme Court of the United States.

Published decisions, case status information, rules and procedures, and other special announcements can be found on the court's website at www .vetapp.gov/. The court's decisions can also be found in West's Veterans Appeals Reporter and on the Westlaw and LEXIS online services. For questions, write the Clerk of the Court, 625 Indiana Avenue, NW, Suite 900, Washington, DC 20004, or call (202) 501-5970.

VETERAN SERVICE OFFICERS (VSO)

Your state, county, or local veteran service organizations have specially trained individuals who can offer transition assistance. A VSO can give you counseling and help with everything from filling out VA claims and enrollment forms to assisting with claims appeals. You can call the VA toll-free number for assistance with contacting the nearest VSO.

VETERAN CENTERS

Vet Centers provide readjustment counseling and outreach services to all veterans who served in any combat zone. Services are also available for their family members for military-related issues. Veterans have earned these benefits through their service, and all are provided at no cost to the veteran or family. Readjustment counseling is a wide range of services provided to combat veterans in the effort to make a satisfying transition from military to civilian life. Services include:

- Individual counseling
- Group counseling
- Marital and family counseling
- Bereavement counseling
- Medical referrals
- Assistance in applying for VA benefits
- Employment counseling
- Guidance and referral
- Alcohol/drug assessments
- Information and referral to community resources
- Military sexual trauma counseling and referral
- Outreach and community education

Contact your nearest Vet Center through the Vet Center Directory at http://www1.va.gov/directory/guide/vetcenter.asp or listings in your local blue pages. The Vet Center staff is available toll free during normal business hours at 1-800-905-4675 (Eastern) and 1-866-496-8838 (Pacific).

STATE-PROVIDED VETERANS BENEFITS

Many states offer veterans benefits. These benefits may include educational grants and scholarships, special exemptions or discounts on fees and taxes, home loans, veteran's homes, free hunting and fishing privileges, and more.

Each state manages its own benefit programs. Go to http://www1.va.gov/vso/index.cfm?template=view&SortCategory=3 to view the directory of websites for each of the individual states that offer veterans benefits.

9

Finances

Your financial situation can change drastically during your transition. Without proper budgeting and planning you could find yourself in deep financial trouble. The following section will give you the information and resources you need to plan for your financial transition from the military.

FINANCIAL PLANNING ASSISTANCE

When you take off your uniform once and for all you might be living on a reduced budget for a while.

Careful financial planning is the key to successful management of a limited income. The earlier you look at your financial needs and come to terms with them, the more time you will have to lessen their impact. If you are having financial problems now or think you may have them in the future, go to your Family Center for assistance. Help can range from individual counseling on money matters to emergency loans.

In addition, the Family Center usually offers group seminars and workshops on several topics:

- Financial planning for transition
- Family budgets and spending plans
- Record keeping
- Insurance
- Credit
- Debt liquidation
- Consumer rights
- Taxes
- Investments

YOUR CRASH COURSE IN FINANCIAL MANAGEMENT

Among the most popular courses offered by the Family Centers are the financial planning seminars. The content of these courses varies from place to place, but you are almost certain to walk away having learned some basic financial planning guidelines.

Here is an eight-step crash course in financial planning. Get a pencil and paper and pull out your checkbook and recent bank account statements. Find your credit card statements, auto loan payment books or other loan coupons, your federal tax return from last year, and any other relevant documentation.

As you go through the "course," use conservative figures and time frames when planning for periods of unemployment. A healthy dose of pessimism is useful here. Should things ultimately turn out much better than you had planned, you will be pleasantly surprised.

Once you understand your budget clearly, you can then concentrate on getting it under control. This will help to make your transition less stressful.

Step 1. List Your Income
Make a list of all the sources of income you expect to have during your transition and when you expect to receive the income (weekly, monthly, quarterly, etc.). Include your pay, if any, as well as any unused vacation, severance pay, and unemployment compensation. Also list any interest income (interest from a bank savings account, for example), spouse's income, alimony or child support, and other income you expect to receive on a regular basis.

Next, compute all of the sources on a monthly basis: If the income is weekly, multiply it by four. If it is quarterly, divide it by three. Be conservative. Estimate the lowest amount you expect to receive from each source of income.

Step 2. List Your Expenses
On a separate list, write down all of your expenses: mortgage; rent; taxes; utilities; food; clothing; insurance (life, health, automobile, homeowners or renters, etc.); car or motorcycle expenses (payments, insurance, registration, gas, maintenance, and repairs); credit card bills; other loans; magazine subscriptions; cable TV; club dues; gifts; job-hunting costs (stationery, printing, dry cleaning, etc.); entertainment and hobby expenses; children's spending money; alimony or child support payments; groceries; personal items; and all other expenses. When listing expenses, take time to think of everything—all the way down to medicines and toothpaste.

Next, list the expense for each item and an average monthly cost. When figuring your average, keep in mind that this is your transition budget. Assume that you will be temporarily unemployed. If the cost is not "fixed" (such as rent or mortgage payments that cannot be avoided), plan on the smallest realistic amount you can get by on.

Step 3. Prioritize Your Expenses

After listing all of your expenses, rate them as high, medium, or low priority. High-priority items are things you and your family cannot do without: food, shelter, clothing. Medium-priority items are important to you but you can exist without them. Low-priority items should be weeded out of the budget process. Example: Rent or mortgage is an "H"(high priority), while piano lessons for your ten-year-old daughter may be an "M" (medium priority), and cable TV fits into the "L" (low priority) range.

Step 4. Assign Budget Responsibilities

If you are married, determine who is going to be in charge of staying within the budget for each item on the expense list. Example: You may take responsibility for the rent and clothing, while your spouse may be responsible for the food budget and music lessons.

Step 5. Establish a Monthly Budget

Subtract your total monthly expenses from your monthly income. If you have more income than expenses, put the extra money in a savings account for emergencies. If your monthly expenses are more than your income, look over the low- and medium-priority items. Work to reduce some and eliminate others.

Step 6. Identify Additional Sources of Income

If, after all possible cuts have been made, expenses are still greater than income, consider ways to bring in additional money. If your spouse does not currently work, he or she may need to begin working at least part time.

Step 7. Seek Help

Even after you have cut your expenses to the bone and uncovered additional income possibilities, you may still be unable to make ends meet. This is sometimes due to outstanding loan amounts and heavy credit payments. As a final measure, talk to the free Consumer Credit Counseling Service in your area to find ways to work with your creditors to delay payments or extend the time for loan repayment. This will assure your creditors that you do intend to pay them off over time, and it will help prevent you from going into bankruptcy.

Step 8. Obtain an Up-to-Date Credit Report

It is important to have an up-to-date credit report on you and your spouse. You should obtain one at least six months before separation or retirement. Go to http://www.annualcreditreport.com/ to get your credit report. Through this website you can receive one free credit report from each of the credit reporting companies every twelve months.

SEPARATION PAY

You may be eligible for additional separation pay. The finance office at your installation can compute the actual amount, if any, owed you.

This benefit is computed on the basis of 10 percent of your yearly base pay when you separate, multiplied by the number of years of active service you have.

Requirements

- If you have finished your first term of enlistment or period of obligated service; *AND*
- You have at least six years of service; *AND*
- You are separating involuntarily; *AND*
- You are not yet eligible for retirement; *AND*
- You are not separating under adverse conditions; *THEN*
- You may be eligible for separation pay.

Separation pay must be listed on the separation orders to be payable. The type of separation and conditions under which you are being separated will determine if you qualify for separation pay. To find out if you qualify, talk with your unit commander and local personnel and finance offices.

UNEMPLOYMENT COMPENSATION FOR MILITARY

Unemployment compensation for separatees is referred to as Unemployment Compensation for Ex-Servicemembers (UCX). Servicemembers separating from active duty may qualify for unemployment compensation if they are unable to find a new job. Unemployment compensation is handled by each state. Receiving separation pay may influence your receipt of unemployment compensation. The unemployment compensation program provides a weekly income check for a limited period of time.

Administration

The program is administered by your state employment office. The requirements and benefits vary from state to state. Because of this, only the office where you apply will be able to tell you the amount and duration of your entitlement. The nearest state employment office is listed in your local telephone directory.

How to Apply

You must apply for UCX shortly after separation. The best time to do this is when you register for work through your state employment office. To speed the process, have the following information available:

- Your DD Form 214, Certificate of Release or Discharge from Active Duty
- Your Social Security card
- Your civilian and military job history or resume

SOCIAL SECURITY

Everyone in the military pays into Social Security. Social Security provides protection in four areas:

- **Retirement income:** Retirement benefits may be paid as early as age sixty-two.

Transition is a good time to ensure that your Social Security account has been properly posted. Check your account now, and check it again every few years. Here's how: Information on Social Security benefits is available from any local Social Security office; these are listed in the telephone book under "U.S. Government." You can also go to http://www.ssa.gov/ or call 1-800-772-1213. Explain that you would like to check your account balance. The Social Security office will send you a form. Fill it out and mail it back. You will receive your account information in a few weeks. Read the statement closely. If there are errors, this is the time to get them corrected.

- **Disability insurance:** Disability benefits are paid at any age to those who qualify.
- **Medicare medical insurance:** Medicare coverage is available at age sixty-five. If you're disabled, then you may be eligible earlier.
- **Survivors' insurance:** Upon your death, benefits are paid to your survivors at any age, assuming they qualify.

SPECIAL LOAN PROGRAMS

Several government agencies help veterans get loans for homes, farms, and businesses. Although the loans are generally made by commercial lenders, government programs make it easier for veterans to borrow the money.

Note: Loan amounts are usually based on highest income being earned at the time of loan approval; therefore, you may want to consider making large purchases (home, farm, or business) prior to separation if your active duty income would be higher than your postservice income.

VA Home Loans

Eligible veterans, including active duty veterans, discharged veterans, and reservists, may obtain loans guaranteed by the Department of Veterans Affairs (VA) to purchase or refinance homes, condominiums, and manufactured homes. Unmarried surviving spouses may also be eligible. VA home loans feature a negotiable interest rate, choice of loan types, limited closing costs, no monthly mortgage insurance premium, and no down payment is required in most cases.

- **Down payment:** A traditional feature of VA home loans is that they typically require no down payment. A down payment is required if the home's purchase price exceeds the reasonable value of the property, the property being purchased is a manufactured home not permanently affixed, or the loan type is a Graduated Payment Mortgage.
- **Verification:** You will find many lenders to choose from, since most mortgage companies, banks, and credit unions participate in this program because the VA guarantees a portion of the loan amount, which protects them from loss if the loan should ever go to foreclosure. The lender will ask you to provide evidence, in the form of a Certificate of Eligibility (COE), that you are eligible to apply for a VA home loan.

In many instances your lender will be able to obtain your COE online in seconds. However, since not all COE requests can be processed online, there will be instances in which the veteran needs to apply for a COE through the Winston-Salem Eligibility Center. To obtain a COE in that manner, VA Form 26-1880, Request for Certificate of Eligibility, would need to be completed. The form and specific instructions can be accessed at http://www.vba.va.gov/pubs/forms/26-1880.pdf.

Realtors: Most real estate agents are also familiar with the VA home loan program and would be happy to answer your questions. This benefit may be used more than once.

More detailed information on VA home loans is available on the Internet at http://www.homeloans.va.gov/veteran.htm.

FHA Mortgage Insurance

The Federal Housing Administration (FHA) of the Department of Housing and Urban Development (HUD) insures mortgage loans for the construction, purchase, and improvement of homes. FHA-insured mortgages allow veterans to borrow with minimum down payments and over longer periods of time.

Application is made directly to any FHA-approved lender; the lender usually serves as the homebuyer's contact with FHA throughout the loan approval process. Any local HUD field office can provide additional information; look in your local telephone directory for the office nearest you.

Business Loans

Business loans are available to veterans through programs of the Small Business Administration (SBA). In addition, SBA offers loans specifically to Vietnam-era and disabled veterans. Contact the nearest SBA office for details.

Rural Loans

The Farmers Home Administration is the rural credit agency of the Department of Agriculture. This agency has both direct and guaranteed loan programs that give preferential processing to veterans' loan applications. To obtain information and applications, contact the nearest office of the Farmers Home Administration. Most are located in rural county seats.

BAD CREDIT REPORTS

Before you separate or retire, obtain a copy of your credit report. Review it thoroughly. This can be accomplished—for free—by going to http://www.annualcreditreport.com/, calling 1-877-322-8228, or writing to Annual Credit Report Request Service, P.O. Box 105281, Atlanta, GA 30348-5281.

If you find any mistakes on your credit report, resolve them before you leave the military. Once you leave the military, you should obtain a copy of your credit report, and review it thoroughly, at least once a year.

Here is additional information on each of the National Credit Reporting Companies:

Experian National Consumer Assistance
(Address can be found on credit report)
1-888-397-3742
http://www.experian.com

EQUIFAX Credit Information Service
P.O. Box 740241
Atlanta, GA 30374
1-800-685-1111
http://www.equifax.com

TRANSUNION
P.O. Box 2000
Chester, PA 19022-2000
1-800-916-8800
http://www.transunion.com

After receiving your credit report, take steps to correct any incorrect information and to add any omitted favorable information. You can do this by pointing out the errors and providing the credit agency with supporting documentation that it may not have in your file.

THE THRIFT SAVINGS PLAN AND
SAVINGS DEPOSIT PROGRAM

Thrift Savings Plan Participants: If you participated in the Uniformed Thrift Savings Plan (TSP) while you were in the service, then you have several options:

- *Leave your money in the TSP.* If your money remains in the TSP, it will continue to accrue earnings. Although you will not be able to make additional contributions, you will be able to make interfund transfers. You must begin withdrawing from your account no later than April 1 of the year following the year you turn age seventy.
- *Receive a single payment.* All or a portion of your account can be transferred to a traditional IRA or eligible employer plan (e.g., a 401(k) plan or your civilian TSP account).*
- *Request a series of monthly payments based on a dollar amount or your life expectancy.* All or a portion of certain monthly payments can be transferred to a traditional IRA or eligible employer plan.*
- *Request a TSP annuity.* You must have at least $3,500 in your account in order to purchase an annuity.

Savings Deposit Plan Participants: If you participated in the Savings Deposit Program (SDP), your funds may be left in an SDP account indefinitely; however, the account will stop accruing interest ninety days after you

---

*Tax-exempt contributions to the TSP are eligible for transfer to a traditional IRA or eligible employer plan only if the financial institution or plan will accept the funds. Funds not accepted will be paid directly to you. If you transfer balances from your uniformed service TSP account to your civilian TSP account, the TSP will not accept tax-exempt money.

return from the combat zone. Generally, withdrawals may only be made upon termination of eligibility for the program.

To make arrangements for withdrawing SDP funds, send a request to the Defense Finance and Accounting Service (DFAS) at:

E-mail: ccl-sdp@dfas.mil
Fax: (216) 522-6924

or mail at:

DFAS-Cleveland
Code PMMCCB
ATTN: Savings Deposit Program
1240 E. 9th Street
Cleveland, OH 44199-2055

Be sure to include your name, social security number, branch of service, eligible tour start and stop dates, and the amount requested.

LEGAL ASSISTANCE FOR SEPARATEES

If you have legal problems, either on or off the installation, help is available at your place of separation. Contact your installation's transition office for referral to a legal assistance officer. **This service is not available to you once you leave the military. Use it while you have it.**

Depending on local installation guidance, legal assistance officers can help you with:

- Will preparation
- Power-of-attorney arrangements
- Loan contract review (home mortgage, auto loan, etc.)
- Debt/credit problems
- Landlord/tenant issues
- Family law
- Tax law
- Estate planning

You may think that you have little or no "estate." However, you may not realize that your car, household goods, and GI insurance are all part of your estate. Talk to your legal assistance officer about reviewing your will, if you have one. If you do not already have a will, now is a good time to make one. Legal assistance officers are well versed in the special issues of military separatees and their families. Ensuring the financial security of your loved ones before you leave the military will not be time wasted.

Retirees can use the base legal office on a space-available basis. Depending on the location, there could be a lengthy wait to see a legal representative. Retirees should contact the base legal office as far in advance as possible to ensure services will be available.

TAXING MATTERS

Federal Income Tax: Notes for Servicemembers

Almost everyone has to pay federal income taxes, but special considerations apply to those in the service.

Filing Extensions

Any U.S. citizen outside the United States or Puerto Rico on April 15 (the tax filing deadline) is allowed an extension until June 15 for filing a federal income tax return for the previous calendar year. This includes filing a joint return by a servicemember and spouse. However, the Internal Revenue Service charges interest on any unpaid amount due on the April 15 deadline.

Where to Obtain a W-2 Form

You can view and print your W-2 from the MyPay website at https://mypay.dfas.mil/mypay.aspx.

You will be able to access myPay and view your W-2 for one year after you are no longer in a pay status or separated.

RESERVE AFFILIATION

When you leave active duty service you have the opportunity to earn cash bonuses and retain many of your military benefits by joining the Selected Reserve or National Guard. The following section will explain your opportunities and possible obligations in the Reserve.

Obligation to Service Continues for Eight Years

When you entered the service, you incurred a military service obligation of eight years. If you are separating prior to fulfilling eight years of service, then some of that obligation probably remains even though you are returning to civilian life. You *must* satisfy that obligation by becoming a member of the Ready Reserve in one of the following categories:

- **Selected Reserve:** You may voluntarily affiliate with the Selected Reserve, either with a National Guard or Reserve unit or a Reserve individual program.
- **Inactive National Guard:** If you served in the Army, you may become a member of the Army National Guard and request transfer to the Inactive National Guard if you are unable to participate in regular unit training.
- **Individual Ready Reserve (IRR):** If you do *not* affiliate with one of the above programs, your service will automatically or involuntarily assign you to the Individual Ready Reserve.

Opportunity for Continued Military Service Beyond Eight Years

If you *have* served eight years or more of active duty, you may no longer have a military service obligation and do not have to affiliate with the National Guard or Reserves. You may, however, elect to continue your military service by affiliating with a Reserve component in one of these categories.

Selected Reserve

You may volunteer to sign an agreement to serve for between one and eight years in a National Guard or Reserve unit, or a Reserve individual program. Upon becoming a member, you may be recalled to active duty in time of war or national emergency. You may also be ordered to active duty involuntarily for up to 270 days, for any single contingency operation, without a declaration of a national emergency. Members participate and train as required by the Reserve category to which they belong. For National Guard and Reserve unit programs, this usually means a minimum of one weekend a month and two weeks of annual training per year. For Reserve individual programs, the training requirement may be somewhat less.

Inactive National Guard

Currently, only the Army maintains an Inactive National Guard. This consists of National Guard personnel in an inactive status; they are attached to a specific National Guard unit but do not participate in training. As a member of the Inactive National Guard, you would be recalled to active duty with your unit. To remain a member, you must muster once a year with your assigned unit.

Individual Ready Reserve

The Individual Ready Reserve consists mainly of individuals who have had training and who have served previously in the active component. Other IRR members come from the Selected Reserve and have some of their military service obligation remaining. As an IRR member, you may be involuntarily recalled upon declaration of a national emergency. Otherwise, participation requirements may include an annual day of muster duty to satisfy statutory screening requirements. IRR members may participate in voluntary temporary tours of active duty and military professional development education programs.

Benefits of Joining a Selected Reserve Unit

You have gained many valuable and unique job skills through formal and on-the-job training while in the service. You should consider using these skills in the National Guard or Reserves. The benefits of joining the Selected Reserve include the following:

- Extra pay
- Opportunity for promotion
- Full-time employment opportunity
- Military retirement opportunity
- TRICARE Reserve Select
- Exchange and commissary privileges
- Morale, welfare, and recreation programs
- Education assistance
- Officer and noncommissioned officer clubs
- Travel (on a space-available basis)
- Servicemens' Group Life Insurance
- Reserve Component Survivors Benefits Plan
- Legal assistance
- Family Centers
- Opportunities for contacts in the civilian community
- Continuation of military ties
- Reserve Component Dental Plan

Priority Placement

Priority placement in a Selected Reserve unit is authorized for "Eligible Involuntary" separatees who apply within one year after their separation. Your installation's retention or personnel office can assist you. If you have already separated, contact the Reserve or National Guard recruiter listed in your local telephone directory.

Standby Reserve

If you have not completed your eight-year military service obligation, you will be transferred to a Reserve component in either the Ready Reserve (Selected Reserve, Individual Ready Reserve, or Inactive National Guard), discussed above, or possibly in the Standby Reserve, under certain conditions.

You may be placed in the Standby Reserve if you still have time remaining to complete your military service obligation and are either:

1. filling a "key" position in a civilian occupation, or
2. have a temporary hardship or disability.

Members of the Standby Reserve have no participation or training requirements, but, in the event of a national emergency, they may be involuntarily recalled to active duty. As the term *standby* implies, these reservists will only be mobilized once it has been determined that there are insufficient numbers of qualified members in the Ready Reserve to do the job. There are no other participation or training requirements.

Contact the Reserve Component Transition Office at your installation to see if you qualify for assignment to the Standby Reserve. If you cannot locate this office, contact your installation's personnel office for assistance.

Where to Sign Up for the Reserves

If you are interested in joining the National Guard or Reserves, keep in mind that there are a limited number of positions available. The sooner you review your options, the better your chances of finding a good position by the time you separate.

While you are in the military: Contact your installation's Reserve Component Transition Office. The staff will provide you with information about your obligations and benefits. In most cases, they will put you in touch with an active duty recruiter. You can access information about opportunities in the Reserve and National Guard online at the websites listed below.

Once you are out: Contact the nearest Reserve or National Guard unit listed in your local telephone directory. Any recruiting office will be happy to refer you to the appropriate recruiter.

Other resources: Many overseas and stateside installations have National Guard and Reserve recruiters located on their facilities.

RESERVE WEBSITES

U.S. Air Force Reserves: http://www.afreserve.com

U.S. Air National Guard: http://www.goang.com

U.S. Army National Guard: http://www.1800goguard.com

U.S. Army Reserves: http://www.usar.army.mil/arweb/pages/default.aspx; http://www.goarmyreserve.com

U.S Coast Guard Reserves: http://www.uscg.mil/hq/reserve/reshmpg.html

U.S. Marine Corps: http://www.marforres.usmc.mil; http://www.mfr.usmc .mil

U.S. Navy Reserve: http://www.navyreserve.com

Appendix 1: Useful Websites

GENERAL TRANSITION-RELATED WEBSITES

A Summary of Veteran's Benefits: http://www.vba.va.gov/bln/21/index.htm

Army Career and Alumni Program (ACAP): http://www.acap.army.mil

Civilian Assistance and Reemployment (CARE): http://www.cpms.osd.mil/care/

Department of Veterans Affairs (DVA): http://www.va.gov

Department of Veterans Affairs Locations: http://www1.va.gov/directory/guide/home.asp?isFlash=1)

Department of Labor: http://www.dol.gov

MilitaryHOMEFRONT: http://www.militaryhomefront.dod.mil

Military Installation Locator: http://www.militaryinstallations.dod.mil/ismart/MHF-MI/

Military OneSource: http://www.militaryonesource.com/skins/MOS/home.aspx

Operation Transition: http://www.dmdc.osd.mil/ot

DoD Transportal: http://www.dodtransportal.org/

Temporary Early Retirement Authority (TERA) Program: http://www.dmdc.osd.mil/tera

National Guard Transitional Assistance Advisors: http://www.guardfamily.org/Public/Application/ResourceFinderSearch.aspx

Air Force Airmen and Family Readiness Center: www.militaryinstallations.dod.mil.

Navy Fleet and Family Support Center: http://www.fssp.navy.mil/

Marines Career Resource Management Center (CRMC)/Transition and Employment Assistance Program Center: http://www.usmc-mccs.org/tamp/index.cfm

Coast Guard Work-Life Division—Transition Assistance: http://www.uscg.mil/hq/g-w/g-wk/wkw/worklife_programs/transition_assistance.htm

Family Center, Chaplain's Office, and Related Resources Finder: http://www.nvti.cudenver.edu/resources/militarybasestap.htm

Marine for Life: http://www.mfl.usmc.mil/

Military Family Network: http://www.emilitary.org/

EMPLOYMENT ASSISTANCE WEBSITES

Employer Support of the Guard and Reserve (ESGR): http://www.esgr.org/

21st Century Workforce Initiative: http://www.dol.gov/21cw/

Department of Labor Resources:
www.careeronestop.org
www.bla.gov
http://www.dol.gov/vets/
www.doleta.gov/programs
www.doleta.gov/jobseekers/building_your_career.cfm

Career OneStop Center: www.ServiceLocator.org.

Transition Bulletin Board (TBB): http://www.dmdc.osd.mil/ot

Federal Job Search: http://www.usajobs.com

DoD Civilian Careers: http://www.go-defense.com/

DoD Job Search: http://www.dod.jobsearch.org

FedWorld Job Resource: http://www.fedworld.gov

Federal Employment Portal: http://www.opm.gov

DoD Civilian Employment: http://www.go-defense.com

Army Civilian Personnel Online: http://www.cpol.army.mil/

U.S. Job Bank: http://www.ajb.dni.us

Career InfoNet: http://www.acinet.org/acinet

Careers in Government: http://www.careersingovernment.com

Vocational Information Center: http://www.khake.com

The Riley Guide: http://www.rileyguide.com

Veterans Employment and Training Service (VETS): http://www.dol.gov/vets/aboutvets/contacts/main.htm

A list of state VETS directors: http://www.dol.gov/dol.vets

DoD Spouse Career Center: http://www.military.com/spouse

Helpful Career Related Resources: http://www.military.com/careers

Army Credentialing Opportunities Online (COOL): https://www.cool.army.mil/

Navy Credentialing Opportunities Online (COOL): https://www.cool.navy.mil/

Helmets to Hardhats (H2H): http://helmetstohardhats.org/

Occupational Information Network (O*NET): http://online.onetcenter.org/

The Encyclopedia of Associations: http://library.dialog.com/bluesheets/html/bl0114.html

National Trade and Professional Associations of the United States: http://www.associationsexecs.com

The Occupational Outlook Handbook: http://www.bls.gov/oco/home.htm

Military and Veteran Service Organizations: http://www.military.com/Community/Subpage/1,14746,GENERAL,00.html

Skills Assessment Resources: http://www.dol.gov/vets/ and http://www.Military.com/careers

DD Form 2586, Verification of Military Experience and Training (VMET): http://www.dmdc.dod.mil/vmet

Troops to Teachers (TTT) Related Links:
  TTT Home Page: http://www.proudtoserveagain.com/
  TTT Self-Determination Eligibility Guide: http://www.proudtoserveagain.com
  TTT Registration: http://www.proudtoserveagain.com

State Employment Office Locator: http://www.naswa.org/links.cfm

ENTREPRENEURSHIP/BUSINESS WEBSITES

U.S. Small Business Administration (SBA): http://www.sba.gov/
SBA Programs, Contacts, and Representatives:

Local SBA District Office Locator: http://www.sba.gov/GC/pcr.html

SBA Government Contract (GC) Office: http://www.sba.gov/GC/indexwhatwedo.html

Subcontracting Opportunities Directory: http://www.sba.gov/GC/indexcontacts-sbsd.html

Procurement Technical Assistance Centers (PTACS): http://www.dla.mil/db/procurem.html

Simplified Acquisition Contracts: http://www.sba.gov/gc/indexprograms-vets.html

Small Business Development Centers (SBDC): http://www.sba.gov/sbdc/sbdcnear.html

Local Women's Business Center (WBC) Locator: http://www.sba.gov/wbc.html

Basic 7(a) Loan Guaranty: http://www.sba.gov/financing/sbaloan/7a.html

Section 8(a) Program: http://www.sba.gov/8abd/

Surety Bond Guarantee Program: http://www.sba.gov/osg/

Federal Agency Procurement Forecast: http://www.sba.gov/GC/forecast.html

Military Reservist Economic Injury Disaster Loan (MREIDL) Program: http://www.sba.gov/disaster_recov/loaninfo/militaryreservist.html

HUBZone Empowerment Contracting Program: https://eweb1.sba.gov/hubzone/internet/

Service-Disabled Veteran-Owned Small Business Concern Program: http://www.sba.gov/gc/indexprograms-vets.html

Veterans Business Outreach Centers (VBOC): http://www.vboc.org/

The Research Foundation of the State University of New York: http://www.nyssbdc.org/vboc

The University of West Florida in Pensacola: http://www.vboc.org

The University of Texas—Pan American: http://www.coserve.org/vboc

Vietnam Veterans of California: http://www.vboc-ca.org

Robert Morris University: www.rmu.edu/vboc

SCORE "Counselors to America's Small Business": http://www.score.org/

Local SCORE Chapter Locator: http://www.score.org/findscore/chapter_maps.html

Office of Small and Disadvantaged Business Utilization: http://www.osdbu.gov/Listofmembers.htm

Center for Veterans Enterprise (CVE): http://www.vetbiz.gov/

Association of Small Business Development Centers (ASBDC): www.asbdc-us.org

International Franchise Association (IFA): www.franchise.org

RELOCATION WEBSITES

Relocation Assistance Office Locator: http://www.militaryinstallations.dod.mil/smart/MHF-MI

"Plan My Move": http://www.militaryhomefront.dod.mil/pls.htmsdb/f?p=107:1:3267731230074301

Chamber of Commerce Locator: http://www.chamberofcommerce.com

Military Personnel Portals:

    Army Knowledge Online (AKO): http://www.army.mil/ako

Navy Knowledge Online (NKO): http://www.nko.mil
Air Force Portal: http://www.my.af.mil
USA Travel Source: http://www.relo.usa.com
Travel and Per Diem Information: https://secureapp2.hqda.pentagon
.mil.perdiem/.
The "It's Your Move" Pamphlet: http://www.apd.army.mil/
"Special Needs" Resources: http://www.militaryhomefront.dod.mil/.

EDUCATION/TRAINING WEBSITES

VA Education Services (GI Bill): http://www.gibill.va.gov/
VA 22-1990 Application for Education Benefits: http://www.vba
.va.gov/pubs/forms/22-1990.pdf
VA Regional Office Finder: http://www1.va.gov/directory/guide/home
.asp
The Defense Activity for Nontraditional Education Support (DANTES):
http://www.dantes.doded.mil/dantes_web/danteshome.asp
Department of Defense Voluntary Education Program: http://apps
.mhf.dod.mil/pls/psgprod/f?p=VOLED:HOME:0
Army (AARTS) Transcript: http://aarts.army.mil
Navy and Marine Corps (SMART) Transcript: http://www.navycollege
.navy.mil
Air Force (CCAF) Transcript: http://www.au.af.mil/au/ccaf/
Coast Guard Institute Transcript: http://www.uscg.mil/hq/cgi/forms.html
Federal Financial Student Aid: http://www.federalstudentaid.ed.gov/
Application Pell Grants or Federal Stafford Loans (FAFSA): http://www
.fafsa.ed.gov/
Veterans' Upward Bound: http://www.veteransupwardbound.org/vetub
.html

HEALTH CARE WEBSITES

TRICARE Reserve Select (TRS) on the Guard/Reserve Portal: https://
www.dmdc.osd.mil/appj/esgr/privacyAction.do.
TRS Point of Contact Information: http://www.tricare.mil/reserve/reserve
select/index.cfm.
TRICARE: http://www.tricare.osd.mil.
TRICARE For Life (TFL): http://www.tricare.mil/tfl

TRICARE Health Benefits Advisors/Beneficiary Counselor and Assistance Coordinators (BCAC) Locator: http://www.tricare.mil/bcacdcao/.

Post-Traumatic Stress Disorder (PTSD) Resources:

DoD Mental Health Self-Assessment Program: http://www.pdhealth.mil/mhsa.asp

National Center for Post-Traumatic Stress Disorder (PTSD): http://www.ncptsd.va.gov/index.html

Ameriforce Deployment Guide: http://www.ameriforce.net/deployment/

Courage to Care: http://www.usuhs.mil/psy/courage.html

Returning Reservists Resources: http://www.usuhs.mil/psy/GuardReserve ReentryWorkplace.pdf

Continued Health Care Benefit Program (CHCBP): http://www.humana-military.com/chcbp/main.htm

CHCBP Enrollment Application: http://www.humana-military.com/chcbp/pdf/dd2837.pdf

VA Home Page: http://www.va.gov/

VA Health Care Enrollment Resources: https://www.1010ez.med.va.gov/sec/vha/1010ez/.

VA Eligibility: http://www.va.gov/healtheligibility/

TRICARE Dental Program: http://www.tricaredentalprogram.com/

TRICARE Retiree Dental Program: http://www.trdp.org/

LIFE INSURANCE WEBSITES

VA Office of Servicemembers' Group Life Insurance (OSGLI): http://www.insurance.va.gov

OSGLI Contact Information: http://www.insurance.va.gov/sgliSite/miscellaneous/contact.htm

Form SGLV 8286, Servicemembers' Group Life Insurance Election & Certificate: http://www.insurance.va.gov/sgliSite/forms/8286.htm

Form SGLV 8286A, Family Coverage Election (FSGLI): http://www.insurancc.va.gov/sgliSite/forms/8286a.pdf

Form SGLV 8714, Application for Veterans' Group Life Insurance: http://www.insurance.va.gov/sgliSite/forms/8714.htm

SGLI Conversion Policy: http://www.insurance.va.gov/sgliSite/conversion/convertingSGLI.htm

VA OSGLI Frequently Asked Questions: http://www.insurance.va.gov/sgliSite/SGLI/deployFAQ.htm

FINANCE-RELATED WEBSITES

Military Installation Finder: http://www.militaryinstallations.dod.mil/ismart/MHF-MI/

Military OneSource: http://militaryonesource.com/skins/MOS/home.asps

AnnualCreditReport.Com: http://www.annualcreditreport.com

Experian National Consumer Assistance: http://www.experian.com

Equifax Credit Information Service: http://www.equifax.com

TransUnion: http://www.transunion.com

VA Home Loan Resources: http://www.homeloans.va.gov/veteran.htm

VA Form 26-1880, Request for Certificate of Eligibility: http://www.vba.va.gov/pubs/forms/26-1880.pdf

Get your W-2 from myPay: https://mypay.dfas.mil/mypay.aspx

VETERANS BENEFIT-RELATED WEBSITES

Department of Veterans Affairs: http://www.va.gov

Vet Center Directory: http://www1.va.gov/directory/guide/vetcenter.asp

State Veterans Benefits Directory: http://www1.va.gov/vso/index.cfm?template=view&SortCategory=3

Health Care Benefits: http://www1.va.gov/health/

Health Care Enrollment—Priority Groups: http://www.va.gov/health eligibility/

Education Benefits: http://www.gibill.va.gov/

Compensation and Pension: http://www.vba.va.gov/bln/21/index.htm

Home Loan Guaranty: http://www.homeloans.va.gov/

Vocational Rehabilitation and Employment (VR&E): http://www.vba.va.gov/bln/vre/index.htm

DVA Life Insurance Programs: http://www.insurance.va.gov/

Appendix 2: Transition Checklists Used as Part of the Recovery Care Coordinator Program

Topic	Requirement	Who/Reference	Action
Privacy Act Statement	Collection of PII from immediate family members and non-dependent family members must be preceded by provision of an appropriate privacy act statement as required by Reference (e). (DoDD 5400.11)	Service/RCC/NMCM—(7.b) DODI	
Servicemember			1. Maintain copy of signed statements. 2. Make appropriate entry into CTP 3. Make entry into MCWIITS
Family			1. Maintain copy of signed statements. 2. Make appropriate entry into CTP 3. Make entry into MCWIITS
Recovery Team Membership	All RTs shall include the RSM's Commander, RSM; an RCC or a Federal recovery coordinator (FRC); an MCCM; and an NMCM.	(RT)(RCC/NMCM)—(Encl 3 4.a) DODI	1. Enter team members into CTP. 2. Make appropriate entry into MCWIITS
RCC Training	Complete uniform core training conducted by WWCTP, and Military Department-specific training conducted by the cognizant wounded warrior program prior to assuming the duties of their positions.	RCC—(Encl 3 c.1) DODI	1. RCCs shall complete and maintain certificates of training for WWCTP and Military Department specific training.
	Complete Military Department-specific training prior to independently assuming the duties of their positions, and comply with continuing education requirements.	RT (RCC/NMCM)—(Encl 3 4.b) DODI	1. RCCs shall complete and maintain certificates or records of service specific training. Additionally, they shall maintain documentation for continuing education.
RCC & RT CTP Development/Maintenance	Collaborate with RCC and other RT members to develop the comprehensive recovery plan (CRP), evaluate its effectiveness in meeting RSM's goals, and readjust it as necessary to accommodate the RSM's changing objectives, abilities, and recovery status.	RT (RCC/NMCM)—(Encl 3 4.b) DODI	1. Document RT actions/reviews in CTP. 2. Make appropriate entries in MCWIITS

Location of care		
Determine the RSM's location of care based primarily on the RSM's medical care needs, with consideration given to the desires of the RSM and family and/or designated caregiver. Provide the RSM and family or designated caregiver options for care locations during development of the CRP that address:		
1. The RSM's medical care and non-medical support needs.	RT (RCC/NMCM)—(Encl 3 4.b) DODI	1. Document RT actions/reviews in CTP 2. Make appropriate entries in MCWIITS
2 Capabilities required for the RSM's care.	RT (RCC/NMCM)—(Encl 3 4.b) DODI	1. Document RT actions/reviews in CTP 2. Make appropriate entries in MCWIITS
3. The availability of DoD, VA, or civilian facilities with appropriate capabilities and accreditation of licensure.	RT (RCC/NMCM)—(Encl 3 4.b) DODI	1. Document RT actions/reviews in CTP 2. Make appropriate entries in MCWIITS
4. Determine the appropriate course of action for the RSM when he or she is located at an MTF, specialty medical care facility, military quarters, or leased housing that is found to be deficient in accordance with Secretary of Defense Memorandum (Reference (i)); this course of action may be temporary or permanent based on the deficiency and the RSM's needs.	RT (RCC/NMCM)—(Encl 3 4.b) DODI	1. Document RT actions/reviews in CTP 2. Make appropriate entries in MCWIITS
5. Reevaluate the needs of the RSM in accordance with the options for care locations if relocation is required.	RT (RCC/NMCM)—(Encl 3 4.b) DODI	1. Document RT actions/reviews in CTP 2. Make appropriate entries in MCWIITS
6. Facilitate the most expeditious appointment available for the RSM for non-urgent care to include appointments for follow-up and/or specialty care, diagnostic referral and studies, and surgery.	RT (RCC/NMCM)—(Encl 3 4.b) DODI	1. Document RT actions/reviews in CTP 2. Make appropriate entries in MCWIITS

Category	Description	Reference	Action
TRICARE Waiver	7. Allow the RSM to waive TRICARE standards for access to care detailed in the TRICARE Management Activity guide (Reference (jj)) when either of these circumstances occur	RT (RCC/NMCM)—(Encl 3 4.b) DODI	1. Document RT actions/reviews in CTP 2. Make appropriate entries in MCWIITS
	a. No appointment is available that meets access stands within DoD MTFs or the TRICARE program	RT (RCC/NMCM)—(Encl 3 4.b) DODI	1. Document RT actions/reviews in CTP 2. Make appropriate entries in MCWIITS
	b. Travel is required beyond the TRICARE catchment area, and the healthcare provider has determined that travel will not adversely affect the health of the RSM.	RT (RCC/NMCM)—(Encl 3 4.b) DODI	1. Document RT actions/reviews in CTP 2. Make appropriate entries in MCWIITS
	8. Document in writing, and maintain in the RSM's records, any situation in which the RSM waives a standard for access to care.	RT (RCC/NMCM)—(Encl 3 4.b) DODI	1. Document RT actions/reviews in CTP 2. Make appropriate entries in MCWIITS
RCC CTP Responsbility	All RSMs enrolled in a Military Department RCP shall receive a CRP. (RSMs assigned an FRC shall also receive a federal individual recovery care.)	RCC—(Encl 4 4.a) DODI	1. RCCs shall complete and maintain a CTP for each servicemember assigned to the RCP. 2. RCCs shall upload all CTPs into MCWIITS.
Development	Have primary responsibility for development of the CRP, in conjunction with the RT, and assist the Commander in overseeing and coordinating the services and resources identified in the CRP.	RCC—(Encl 3 c.2) DODI	1. RCCs shall complete and maintain a CTP for each servicemember assigned to the RCP. 2. RCCs shall upload all CTPs into MCWIITS when initially developed.
	The RSM, family or designated caregiver, and RT members will create steps for accomplishing plan goals which must be specific, measurable, and achievable within an agreed upon time frame. In addition to the action to be taken, action steps shall contain these data elements:	RCC—(Encl 4 4.a) DODI	1. In development of the CTP, RCCs should ensure that goals are specific, measurable and achievable.
	1. An indentified point of contact for each step	RCC—(Encl 4 4.a) DODI	1. CTP entry as required.

	2. A list of the support and resources available to the RSM and family or designated caregiver for each action, including the location of the support and resources.	RCC—(Encl 4 4.a) DODI	1. CTP entry as required.
	The RSM and family or designated caregiver, and the RCC shall review the CRP and sign the document, demonstrating their understanding of the plan and commitment to its implementation.	RCC—(Encl 4 4.b) DODI	1. Document in CTP. 2. Document in MCWIITS that RSM and/or family member has reviewed and understands the plan.
Provide Copy to RSM & Family	Provide a hard copy of the CRP to the RSM and family and/or designated caregiver upon completion and whenever changes are made to the document.	RCC—(Encl 3 c.5) DODI	1. Ensure RSM and/or family receives hard copy of CTP. 2. Annotate in MCWIITS same.
Review and Update	Review and update the CRP in person (when possible) with the RSM and family or designated caregiver as frequently as necessary based on the RSM's needs and during transition phases in the RSM's care (change in location or familial, marital, financial, job, medical, or retirement status).	RCC—(Encl 3 c.5) DODI	1. Update CTP accordingly and also document in MCWIITS significant changes that other members of the RT or military leadership should be made aware of or have access to.
Facilitate and monitor servies for RSM identified in CTP	Facilitate and monitor the execution of services for the RSM across the continuum of care as documented in the recovery plan, to include services available from:	RCC—(Encl 3 c.6) DODI	1. Update CTP accordingly and also document in MCWIITS significant changes that other members of the RT or military leadership should be made aware of or have access to.
	1. Department of Defense	RCC—(Encl 3 c.6) DODI	
	2. VA	RCC—(Encl 3 c.6) DODI	
	3. Department of Labor	RCC—(Encl 3 c.6) DODI	
	4. Social Security Administration.	RCC—(Encl 3 c.6) DODI	

Category	Description	Reference	Action
Advice and Training Services	Advice and training services include, but are not limited to, financial counseling, spouse employment assistance, respite care information, and childcare assistance. When the family has arrived at the treatment facility, the NMCM, RCC, or FRC should provide information on services and resources available through the National Resource Directory, the Wounded Warrior Resource Center Call Center and Web Site, the Wounded, Ill, and Injured Compensation Benefits Handbook.	RCC/NMCM—(Encl 4 5.c) DODI	1. Update CTP accordingly and also document in MCWIITS significant changes that other members of the RT or military leadership should be made aware of or have access to.
Financial Assistance and Job Placement Services	Identify any loss of income and financial challenges facing the RSM's family. Ensure the recovery plan identifies benefits, compensation, services (such as job placement services), and resources from Federal, State, and local agencies and non-profit organizations for which the RSM's family is eligible.	RT/RCC/NMCM—(Encl 4 5.d) DODI	1. Update CTP accordingly and also document in MCWIITS significant changes that other members of the RT or military leadership should be made aware of or have access to.
Transition: DOD to VA care	Prior to transition of the RSM to the VA, the RCC (assisted by the RT) shall ensure that all appropriate care coordination activities, both medical and non-medical, have been completed, including:	RCC/RT—(Encl 5 1.a) DODI	1. Update CTP accordingly and also document in MCWIITS significant changes that other members of the RT or military leadership should be made aware of or have access to.
	1. Notification to the appropriate VA point of contact (such as Transition Patient Advocate) when the RSM begins physical disability evaluation process, as applicable.	RCC/RT—(Encl 5 1.a) DODI	1. Annotate in CTP 2. Annotate in MCWIITS
	2. Scheduling initial appointments with the Veterans Health Administration system.	RCC/RT—(Encl 5 1.a) DODI	1. Coordinate with RT and document as required.
	3. Transmittal of the RSM's military service record and health record to the VA. The transmittal shall include:	RCC/RT—(Encl 5 1.a) DODI	1. Coordinate with RT and document as required.

a. The RSM's authorization (or that of an individual legally recognized to make medical decisions on behalf of the RSM) for transmittal in accordance with Public Law 104-191 (Reference (k)). The RSM may have authorized release of his or her medical records if he or she applied for benefits prior to this point in the transition. Is so, a copy of that authorization shall be included with the records.	RCC/RT—(Encl 5 1.a) DODI	1. Coordinate with RT and document as required.
b. The RSM's address and contact information	RCC/RT—(Encl 5 1.a) DODI	1. Coordinate with RT and document as required.
c. The RSM' DD Form 214, "Certificate of Release or Discharge from Active Duty," which shall be transmitted electronically when possible, and in compliance with Reference (d).	RCC/RT—(Encl 5 1.a) DODI	1. Coordinate with RT and document as required.
d. The results of any PEB.	RCC/RT—(Encl 5 1.a) DODI	1. Coordinate with RT and document as required.
e. A determination of the RSM's entitlement to transitional health care, a conversion health policy, or other health benefits through the Department of Defense, as explained in section 1145 of Title 10, United States Code (Reference (l)).	RCC/RT—(Encl 5 1.a) DODI	1. Coordinate with RT and document as required.
f. A copy of requests for assistance from the VA, or of applications made by the RSM for healthcare, compensation and vocational rehabilitation, disability, education benefits, or other benefits for which he or she may be eligible pursuant to laws administered by the Secretary of Veterans Affairs.	RCC/RT—(Encl 5 1.a) DODI	1. Coordinate with RT and document as required.

4. Transmittal of the RSM's address and contact information to the department or agency for veteran's affairs of the State in which the RSM intends to reside after retirement or separation.	RCC/RT—(Encl 5 1.a) DODI	1. Coordinate with RT and document as required.
5. Update the CRP for the RSM's transition that shall included standardized elements of care, treatment requirements, and accountability for the plan. The CRP shall also include:		
a. Detailed instructions for the transition from the DoD disability evaluation system to the VA system.	RCC/RT—(Encl 5 1.a) DODI	1. Coordinate with RT and document as required.
b. The recommended schedule and milestones for the RSMs transition from military service.	RCC/RT—(Encl 5 1.a) DODI	1. Coordinate with RT and document as required.
c. Information and guidance designed to assist the RSM in understanding and meeting the schedule and milestones.	RCC/RT—(Encl 5 1.a) DODI	1. Coordinate with RT and document as required.
6. The RCC and RT shall:	RCC/RT—(Encl 5 1.a) DODI	1. Coordinate with RT and document as required.
a. Consider the desires of the RSM and the family or designated caregiver when determining the location of the RSM's care, treatment, and rehabilitation.	RCC/RT—(Encl 5 1.a) DODI	1. Coordinate with RT and document as required.
b. Coordinate the transfer to the VA by direct communication between appropriate medical and non-medical staff of the losing and gaining facilities (e.g. MCCM to accepting physician).	RCC/RT—(Encl 5 1.a) DODI	1. Coordinate with RT and document as required.

Transition: DOD to Civilian care	Prior to transition of the RSM to a civilian medical care facility, the RCC (assisted by the RT) shall ensure that all care coordination activities, both medical and non-medical, have been completed, including:	RCC/RT—(Encl 5 2.a) DODI	1. Update CTP accordingly and also document in MCWIITS significant changes that other members of the RT or military leadership should be made aware of or have access to.
	1. Appointment scheduling with civilian medical care facility providers	RCC/RT—(Encl 5 2.a) DODI	1. Coordinate with RT and document as required.
	2. Transmittal of the RSM's health record to the civilian medical care facility. The transmittal shall include:	RCC/RT—(Encl 5 2.a) DODI	1. Coordinate with RT and document as required.
	a. The RSM's authorization (or that of an individual legally recognized to make medical decisions on behalf of the RSM) for the transmittal in accordance with Reference (i).	RCC/RT—(Encl 5 2.a) DODI	1. Coordinate with RT and document as required.
	b. A determination of the RSM's entitlement to transitional health care, a conversion health policy, or other health benefits through the Department of Defense, as explained in section 1145 of Reference (l).	RCC/RT—(Encl 5 2.a) DODI	1. Coordinate with RT and document as required.
	3. Transmittal of the RSM's address and contact information.	RCC/RT—(Encl 5 2.a) DODI	1. Coordinate with RT and document as required.
	4. Preparation of detailed plans for the RSM's transition, to include standardized elements of care, treatment requirements, and accountability of the CRP.	RCC/RT—(Encl 5 2.a) DODI	1. Coordinate with RT and document as required.
	5. The RCC and RT shall:	RCC/RT—(Encl 5 2.a) DODI	1. Coordinate with RT and document as required.
	a. Consider the desires of the RSM and the family or designated caregiver when determining the location of the RSM's care, treatment, and rehabilitation.	RCC/RT—(Encl 5 2.a) DODI	1. Coordinate with RT and document as required.

	b. Coordinate the transfer by direct communication between the appropriate medical and non-medical staff of the losing and gaining facilities (e.g. RCC to FRC, MCCM to accepting physician).	RCC/RT—(Encl 5 2.a) DODI	
Medical Separation or Retirement	An RSM who is enrolled in the RCP and subsequently placed on the temporary disability retired list shall continue to receive the support of an RCC, including implementation of the recovery plan, until such time as the wounded warrior program determines that the services and resources necessary to meet indentified needs are in place through non-DoD programs.	Service/CO WWP/RCC—(Encl 5 4.b) DODI	1. Coordinate with RT and document as required.
Transition from DoD Care	The RT shall provide transition support to the RSM and family or designated caregiver before, during, and after relocation from one treatment or rehabilitation facility to another or from one care provider to another. Transition preparation will occur with sufficient advance notice and information that the upcoming change in location or caregiver is anticipated by the RSM and family or designated caregiver, and will be documented in the CRP.	RT/RCC—(Encl 5 5.a) DODI	1. Coordinate with RT and document as required.
Separation or Retirement	Once the PEB determines that the RSM will not return to duty:	RT/RCC—(Encl 5 5.b) DODI	1. Coordinate with RT and document as required.
	1. the RT shall:	RT/RCC—(Encl 5 5.b) DODI	
	a. Work with the RSM and family or designated caregiver to prepare for the transition to retirement and veteran status.	RT/RCC—(Encl 5 5.b) DODI	1. Coordinate with RT and document as required.
	b. Ensure transition plans are written prior to the time of separation for RSMs being retired or separated pursuant to chapter 61 of Reference (l).	RT/RCC—(Encl 5 5.b) DODI	1. Coordinate with RT and document as required.

	2. The RCC or FRC shall:	RT/RCC—(Encl 5 5.b) DODI	
	a. Discuss with the RSM his or her short- and long-term personal and professional goals such as employment, education, and vocational training, and the rehabilitation needed to meet those goals; identify the options and transition activities in the CRP.	RT/RCC—(Encl 5 5.b) DODI	1. Document discussions in CTP. 2. Annotate in MCWIITS
	b. Ensure the RSM, as appropriate, has received the mandatory pre-separation counseling and has the opportunity to attend the VA benefits briefing and to participate in the Disabled Transition Assistance Program (TAP) and the Department of Labor TAP Employment Workshop. Encourage the RSM to establish a TAP account through the Internet.	RT/RCC—(Encl 5 5.b) DODI	1. Document discussions in CTP. 2. Annotate in MCWIITS
	c. Ensure the RC RSMs have the opportunity to participate in the Benefits Delivery at Discharge Program as appropriate.	RT/RCC—(Encl 5 5.b) DODI	1. Advise RSM. 2. Annotate in MCWIITS. 3. CTP Annotation
CTP Transfer	Coordinate the transfer of an updated CRP to, and directly communicate with, appropriate medical and non-medical personnel should the RSM be moved to a different location for care.	RCC—(Encl 3 c.7) DODI	1. All transfers of cases will be approved by the Battalion Operations Officer. 2. RCC will coordinate with the receiving RCC to ensure that a appropriate turnover is conducted. 3. Tranferring RCC will annotate in MCWIITS that the turnover is complete and case is transferred to receiving RCC (by name). 4. Receiving RCC will acknowledge repsonsbility for the case and completion of turnover in MCWIITS as well
CTP Closure/Suspense	Close out the CRP when the RSM has met all goals or declines further support and retain all documents according to applicable Military Department policies.	RCC—(Encl 3 c.8) DODI	1. Command review and concurrence is required first. 2. Maintain documentation. 3. Annotate in MCWITTS that command (cite specifically who) concurs with suspending the case.

RSM & Family Medical Care Access	Ensure, in coordination with the Secretary of the Military Department concerned, that the RSM and family and/or designated caregiver have access to all medical and non-medical services throughout the continuum of care.	RCC—(Encl 3 c.3) DODI	1. Coordinate with RT or others as appropriate to ensure accomplishment of this task. 2. Annotate problems associated with accomplishing this task in MCWIITS
Medical Support for Non-Dependent Family Members	The RCC or FRC, MCCM, and NMCM, in coordination with the Secretary of the Military Department concerned or designee, shall facilitate non-dependent family member access to medical care at DoD military treatment facilities. The RCC or FRC, MCCM, and NMCM shall facilitate non-dependent family member access to non-Federal care providers as needed (not at Government expense). In general, medical care and counseling may be provided at a DoD MTF on a space-available basis when:	RCC/NMCM—(Encl 4 5.b) DODI	1. Coordinate with RT or others as appropriate to ensure accomplishment of this task. 2. Annotate problems associated with accomplishing this task in MCWIITS
	1. The family member is on invitational travel orders to care for the RSM.	RCC/NMCM—(Encl 4 5.b) DODI	
	2. The family member is issued non-medical attendant orders to care for the RSM.	RCC/NMCM—(Encl 4 5.b) DODI	
	3. The family member is receiving per diem payments from the Department of Defense while caring for the RSM.	RCC/NMCM—(Encl 4 5.b) DODI	
RSM Medical Care	Minimize delays and gaps in treatment and services.	RCC—(Encl 3 c.4) DODI	1. Annotate problems associated with accomplishing this task in MCWIITS

Appendix 3: Guide to Entrepreneurship

The mission of the U.S. Small Business Administration (SBA) is to maintain and strengthen the nation's economy by aiding, counseling, assisting, and protecting the interests of small businesses and by helping families and businesses recover from national disasters.

The mission of the SBA Office of Veterans Business Development is to conduct comprehensive outreach to veterans, service-disabled veterans, and Reserve and National Guard small business owners; formulate, execute, and promote policies and programs of the Administration; and act as an ombudsman for full consideration of veterans in all programs of the Administration. In carrying out its mission, SBA offers programs and services designed to assist small business owners and entrepreneurs in starting, managing, and growing successful small business concerns that are a source of competitive American strength in the global economy. These programs and services are defined by four distinctly identifiable phases of successful entrepreneurial development:

- Entrepreneurial self-analysis
- Resources to assist entrepreneurs and small business owners
- Capital and financing resources
- Government contracting resources

To learn more about the programs, services, and business assistance tools SBA offers small business owners and entrepreneurs, as well as business and technical assistance specific to veteran and service-disabled veteran small business owners/entrepreneurs and Reserve component members, explore the links below.

ENTREPRENEURIAL SELF-ANALYSIS

Phase 1 Entrepreneurial Self-Analysis

This link provides access to entrepreneurial tests that will assist you in determining if owning a business is right for you.

http://www.sba.gov/starting_business/startup/areyouready.html

ENTREPRENEURIAL DEVELOPMENT RESOURCES

Phase 2 Resources to Assist in Starting, Managing, and Growing Successful Small Business Concerns

These links provide access to SBA's network of resource partners that can assist you in starting, managing, and growing successful small business concerns. Included in this network are centers charged with providing assistance specific to veteran and service-disabled veteran business owners/entrepreneurs, as well as tools specifically designed to aid self-employed members of the Reserve and National Guard balance successful business ownership with Title 10 activations and deployment, including restarting or reestablishing their businesses upon deactivation from active duty.

Veterans Business Outreach Centers (VBO Centers): http://www.sba.gov/VETS/vbop.html

Veteran Business Development Officers (VBD Officers): http://www.sba.gov/VETS/reps.html

Small Business Development Centers (SBDCs): http://www.sba.gov/sbdc/sbdcnear.html

SCORE: http://www.score.org/findscore/

Women's Business Centers: http://www.sba.gov/wbc.html/

Native American Affairs: http://www.sba.gov/naa/

Small Business Training Network: http://www.sba.gov/training/

Reserve and Guard Tools: http://www.sba.gov/reservists

Hire a Veteran: http://hirevetsfirst.dol.gov.

Phase 3 Capital and Financing Resources

These links provide access to the various loan programs SBA offers small business owners and aspiring entrepreneurs. By following the links, a synopsis on the Agency's loan programs follows along with information on how to apply for an SBA-backed loan and criteria for qualifying.

Basic 7(a) Loan Program: http://www.sba.gov/financing/index.html
CDC/504 Loan Program: http://www.sba.gov/financing/sbaloan/cdc504.html
Microloans: http://www.sba.gov/financing/sbaloan/microloans.html
Surety Bond: http://www.sba.gov/financing/bonds/whatis.html
International Trade: http://www.sba.gov/oit
Military Reservists Economic Injury Disaster Loans: http://www.sba.gov/
disaster_recov/loaninfo/militaryreservist.html
Small Business Investment Corporations: http://www.sba.gov/INV/

Phase 4 Government Contracting Resources

These links provide information on the various government contracting programs SBA offers in assisting small business owners and entrepreneurs in bidding on and winning federal government contracts.

Government Contracting for Veteran Business Owners: http://www.sba
.gov/GC/indexprograms-vets-html
HUBZone Program: http://www.sba.gov/hubzone
8(a) Business Development Program: http://www.sba.gov/8abd
Technology—SBIR/STTR Program: http://www.sba.gov/sbir
Contract Assistance for Women-owned Businesses: http://www.sba.gov/
GC/indexprograms-cawbo.html
Small Disadvantaged Businesses: http://www.sba.gov/sdb/
Procurement Center Representatives: http://www.sba.gov/GC/pcr.html
Commercial Market Representatives: http://www.sba.gov/GC/indexcontact-crms.html
Procurement Technical Assistance Centers: http://www.aptac-us.org; http://www.dla.mil/db/procurem.htm

OTHER RESOURCES

SBA Office of Advocacy: http://www.sba/gov/ADVO
SBA Office of Ombudsman: http://www.sba.gov/ombudsman
Department of Veterans Affairs: http://www.va.gov
Vocational Rehabilitation and Employment Services: http://www.vba.gov/
bln/vre
Department of Labor: http://www.dol.gov
Office of Veterans Employment and Training Services: http://www.dol.gov/
vets/programs/empserv/employment_services_fshtm
Office of Disability Policy Initiatives: http://www.dol.gov/odep
National Veterans Business Development Corporation: http://www.vets
corp.org

Appendix 4: VA Facilities

VA Facilities Nationwide

Station ID	Facility	Address	State	Phone
691	VA Greater Los Angeles Healthcare System (GLA)	11301 Wilshire Boulevard, Los Angeles, CA 90073	CA	310-478-3711 800-952-4852
605	VA Loma Linda Healthcare System	11201 Benton Street, Loma Linda, CA 92357	CA	909-825-7084 909-825-7084
600	VA Long Beach Healthcare System	5901 E. 7th Street, Long Beach, CA 90822	CA	562-826-8000 888-769-8387
664	VA San Diego Healthcare System	3350 La Jolla Village Drive, San Diego, CA 92161	CA	858-552-8585 858-552-8585
593	VA Southern Nevada Healthcare System (VASNHS)	901 Rancho Lane, Las Vegas, NV 89106 Mailing Address: P.O. Box 360001, North Las Vegas, NV 89036	NV	702-636-3000 702-636-3000
605	Blythe Telehealth Clinic	205 N. 1st Street, Suite C, Blythe, CA 92225	CA	760-619-4243
691GA	Los Angeles Ambulatory Care Center	351 East Temple Street, Los Angeles, CA 90012	CA	213-253-2677
664	Mission Valley	8810 Rio San Diego Drive, San Diego, CA 92108	CA	619-400-5000
664	Oceanside	1300 Rancho del Oro Road, Oceanside, CA 92056	CA	760-643-2000
691GB	Santa Barbara Community Based Outpatient Clinic	4440 Calle Real, Santa Barbara, CA 93110	CA	805-683-1491
691A4	Sepulveda Outpatient Clinic and Nursing Home	16111 Plummer Street, North Hills, CA 91343	CA	818-891-7711 800-516-4567

691	VA West Los Angeles Healthcare Center	11301 Wilshire Boulevard, Los Angeles, CA 90073	CA	310-268-3526
600GA	Anaheim	Professional Center, 3rd Floor, Suite 303, 1801 W. Romneya Drive, Anaheim, CA 92801	CA	714-780-5400
691GD	Bakersfield Community Based Outpatient Clinic	1801 Westwind Drive, Bakersfield, CA 93301	CA	661-632-1800
664GC	Chula Vista	835 3rd Avenue, Chula Vista, CA 91910	CA	619-409-1600
605GD	Corona	800 Magnolia Avenue, #101, Corona, CA 92879	CA	951-817-8820
593	East Clinic/Las Vegas	3131 LaCanada Street, Las Vegas, NV 89109	NV	702-636-6360
691GF	East Los Angeles	5426 E. Olympic Boulevard, City of Commerce, CA 90040	CA	323-725-7557
664GD	Escondido	815 East Pennsylvania Avenue, Escondido, CA 92025	CA	760-466-7020
691	Gardena	1251 Redondo Beach Boulevard, 3rd Floor, Gardena, CA 90247	CA	310-851-4705
593	Healthcare for the Homeless Vets	926 West Owens Avenue, Las Vegas, NV 89106	NV	702-636-4077
664GA	Imperial Valley	1600 South Imperial Avenue, El Centro, CA 92243	CA	760-352-1506
600GE	Laguna Hills	25292 McIntyre Street, Laguna Hills, CA 92653	CA	949-269-0700
691	Lancaster Community Based Outpatient Clinic	547 West Lancaster Boulevard, Lancaster, CA 93536	CA	661-729-8655 661-729-8655
593	Northwest Clinic	2410 Fire Mesa, Las Vegas, NV 89129	NV	702-636-6320
691GM	Oxnard	2000 Outlet Center Drive, Suite 225, Oxnard, CA 93036	CA	805-604-6960
593	Pahrump Community Based Outpatient Clinic	2100 E. Calvada Boulevard, Pahrump, NV 89048	NV	775-727-7535
605	Palm Desert	41-990 Cook Street, Building F, Ste. 1004, Palm Desert, CA 92211	CA	760-341-5570
69G	Pasadena	420 W. Las Tunas Drive, San Gabriel, CA 91776	CA	626-289-5973
605	Rancho Cucamonga	8599 Haven Avenue, Suite 102, Rancho Cucamonga, CA 91730	CA	909-946-5348
691GK	San Luis Obispo–Pacific Medical Plaza	1288 Morro Street, Suite 200, San Luis Obispo, CA 93401	CA	805-543-1233

600GB	Santa Ana–Bristol Medical Center	2740 S. Bristol Street, 1st Floor, Suite 101, Santa Ana, CA 92704	CA	714-825-3500
691	Santa Maria Community Based Outpatient Clinic	1550 East Main Street, Santa Maria, CA 93454	CA	805-354-6000
593	Southwest Clinic	3880 S. Jones Boulevard, Las Vegas, NV 89103	NV	702-636-6390
605GB	Sun City	28125 Bradley Road, Suite 130, Sun City, CA 92586	CA	951-672-1931
691	Ventura Community Based Outpatient Clinic	120 N. Ashwood Avenue, Ventura, CA 93003	CA	805-658-5800
605	Victorville	12138 Industrial Boulevard, Suite 120, Victorville, CA 92392	CA	760-951-2599
600GC	Villages at Cabrillo	2001 River Avenue, Building 28, Long Beach, CA 90806	CA	562-388-8000
593	West Clinic	630 S. Rancho Road, Las Vegas, NV 89106	NV	702-636-6355
600GD	Whittier/Santa Fe Springs Clinic	10210 r & Day Road, Santa Fe Springs, CA 90670	CA	562-826-8000
0603	Antelope Valley Vet Center	38925 Trade Center Drive, Suite J, Palmdale, CA 93551	CA	661-267-1026
0614	Chula Vista Vet Center	180 Otay Lakes Road, Suite 108, Bonita, CA 91902-2439	CA	858-642-1500
0611	Corona Vet Center	800 Magnolia Avenue, Suite 110, Corona, CA 92879	CA	951-734-0525
0623	East Los Angeles Vet Center	5400 E. Olympic Boulevard, #140, Commerce, CA 90022	CA	323-728-9966
0534	Henderson Vet Center	400 North Stephanie, Suite 180, Henderson, NV 89014	NV	702-791-9100
0613	High Desert Vet Center	15095 Amargosa Road, Suite 107, Victorville, CA 92394	CA	760-261-5925
0505	Las Vegas Vet Center	1919 S. Jones Boulevard, Suite A, Las Vegas, NV 89146	NV	702-251-7873
0606	Los Angeles Veterans Resource Center	1045 W. Redondo Beach Boulevard, Suite 150, Gardena, CA 90247	CA	310-767-1221
0624	North Orange County Vet Center	12453 Lewis Street, Suite 101, Garden Grove, CA 92840	CA	714-776-0161
0637	San Bernardino Vet Center	1325 E. Cooley Drive, Suite 101, Colton, CA 92324	CA	909-801-5762
0618	San Diego Vet Center	2790 Truxtun Road, Suite 130, San Diego, CA 92106	CA	858-642-1500

0642	San Marcos Vet Center	One Civic Center Drive, Suite 140, San Marcos, CA 92069	CA	760-744-6914
0605	Sepulveda Vet Center	9737 Haskell Avenue, Sepulveda, CA 91343	CA	818-892-9227
0604V	South Orange County Vet Center	26431 Crown Valley Parkway, Suite 100, Mission Viejo, CA 92691	CA	949-348-6700
0608	Temecula Vet Center	40935 County Center Drive, Suite A, Temecula, CA 92591	CA	951-302-4849
0643	Ventura Vet Center	790 E. Santa Clara Street, Suite 100, Ventura, CA 93001	CA	805-585-1860
0607	West Los Angeles Vet Center	5730 Uplander Way, Suite 100, Culver City, CA 90230	CA	310-641-0326
593	Mike O'Callaghan Federal Hospital	4700 N. Las Vegas Boulevard, Nellis AFB, NV 89191-6601	NV	702-653-2260
593	Readjustment Counseling Services (Vet Center–Henderson)	400 North Stephanie Street, Suite 180, Henderson, NV 89014	NV	702-791-9100
593	Readjustment Counseling Services (Vet Center–Las Vegas)	1919 S. Jones, Suite A, Las Vegas, NV 89146	NV	702-251-7873

Veterans Health Administration: VISN 23: VA Midwest Health Care Network

Station ID	Facility	Address	State	Phone
10N23	VISN 23: VA Midwest Health Care Network	5445 Minnehaha Avenue, S. Minneapolis, MN 55417-2300	MN	612-725-1968
636A6	Des Moines Division–VA Central Iowa Health Care System	3600 30th Street, Des Moines, IA 50310-5774	IA	515-699-5999 800-294-8387
437	Fargo VA Medical Center	2101 Elm Street, N. Fargo, ND 58102	ND	701-232-3241 701-232-3241
636A8	Iowa City VA Medical Center	601 Highway 6 West, Iowa City, IA 52246-2208	IA	319-338-0581 319-338-0581
618	Minneapolis VA Health Care System	One Veterans Drive, Minneapolis, MN 55417	MN	612-725-2000 866-414-5058
636	Omaha–VA Nebraska-Western Iowa Health Care System	4101 Woolworth Avenue, Omaha, NE 68105	NE	402-346-8800 402-346-8800
438	Sioux Falls VA Medical Center	2501 W. 22nd Street, P.O. Box 5046, Sioux Falls, SD 57117-5046	SD	605-336-3230
656	St. Cloud VA Medical Center	4801 Veterans Drive, St. Cloud, MN 56303	MN	320-252-1670 800-247-1739

568A4	VA Black Hills Health Care System–Hot Springs Campus	500 North 5th Street, Hot Springs, SD 57747	SD	605-745-2000 605-745-2000
568	VA Black Hills Health Care System–Fort Meade Campus	113 Comanche Road, Fort Meade, SD 57741	SD	605-347-2511 605-347-2511
638A8	Cedar Rapids Community Based Outpatient Clinic	2230 Wiley Boulevard, SW, Cedar Rapids, IA 52404	IA	319-369-4340
636A8	Coralville Outpatient Clinic	520 10 Avenue, Suite 200, Coralville, IA 52441	IA	319-358-2406
437	Dickinson VA Community Based Outpatient Clinic	528 21st Street W., Suite F, Dickinson, ND 58601	ND	701-483-1850
437	Jamestown VA Community Based Outpatient Clinic	Jamestown Hospital, 419 5th Street NE, Jamestown, ND 58401	ND	701-952-4787
438GD	Aberdeen VA Clinic	2391 8th Avenue NE, Suite 225, Aberdeen, SD 57401	SD	605-229-3500
656	Alexandria Community Based Outpatient Clinic	515 22nd Avenue East, Alexandria, MN 56308	MN	320-759-2640
568HC	Alliance VA Clinic	Closed on Nov 8, 2010 Alliance, NE 69301	NE	
636	Bellevue Community Based Outpatient Clinic	2501 Capehart Road, Bellevue, NE 68113	NE	402-591-4500
437GE	Bemidji VA Community Based Outpatient Clinic	705 5th Street NW, Suite B, Bemidji, MN 56601	MN	218-755-6360
636GF	Bettendorf VA Clinic	2979 Victoria Street, Bettendorf, IA 52722	IA	563-332-8528
437GB	Bismarck VA Community Based Outpatient Clinic	Gateway Mall, 2700 State Street, Suite 5, Bismarck, ND 58503	ND	701-221-9169
656GA	Brainerd VA Clinic	722 NW 7th Street, Brainerd, MN 56401	MN	218-855-1115
618GE	Chippewa Valley VA Clinic	2503 County Highway I, Chippewa Falls, WI 54729	WI	715-720-3780
636GJ	Dubuque VA Clinic	200 Mercy Drive, Suite 106, Dubuque, IA 52001	IA	563-588-5520
568HM	Eagle Butte VA Clinic	Prairie Community Health, 8000 Highway 212, Eagle Butte, SD 57625	SD	605-964-8000
568HM	Faith VA Clinic	Prairie Community Health, 8000 Highway 212, Eagle Butte, SD 57625	SD	605-967-2644
437GC	Fergus Falls VA Community Based Outpatient Clinic	Veterans Home, 1821 North Park Street, Fergus Falls, MN 56537	MN	218-739-1400
636GK	Fort Dodge VA Clinic	2419 2nd Avenue N, Fort Dodge, IA 50501	IA	515-576-2235 877-578-8846
636GI	Galesburg VA Clinic	387 East Grove, Galesburg, IL 61401	IL	309-343-0311
568HB	Gordon VA Clinic	300 East 8th Street, Gordon, NE 69343	NE	308-282-0362

437GA	Grafton VA Community Based Outpatient Clinic	ND St. Developmental Ctr., Health Service Building, West Sixth Street, Grafton, ND 58237	ND	701-352-4059
437GI	Grand Forks VA Community Based Outpatient Clinic	3221 32nd Avenue South, Suite 700, Grand Forks, ND 58201	ND	701-335-4380
636A4	Grand Island Community Based Outpatient Clinic	2201 N. Broadwell Avenue, Grand Island, NE 68803-2196	NE	308-382-3660
618GH	Hayward VA Clinic	15954 River's Edge Drive, Suite 103, Hayward, WI 54843	WI	715-934-5454
618GB	Hibbing VA Clinic	990 West 41st Street, Suite 78, Hibbing, MN 55746	MN	218-263-9698
636	Holdrege Community Based Outpatient Clinic	1118 Burlington Street, Holdrege, NE 68949	NE	308-995-3760
568FM	Isabel Community Based Outpatient Clinic	Prairie Community Health, 8000 Highway 212, Eagle Butte, SD 57625	SD	605-466-2120
636A7	Knoxville VA Clinic	1515 W. Pleasant Street, Knoxville, IA 50138	IA	641-828-5019 641-828-5019
636A5	Lincoln Community Based Outpatient Clinic	600 South 70th Street, Lincoln, NE 68510	NE	402-489-3802
618	Mankato Community Based Outpatient Clinic	1600 E. Madison Avenue, Suite 103, Mankato, MN 56002	MN	507-387-2348
618GD	Maplewood VA Clinic	2785 White Bear Avenue, Suite 210, Maplewood, MN 55109	MN	651-290-3040
636	Marshalltown Community Based Outpatient Clinic	101 Iowa Avenue, Marshalltown, IA 50158	IA	641-754-6700 877-424-4404
636GC	Mason City VA Clinic	520 S. Pierce, Suite 150, Mason City, IA 50401	IA	800-351-4671 800-351-4671
568HK	McLaughlin VA Clinic	Veterans Industries, Sales Barn Road, P.O. Box 519, McLaughlin, SD 57642	SD	605-347-2511 X 7161
437GD	Minot VA Community Based Outpatient Clinic	5th Medical Group, 10 Missile Avenue, Minot, ND 58705	ND	701-727-9800
568HS	Mission Community Based Outpatient Clinic	Horizon Health Care, Inc., 153 Main Street, Mission, SD 57555	SD	605-856-2295
656GB	Montevideo VA Clinic	1025 North 13th Street, Montevideo, MN 56265	MN	320-269-2222
568HA	Newcastle VA Clinic	1124 Washington Boulevard, Newcastle, WY 57555	WY	307-745-4491
636GA	Norfolk Community Based Outpatient Clinic	710 S 13th, Suite 1200, Norfolk, NE 68701	NE	402-370-4570
636GB	North Platte Community Based Outpatient Clinic	600 East Francis, Suite 3, North Platte, NE 69101	NE	308-532-6906

568GB	Pierre VA Clinic	Linn Medical Clinic, 1601 North Harrison, Suite 6, Pierre, SD 57501	SD	605-945-1710
568HF	Pine Ridge VA Clinic	Next to Dialysis Building across from IHS Hospital, Pine Ridge, SD 57770	SD	605-867-2393 X 4033
636GG	Quincy VA Clinic	721 Broadway Street, Quincy, IL 62301	IL	217-224-3366
568GA	Rapid City VA Clinic	3525 5th Street, Rapid City, SD 57701	SD	605-718-1095
618	Rice Lake VA Clinic	2700A College Drive, Rice Lake, WI 54843	WI	715-236-3355
618GG	Rochester VA Clinic	3900 55th Street NW, Rochester, MN 55901	MN	507-252-0885
568HB	Rushville VA Clinic	Rushville Rural Health Clinic, 307 Conrad Street, Rushville, NE 69360	NE	605-745-2000 X 2474
568HH	Scottsbluff Community Based Outpatient Clinic	1720 E. Portal Place, Scottsbluff, NE 69361	NE	308-220-3930
636	Shenandoah Community Based Outpatient Clinic	512 S. Fremont, Shenandoah, IA 51601	IA	712-246-0092
438GC	Sioux City VA Clinic	1551 Indian Hills Drive, Suite 214, Sioux City, IA 51104	IA	712-258-4700
618GA	South Central VA Clinic (St. James)	St. James Medical Center, 1101 Moultin and Parsons Drive, St. James, MN 56081	MN	507-375-3391
438GA	Spirit Lake VA Clinic	1310 Lake Street, Spirit Lake, IA 51360	IA	712-336-6400
618BY	Twin Ports VA Clinic	3520 Tower Avenue, Superior, WI 54880	WI	715-392-9711
438GE	Wagner Community Based Outpatient Clinic	400 West Highway 46, Wagner, SD 57380	SD	605-384-2340
636GH	Waterloo VA Clinic	1015 S. Hackett Road, Waterloo, IA 50701	IA	319-235-1230
438GF	Watertown Community Based Outpatient Clinic	1900 W. Kemp (temporary location), Watertown, SD 57201	SD	
437GF	Williston VA Community Based Outpatient Clinic	205 Main Street, Williston, ND 58802	ND	701-572-2470
568HP	Winner VA Clinic	1436 East 10th Street, Winner, SD 57580	SD	605-842-2443
04041	Bismarck Vet Center Outstation	1684 Capital Way, Bismarck, ND 58501	ND	701-224-9751
0439V	Brooklyn Park Vet Center	7001 78th Avenue North, Suite 300, Brooklyn Park, MN 55445	MN	763-503-2220
0431	Cedar Rapids Vet Center Satellite	1642 42nd Street NE, Cedar Rapids, IA 52402	IA	319-378-0016

0405	Des Moines Vet Center	2600 Martin Luther King Parkway, Des Moines, IA 50310	IA	515-284-4929
0429	Duluth Vet Center	405 E. Superior Street, Duluth, MN 55802	MN	218-722-8654
0406	Fargo Vet Center	3310 Fiechtner Drive, Suite 100, Fargo, ND 58103-8730	ND	701-237-0942
0427	Lincoln Vet Center	3119 O Street, Suite A, Lincoln, NE 68510	NE	402-476-9736
0404	Minot Vet Center	1400 20th Avenue SW, Minot, ND 58701	ND	701-852-0177
0424	Omaha Vet Center	2428 Cuming Street, Omaha, NE 68131-1600	NE	402-346-6735
04231	Pine Ridge Vet Center Outstation	P.O. Box 910, 105 E. Highway 18, Martin, SD 57747	SD	605-685-1300
0430	Quad Cities Vet Center	1529 46th Avenue #6, Moline, IL 61265	IL	309-762-6955
0423	Rapid City Vet Center	621 6th St., Suite 101, Rapid City, SD 57701	SD	605-348-0077
0428	Sioux City Vet Center	1551 Indian Hills Drive, Suite 214, Sioux City, IA 51104	IA	712-255-3808
0425	Sioux Falls Vet Center	601 S. Cliff Avenue, Suite C, Sioux Falls, SD 57104	SD	605-330-4552
0416	St. Paul Veterans Resource Center	550 County Road D, Suite 10, New Brighton, MN 55112	MN	651-644-4022

Veterans Benefits Administration: Eastern Area Office

Station ID	Facility	Address	State	Phone
xxx	Eastern Area Office	P.O. Box 303, Ann Arbor, MI 48105	MI	800-827-1000
313	Baltimore Regional Office	31 Hopkins Plaza, Baltimore, MD 21201	MD	800-827-1000
301	Boston VA Regional Office	JFK Federal Building, Boston, MA 02203	MA	800-827-1000
307	Buffalo Regional Office	130 S. Elmwood Avenue, Buffalo, NY 14202-2478	NY	800-827-1000
325	Cleveland Regional Office	A. J. Celebrezze Federal Building, 1240 East 9th Street, Cleveland, OH 44199	OH	800-827-1000
329	Detroit Regional Office	Patrick V. McNamara Federal Building, 477 Michigan Avenue, Detroit, MI 48226	MI	800-827-1000

308	Hartford Regional Office	555 Willard Avenue, Newington, CT 06111 Mailing Address: P.O. Box 310909, Newington, CT 06131	CT	800-827-1000
326	Indianapolis Regional Office	575 N Pennsylvania Stsreet, Indianapolis, IN 46204	IN	800-827-1000
373	Manchester Regional Office	Norris Cotton Federal Building, 275 Chestnut Street, Manchester, NH 03101	NH	800-827-1000
306	New York Regional Office	245 W. Houston Street, New York, NY 10014	NY	800-827-1000
309	Newark Regional Office	20 Washington Place, Newark, NJ 07102	NJ	800-827-1000
310	Philadelphia Regional Office and Insurance Center	5000 Wissahickon Avenue, Philadelphia, PA 19101	PA	800-827-1000
311	Pittsburgh Regional Office	1000 Liberty Avenue, Pittsburgh, PA 15222	PA	800-827-1000
304	Providence Regional Office	380 Westminster Street, Providence, RI 02903	RI	800-827-1000
402	Togus VA Medical/ Regional Office Center	1 VA Center, Augusta, ME 04330	ME	800-827-1000
405	White River Junction Regional Office	215 North Main Street, White River Junction, VT 05009	VT	800-827-1000
460	Wilmington Regional Office	1601 Kirkwood Highway, Wilmington, DE 19805	DE	800-827-1000
313	Intake Site at Aberdeen Proving Ground	APG Retirement Services Offices, Susquehanna Avenue, Building 4305, Room 243A, Aberdeen Proving Ground, MD 21005	MD	
313	Intake Site at Annapolis Naval Station/USNA	Navy Fleet & Family Support Center, 348 Kinkaid Road, Annapolis, MD 21402	MD	
313	Intake Site at Bethesda National Naval Hospital (No MOU)	10411 Motor City Drive, 5th Floor, Bethesda, MD, 20817	MD	
402	Intake Site at Brunswick Naval Air Station	Fleet & Family Support Services, Brunswick, ME 04011	ME	
310	Intake Site at Carlisle Barracks	Army Community Services, Building 46, Room 118, Carlisle, PA 17013	PA	
308	Intake Site at Coast Guard Academy	15 Mohegan Avenue, Monroe Hall, New London, CT 06320	CT	

313	Intake Site at Curtis Bay Coast Guard	U.S. Coast Guard Yard Clinic, 2401 Hawkins Point Road, Baltimore, MD 21226	MD
313	Intake Site at Dahlgren Naval Station WC	Fleet & Family Service Support Center, 6027 School House Lane, Dahlgren, VA 22448	VA
310	Intake Site at Dover Air Force Base	Airman & Family Readiness Center, Dover AFB, DE 19902	DE
309	Intake Site at Earle Naval Weapons	NWS Earle Fleet & Family Support Center, 201 Highway 34, Building C59, Colt's Neck, NJ 07722	NJ
313	Intake Site at Fort Detrick	Community Support Center, 1520 Freedman Drive, Room 123, Fort Detrick, MD 21702	MD
310	Intake Site at Fort Dix	HQ, U.S. Army Garrison, HRM, Building 5418, Fort Dix, NJ 08640	NJ
307	Intake Site at Fort Drum	Fort Drum Outbased Office/Department of VA, Fort Drum, NY	NY
313	Intake Site at Fort Meade	Kimbrough Ambulatory Care Center, 3rd Floor, Room 3A04, Fort Meade, MD 20755	MD
309	Intake Site at Fort Monmouth	Army Career and Alumni Program (ACAP), Fort Monmouth, NJ	NJ
313	Intake Site at Indian Head Naval Surface Warfare Center	Fleet & Family Support Center, 12 Strauss Avenue, Indian Head, MD 20640	MD
310	Intake Site at Lakehurst Naval Air Engineering Station	Fleet & Family Support Center, Lakehurst, NJ 08733	NJ
310	Intake Site at McGuire Air Force Base	Family Support Center, McGuire AFB, NJ 08641	NJ
310	Intake Site at New Cumberland Defense Distribution Center	Family Services, DDSP-HF, New Cumberland, PA 17070	PA
313	Intake Site at Patuxent River Naval Air Station	Navy Family Service Center, Building 2090, 21993 Bundy Road, NASFS NAS, Patuxent River, MD 20670	MD
373	Intake Site at Portsmouth Naval Shipyard/Naval Ambulatory Care Center	Manchester VA Regional Office, Manchester, NH 03101	NH

308	Intake Site at U.S. Naval Submarine Base New London at Groton	Fleet & Family Support Center, Building 83, Groton, CT 06349	CT
310	Intake Site at Willow Grove	Fleet & Family Support Center, Willow Grove, PA 19090	PA
325	Intake Site at Wright-Patterson Air Force Base	VA/DOD Transition Office, 4881 Sugar Maple Drive, Wright-Patterson Air Force Base, OH 45433	OH

Veterans Benefits Administration: Southern Area Office

Station ID	Facility	Address	State	Phone
316	Atlanta Regional Office	1700 Clairmont Road, Decatur, GA 30033	GA	800-827-1000
319	Columbia Regional Office	6437 Garners Ferry Road, Columbia, SC 29209	SC	800-827-1000
315	Huntington Regional Office	640 Fourth Avenue, Huntington, WV 25701	WV	800-827-1000
323	Jackson Regional Office	1600 E. Woodrow Wilson Avenue, Jackson, MS 39216	MS	800-827-1000
327	Louisville Regional Office	321 West Main Street, Suite 390, Louisville, KY 40202	KY	
322	Montgomery Regional Office	345 Perry Hill Road, Montgomery, AL 36109	AL	800-827-1000
320	Nashville Regional Office	110 9th Avenue South, Nashville, TN 37203	TN	800-827-1000
314	Roanoke Regional Office	210 Franklin Road SW, Roanoke, VA 24011	VA	800-827-1000
355	San Juan Regional Office	150 Carlos Chardon Avenue, Hato Rey, PR 00918	PR	800-827-1000
317	St. Petersburg Regional Office	9500 Bay Pines Boulevard, St. Petersburg, FL 33708 Mailing Address: P.O. Box 1437, St. Petersburg, FL 33731	FL	800-827-1000
372	Washington D.C. Regional Office	1722 I Street N.W., Washington DC, 20421	DC	800-827-1000
318	Winston-Salem Regional Office	Federal Building, 251 N. Main Street, Winston-Salem, NC 27155	NC	800-827-1000
372	Intake Site at Andrews Air Force Base	Airman & Family Readiness Center, 316 MSS/DPF, Andrews AFB, MD 20762	MD	

372	Intake Site at Bolling Air Force Base	Airman & Family Readiness Center, 118 Brookley Avenue, Building 13, Suite 100, Bolling AFB, Washington, DC 20032	DC
318	Intake Site at Camp Lejeune	Department of VA–Benefits, Delivery at Discharge, Camp Lejeune, NC	NC
319	Intake Site at Charleston Air Force Base	Airman & Family Readiness Center, Building #500, Charleston, SC 29404	SC
318	Intake Site at Cherry Point MCAS	Camp Lejeune Department of VA–Benefits, Delivery at Discharge, Camp Lejeune, NC 28547	NC
317	Intake Site at Corry Station	VA Joint Ambulatory Care, Center Pensacola, FL 32507	FL
372	Intake Site at DC Coast Guard	Coast Guard Headquarters, 2100 Second Street, SW, Washington, DC 20593	DC
317	Intake Site at Eglin Air Force Base	Airman & Family Readiness Support Center, Fort Walton, Beach, FL 32542	FL
372	Intake Site at Fort Belvoir	5th Street & Gunston Road, Building #1467, Fort Belvoir, VA 22060	VA
316	Intake Site at Fort Benning	Department of Veterans Affairs, Building 2617, Fort Benning, GA	GA
318	Intake Site at Fort Bragg	Soldier Support Center/ VA Outbase Office, Fort Bragg, NC 28307	NC
320	Intake Site at Fort Campbell	Lee Soldier & Family Support Center, Fort Campbell, KY	KY
314	Intake Site at Fort Eustis	210 Franklin Road SW, Roanoke, VA 24011	VA 800-827-1000
316	Intake Site at Fort Gordon	Department of Veterans Affairs, Building 33800, Fort Gordon, GA	GA
319	Intake Site at Fort Jackson	VA Predischarge Program, Building #4600, Education Center, Strom Thurmond Boulevard, Fort Jackson, SC	SC
327	Intake Site at Fort Knox	Department of Veterans Affairs www.knox.army.mil/acap/va.htm Fort Knox, KY	KY
314	Intake Site at Fort Lee	1403 Mahone Avenue, Fort Lee, VA 23801	VA
372	Intake Site at Fort Myer	126 Forest Circle, Building 230, Fort Myer, VA 22211	VA

322	Intake Site at Fort Rucker	ACAP Center, Fort Rucker, AL 36362	AL
316	Intake Site at Fort Stewart/ Hunter Army Airfield	Audie Murphy Soldier Center (3 ID Welcome Center), Fort Stewart, GA	GA
317	Intake Site at Hurlburt Field	Airman & Family Readiness Center, Hulburt Field, FL 32544	FL
323	Intake Site at Keesler Air Force Base	VA Medical Center, 400 Veterans Avenue, Building 2, Room 1040, Biloxi, MS 39532	MS
317	Intake Site at Key West Coast Guard	NAS Key West & USCG Group Key West, Key West, FL 33040	FL
317	Intake Site at Kings Bay Naval Submarine Base	Fleet & Family Support Center, Naval 1063 USS Tennessee Avenue, Building 1051, Kings Bay, GA 3154	GA
314	Intake Site at Langley Air Force Base	Airman & Family Readiness Center, 45 Nealy Avenue, Building 15, Suite 100, Hampton, VA 23665	VA
314	Intake Site at Little Creek Naval Amphibious Base	Fleet & Family Support Center, Norfolk, VA 23511	VA
317	Intake Site at MacDill Air Force Base	Base Hospital, 2nd Floor, Room C 277, Tampa, FL 33621	FL
319	Intake Site at Marine Corps Air Station	Building 807 CRMC, MCAS, Beaufort, SC	SC
322	Intake Site at Maxwell Air Force Base	Maxwell-Gunter Transition Services, Maxwell AFB, AL 36112	AL
317	Intake Site at Mayport Naval Station	Branch Medical Clinic, Mayport, FL 32228	FL
317	Intake Site at NAS Jacksonville	Department of Veterans Affairs, Jacksonville, FL 32217	FL
317	Intake Site at NAS Key West	NAS Key West & USCG Group Key West, Key West, FL 33040	FL
317	Intake Site at NAS Pensacola	Fleet & Family Support Center, Pensacola, FL	FL
317	Intake Site at NAS Whiting Field	Fleet & Family Support Center, Milton, FL	FL
317	Intake Site at Naval Hospital Pensacola	Pensacola, FL	FL
317	Intake Site at Naval Support Activity–Panama City	Fleet & Family Support Center, Panama City, FL 32407	FL

319	Intake Site at Navy Weapons Station	Fleet & Family Support Center, 1005 Jefferson Avenue, Building 775, Goose Creek, SC 29445	SC
318	Intake Site at New River MCAS	Camp Lejeune Department of VA–Benefits Delivery at Discharge, Camp Lejeune, NC 28547	NC
314	Intake Site at Norfolk NB	Regional TAP Office, Building U93, Norfolk, VA 23511	VA
314	Intake Site at Oceana Naval Air Station	Fleet & Family Support Center, Norfolk, VA 23511	VA
319	Intake Site at Parris Island	Marine Corps Recruit Depot, Building 923, CRMC, Parris Island, SC	SC
317	Intake Site at Patrick Air Force Base	VA Office of Public Contact, Viera, FL 32940	FL
372	Intake Site at Pentagon (Air Force)	11MSS/DPF, RM 5C1049, 1565 AF, Pentagon, Washington, DC 20330	DC
318	Intake Site at Pope Air Force Base	Family Support Center, Seymour-Johnson AFB, NC 28307	NC
314	Intake Site at Portsmouth Coast Guard	Fleet & Family Support Center, Norfolk, VA 23511	VA
314	Intake Site at Portsmouth Naval Hospital	Fleet & Family Support Center, Norfolk, VA 23511	VA
322	Intake Site at Redstone Arsenal	Military Personnel Office, Redstone Arsenal, AL 35758	AL
318	Intake Site at Seymour Johnson Air Force Base	Family Support Center, Seymour-Johnson AFB, NC 27531	NC
319	Intake Site at Shaw Air Force Base	VA Predischarge Office, Airman Family Readiness, Flight Building, 1127 Stuart Avenue, Sumter, SC 29152	SC
317	Intake Site at Tyndall Air Force Base	325 FSS/FSFR, Tyndall AFB, FL	FL
317	Intake Site at U.S. Coast Guard Group Miami	USCG Health, Safety and Work-Life Field Office, Miami, FL 33177	FL
317	Intake Site at U.S. Southern Command	U.S. Army Garrison-Miami, Southern Command Family Support Center, Doral, FL	FL
372	Intake Site at Walter Reed Army Medical Center	Department of Veterans Affairs, 6900 Georgia Avenue NW, Abrams Hall (Building 14), Room 2042, Washington, DC 20307	DC

Veterans Benefits Administration: Central Area Office

Station ID	Facility	Address	State	Phone
394	Central Area Office	Federal Building, 125 South Main Street, Muskogee, OK 74401-7025	OK	800-827-1000
328	Chicago Regional Office	2122 W. Taylor Street, Chicago, IL 60612	IL	800-827-1000
333	Des Moines Regional Office	210 Walnut Street, Des Moines, IA 50309	IA	800-827-1000
437	Fargo Regional Office	2101 Elm Street, Fargo, ND 58102-2417	ND	701-451-4600
362	Houston Regional Office	6900 Almeda Road, Houston, TX 77030	TX	800-827-1000
334	Lincoln Regional Office	3800 Village Drive, Lincoln, NE 68501-5816 Mailing Address: P.O. Box 85816, Lincoln, NE 68501-5816	NE	800-827-1000
330	Milwaukee Regional Office	5400 West National Avenue, Milwaukee, WI 53214	WI	800-827-1000 800-827-1000
351	Muskogee Regional Office	125 South Main Street, Muskogee, OK 74401	OK	800-827-1000
321	New Orleans Regional Office	1250 Poydras Street, New Orleans, LA 70113	LA	800-827-1000
350	North Little Rock Regional Office	2200 Fort Roots Drive, Building 65, North Little Rock, AR 72114-1756	AR	800-827-1000
438	Sioux Falls Regional Office	2501 W 22nd Street, Sioux Falls, SD 57117	SD	800-827-1000
331	St. Louis Regional Office	400 South 18th Street, St. Louis, MO 63103	MO	800-827-1000
335	St. Paul Regional Office	1 Federal Drive, Fort Snelling, St. Paul, MN 55111-4050	MN	800-827-1000
349	Waco Regional Office	1 Veterans Plaza, 701 Clay Avenue, Waco, TX 76799	TX	
452	Wichita Regional Office	5500 E. Kellogg Wichita, KS 67211	KS	800-827-1000
376	VA Records Management Center	4300 Goodfellow Boulevard, Building 104, St. Louis, MO 63120 Mailing Address: P.O. Box 5020 St. Louis, MO 63115	MO	314-538-4500
351	Intake Site at Altus Air Force Base	Transition Assistance Program (TAP) Manager, Altus AFB, OK 73521	OK	
321	Intake Site at Barksdale Air Force Base	Department of Veterans Affairs, New Orleans, LA 70113	LA	

362	Intake Site at Brooks Air Force Base	San Antonio Outbased VSC Office/Frank Tejeda Outpatient Clinic, San Antonio, TX 78240	TX
362	Intake Site at Corpus Christi Naval Air Station	Corpus Christi VSC Office, Corpus Christi, TX 78411	TX
349	Intake Site at Dyess Air Force Base	Airman & Family Readiness Flight, Dyess AFB, TX	TX
349	Intake Site at Fort Bliss	El Paso Outbased Benefits Office, El Paso, TX	TX
349	Intake Site at Fort Hood	Copeland Soldiers Service Center/VA Intake Site, Fort Hood, TX	TX
452	Intake Site at Fort Leavenworth	Transition Service, Manager/Army Career and Alumni Program Office, Fort Leavenworth, KS 66027	KS
331	Intake Site at Fort Leonard Wood	Department of Veterans Affairs, Fort Leonardwood, MO	MO
321	Intake Site at Fort Polk	Bayne Jones Army Community Hospital, 1585 3rd Street, Room 1221, Fort Polk, LA 71459	LA
452	Intake Site at Fort Riley	VA Military Services, Coordinators Office, Fort Riley, KS 66442	KS
362	Intake Site at Fort Sam Houston	Brooke Army Medical Center/Center for the Intrepid, Room 303, Fort Sam Houston, TX 78234	TX
351	Intake Site at Fort Sill	VA BDD, Office Building 4700, Suite 317, Mow-Way Road, Fort Sill, OK 73503	OK
349	Intake Site at Goodfellow Air Force Base	Airman & Family, Readiness Flight, Goodfellow AFB, TX	TX
328	Intake Site at Great Lakes Naval Station	BDD Intake Site/VA Medical Center, North Chicago, IL	IL
362	Intake Site at Lackland Air Force Base	San Antonio Outbased VSC Office/Frank Tejeda Outpatient Clinic, San Antonio, TX 78240	TX
362	Intake Site at Laughlin Air Force Base (No MOU)	San Antonio Outbased VSC Office/Frank Tejeda Outpatient Clinic, San Antonio, TX 78240	TX
350	Intake Site at Little Rock Air Force Base	Little Rock VA Regional Office, North Little Rock, AR 72114	AR

321	Intake Site at NSA (No MOU)	Department of Veterans Affairs, New Orleans, LA 70113	LA
334	Intake Site at Offutt Air Force Base	Military Services Coordinator, Offutt AFB, NE	NE
362	Intake Site at Randolph Air Force Base	San Antonio Outbased VSC Office/Frank Tejeda Outpatient Clinic, San Antonio, TX 78240	TX
328	Intake Site at Scott Air Force Base	Fleet & Family Support, Call (847) 688-3603, Scott AFB, IL 62225	IL
351	Intake Site at Sheppard Air Force Base	Transition Assistance Program (TAP) Manager, Fort Sill, OK 73611	OK
351	Intake Site at Tinker Air Force Base	BDD Office/Tinker Clinic, Tinker AFB, OK 73145	OK
351	Intake Site at Vance Air Force Base	Airman & Family Readiness Support Center, Enid, OK 73703	OK
331	Intake Site at Whiteman Air Force Base	Airman & Family Readiness Support Center, Whiteman AFB, MO	MO

Veterans Benefits Administration: Western Area Office

Station ID	Facility	Address	State	Phone
999	Western Area Office	3333 North Central Avenue, Suite 3026, Phoenix, AZ 85012-2402	AZ	800-827-1000
340	Albuquerque Regional Office	500 Gold Avenue, S.W., Albuquerque, NM 87102	NM	800-827-1000
463	Anchorage Regional Office	1201 North Muldoon Road, Anchorage, AK 99504	AK	800-827-1000
347	Boise Regional Office	444 W. Fort Street, Boise, ID 83702-4531	ID	
442	Cheyenne VA Medical / Regional Office Center	2360 E. Pershing Boulevard, Cheyenne, WY 82001	WY	800-827-1000
339	Denver Regional Office	155 Van Gordon Street, Lakewood, CO 80228	CO	800-827-1000
436	Fort Harrison Regional Office	3633 Veterans Drive, Fort Harrison, MT 59636-0188	MT	800-827-1000
459	Honolulu Regional Office	459 Patterson Road, E-Wing, Honolulu, HI 96819-1522	HI	800-827-1000
344	Los Angeles Regional Office	Federal Building, 11000 Wilshire Boulevard, Los Angeles, CA 90024	CA	800-827-1000

358	Manila Regional Office	1131 Roxas Boulevard, Ermita 0930, Manila, PI 96440	PI	632-301-2000
343	Oakland Regional Office	1301 Clay Street, Room 1300, North Oakland, CA 94612	CA	800-827-1000
345	Phoenix Regional Office	3333 North Central Avenue, Phoenix, AZ 85012	AZ	800-827-1000
348	Portland Regional Office	100 SW Main Street, Floor 2, Portland, OR 97204	OR	800-827-1000
354	Reno Regional Office	5460 Reno Corporate Drive, Reno, NV 89511	NV	
341	Salt Lake City Regional Office	550 Foothill Drive, Salt Lake City, UT 84158	UT	800-827-1000
377	San Diego Regional Office	8810 Rio San Diego Drive, San Diego, CA 92108	CA	800-827-1000
346	Seattle Regional Office	915 2nd Avenue, Seattle, WA 98174	WA	800-827-1000
346	Intake Site at Bangor Sub Base	West Sound/Bremerton Preseparation Office, 262 Burwell Street, Bremerton, WA 98337	WA	
339	Intake Site at Buckley Air Force Base	VA Regional Office, 155 Van Gordon Street, Lakewood, CO 80225	CO	
377	Intake Site at Camp Pendleton	VA Predischarge Center, Building 13150, Room 226, Camp Pendleton, CA 92055	CA	
377	Intake Site at Camp Pendleton Wounded Warrior Transition Center	Wounded Warrior Career Transition Center (WWCTC), Building 278807T, Santa Margarita Road, Camp Pendleton, CA 92055	CA	
359	Intake Site at Camp Smith	Department of Veterans Affairs, 459 Patterson Road, 1st Floor (E-Wing), Honolulu, HI 96819	HI	
344	Intake Site at China Lake Naval Air Weapons Station	Family Service Center, China Lake, CA 93555	CA	
345	Intake Site at Davis-Monthan Air Force Base	Benefits Counseling Office, Tucson, AZ 85723	AZ	
344	Intake Site at Edwards Air Force Base	Family Support Center, Edwards AFB, CA 93524	CA	
363	Intake Site at Eielson Air Force Base	Department of Veterans Affairs (VARO), Anchorage, AK 99508	AK	
363	Intake Site at Elmendorf Air Force Base	Department of Veterans Affairs (VARO), Anchorage, AK 99508	AK	

346	Intake Site at Everett Naval Station	West Sound/Bremerton Preseparation Office, 262 Burwell Street, Bremerton, WA 98337	WA
442	Intake Site at F. E. Warren Air Force Base	Department of Veterans Affairs 442/214, 2360 E. Pershing Boulevard, Cheyenne, WY 82001	WY
346	Intake Site at Fairchild Air Force Base	Airman & Family Readiness Center, Fairchild AFB, WA 99011	WA
339	Intake Site at Fort Carson	1661 O'Connell Boulevard, Fort Carson, CO 80913	CO
345	Intake Site at Fort Huachuca	ACAP Center (ATZS-ESD-A), Building 22420, Room 1, Butler Road, Fort Huachuca, AZ 85613	AZ
344	Intake Site at Fort Irwin	Army Career and Alumni Program (ACAP), Fort Irwin, CA 92310	CA
346	Intake Site at Fort Lewis	Waller Hall, Building 2140, Room 700, Fort Lewis, WA 98433	WA
363	Intake Site at Fort Richardson	Department of Veterans Affairs (VARO), Anchorage, AK 99508	AK
359	Intake Site at Fort Shafter	Department of Veterans Affairs, 459 Patterson Road, 1st Floor (E-Wing), Honolulu, HI 96819	HI
363	Intake Site at Fort Wainwright	Department of Veterans Affairs (VARO), Anchorage, AK 99508	AK
459	Intake Site at Guam Benefits Office	Reflection Center, Suite 202, 222 Chalan Santo Papa Street, Hagatna, GU 96910	GU
359	Intake Site at Hickam Air Force Base	Department of Veterans Affairs, 459 Patterson Road, 1st Floor (E-Wing), Honolulu, HI 96819	HI
341	Intake Site at Hill Air Force Base	Airman Family Readiness Center, 5837 D Avenue, Building 150, Hill AFB, UT 84074	UT
363	Intake Site at Ketchika Coast Guard	Department of Veterans Affairs (VARO), Anchorage, AK 99508	AK
340	Intake Site at Kirtland Air Force Base	Airman & Family Readiness Center, Support Building 20245, Suite 126, Kirtland AFB, NM 87117	NM

346	Intake Site at Kitsap Naval Base	West Sound/Bremerton Preseparation Office, 262 Burwell Street, Bremerton, WA 98337	WA
363	Intake Site at Kodiak Coast Guard	Depatment of Veterans Affairs (VARO), Anchorage, AK 99508	AK
343	Intake Site at Lemoore Naval Air Station	Kings County Veterans Service Representative, Lemoore, CA 93246	CA
344	Intake Site at Los Angeles Air Force Base	Family Support Center, El Segundo, CA 90245	CA
344	Intake Site at Los Angeles San Pedro Coast Guard	Work Life Center, Building #38, San Pedro, CA 90731	CA
345	Intake Site at Luke Air Force Base	56 MSS/DFB Building 1113, 7282 N 137th Avenue, Luke AFB, AZ 85309	AZ
436	Intake Site at Malmstrom Air Force Base	VA Regional Office, 3633 Veterans Drive, Fort Harrison, MT 59636	MT
377	Intake Site at Marine Corps Air Station, Miramar	VA Predischarge Center, Building 5305, Miramar Way, San Diego, CA 92121	CA
359	Intake Site at Marine Corps Base Hawaii	Department of Veterans Affairs, 459 Patterson Road, 1st Floor (E-Wing), Honolulu, HI 96819	HI
377	Intake Site at Marine Corps Recruit Depot (MCRD)	Veterans Affairs Assistance Program, 8810 Rio San Diego Drive, San Diego, CA 92108	CA
346	Intake Site at McChord Air Force Base	Waller Hall, Building, 2140, Room 700, Fort Lewis, WA 98433	WA
347	Intake Site at Mountain Home Air Force Base	575 Gunfighter Avenue, Building 180, Mountain Home AFB, ID 83648	ID
377	Intake Site at Naval Base San Diego	VA Predischarge Center, 3115 Dolphin Alley, Building #270, Room 210, San Diego, CA 92136	CA
377	Intake Site at Naval Hospital Camp Pendleton	DES Office, Naval Hospital, Lower Level, Santa Margarita Road, Camp Pendleton, CA 92055	CA
377	Intake Site at Naval Medical Center San Diego	Balboa Career Transition Center (BCTC), Balboa Hospital Building 26, #3B, San Diego, CA 92134	CA

359	Intake Site at Pearl Harbor Naval Base	Department of Veterans Affairs, 459 Patterson Road, 1st Floor (E-Wing), Honolulu, HI 96819	HI
339	Intake Site at Peterson Air Force Base	1627 Evans Street, Building 1219, Room VA1, Fort Carson, CO 80913	CO
344	Intake Site at Port Hueneme NCBC	Family Support Center, Port Hueneme, CA 93043	CA
344	Intake Site at Port Mugu Naval Air Station	Family Support Center, Port Hueneme, CA 93043	CA
359	Intake Site at Sand Island Coast Guard	Department of Veterans Affairs, 459 Patterson Road, 1st Floor (E-Wing), Honolulu, HI 96819	HI
359	Intake Site at Schofield Barracks	Department of Veterans Affairs, 459 Patterson Road, 1st Floor (E-Wing), Honolulu, HI 96819	HI
339	Intake Site at Schriever Air Force Base	1628 Evans Street, Building 1219, Room VA1, Fort Carson, CO 80913	CO
363	Intake Site at Sitka Coast Guard	Department of Veterans Affairs (VARO), Anchorage, AK 99508	AK
343	Intake Site at Travis Air Force Base	Travis Airman & Family Readiness Center, Travis AFB, CA 94535	CA
359	Intake Site at Tripler Army Medical Center (First Floor/E-Wing)	Department of Veterans Affairs, 459 Patterson Road, 1st Floor (E-Wing), Honolulu, HI 96819	HI
344	Intake Site at Twenty-nine Palms Marine Corps Combat Center	Marine Corps Air Ground Combat Center, Buildings 1437, Twentynine Palms, CA 92277	CA
339	Intake Site at United States Air Force Academy	1629 Evans Street, Building 1219, Room VA1, Fort Carson, CO 80913	CO
344	Intake Site at Vandenberg Air Force Base	Airman & Family Readiness Center, Vandenberg AFB, CA 93437	CA
346	Intake Site at Whidbey Island Naval Air Station	West Sound/Bremerton Preseparation Office, 262 Burwell Street, Bremerton, WA 98337	WA

National Cemetery Administration: Denver Memorial Service Network

Station ID	Facility	Address	State	Phone
789	Denver Memorial Service Network	155 Van Gordon Street, Lakewood, CO 80228 Mailing Address: P.O. Box 25126, Denver, CO 80225	CO	303-914-5720
884	Black Hills National Cemetery	20901 Pleasant Valley Drive, Sturgis, SD 57785	SD	605-347-3830
916	Dallas-Fort Worth National Cemetery	2000 Mountain Creek Parkway, Dallas, TX 75211	TX	214-467-3374
885	Fort Bayard National Cemetery	200 Camino De Paz, Fort Bayard, NM 88036 Mailing Address: P.O. Box 189, Fort Bayard, NM 88036	NM	915-564-0201
886	Fort Bliss National Cemetery	P.O. Box 6342, 5200 Fred Wilson Road, El Paso, TX 79906	TX	915-564-0201
844	Fort Gibson National Cemetery	1423 Cemetery Road, Fort Gibson, OK 74434	OK	918-478-2334
887	Fort Leavenworth National Cemetery	Hancock Biddle Street, Fort Leavenworth, KS 66027	KS	913-758-4105
888	Fort Logan National Cemetery	4400 W. Kenyon Avenue, Denver, CO 80236	CO	303-761-0117
889	Fort Lyon National Cemetery	15700 County Road HH, Las Animas, CO 81054	CO	303-761-0117
890	Fort McPherson National Cemetery	12004 South Spur 56A, Maxwell, NE 69151	NE	308-582-4433
891	Fort Meade National Cemetery	Old Stone Road, Sturgis, SD 57785	SD	605-347-3830
846	Fort Sam Houston National Cemetery	1520 Harry Wurzbach Road, San Antonio, TX 78209	TX	210-820-3891
893	Fort Scott National Cemetery	900 East National Avenue, Fort Scott, KS 66701	KS	620-223-2840
920	Fort Sill National Cemetery	2648 NE Jake Dunn Road, Elgin, OK 73538	OK	580-492-3200
896	Hot Springs National Cemetery	VA Medical Center Hot Springs, SD 57747	SD	605-347-3830
851	Houston National Cemetery	10410 Veterans Memorial Drive, Houston, TX 77038	TX	281-447-8686
854	Kerrville National Cemetery	VA Medical Center, 3600 Memorial Boulevard, Kerrville, TX 78028	TX	210-820-3891
897	Leavenworth National Cemetery	150 Muncie Road, Leavenworth, KS 66048	KS	913-758-4105
877	San Antonio National Cemetery	517 Paso Hondo Street, San Antonio, TX 78202	TX	210-820-3891
904	Santa Fe National Cemetery	501 North Guadalupe Street, Santa Fe, NM 87501	NM	505-988-6400

National Cemetery Administration: Philadelphia Memorial Service Network

Station ID	Facility	Address	State	Phone
826	Alexandria National Cemetery	1450 Wilkes Street, Alexandria, VA 22314	VA	
801	Annapolis National Cemetery	800 West Street, Annapolis, MD 21401	MD	410-644-9696
827	Ball's Bluff National Cemetery	Route 7, Leesburg, VA 22075	VA	540-825-0027
802	Baltimore National Cemetery	5501 Frederick Avenue, Baltimore, MD 21228	MD	410-644-9696
803	Bath National Cemetery	VA Medical Center, San Juan Avenue, Bath, NY 14810	NY	607-664-4853
804	Beverly National Cemetery	916 Bridgeboro Road, Beverly, NJ 08010	NJ	215-504-5610
805	Calverton National Cemetery	210 Princeton Boulevard, Calverton, NY 11933	NY	631-727-5410
836	City Point National Cemetery	10th Avenue and Davis Street, Hopewell, VA 23860	VA	804-795-2031
837	Cold Harbor National Cemetery	6038 Cold Harbor Road, Mechanicsville, VA 23111	VA	804-795-2031
839	Culpeper National Cemetery	305 US Avenue, Culpeper, VA 22701	VA	540-825-0027
808	Cypress Hills National Cemetery	625 Jamaica Avenue, Brooklyn, NY 11208	NY	631-454-4949
811	Finn's Point National Cemetery	Fort Mott Road, Salem, NJ 08079	NJ	215-504-5610
845	Fort Harrison National Cemetery	8620 Varina Road, Richmond, VA 23231	VA	804-795-2031
917	Gerald B. H. Solomon Saratoga National Cemetery	200 Duell Road, Schuylerville, NY 12871-1721	NY	518-581-9128
848	Glendale National Cemetery	8301 Willis Church Road, Richmond, VA 23231	VA	804-795-2031
812	Grafton National Cemetery	431 Walnut Street, Grafton, WV 26354	WV	304-265-2044
849	Hampton National Cemetery	Cemetery Road, at Marshall Avenue, Hampton, VA 23669	VA	757-723-7104
850	Hampton National Cemetery (VAMC)	VA Medical Center, Emancipation Drive, Hampton, VA 23667	VA	757-723-7104
813	Indiantown Gap National Cemetery	RR2, Box 484, Indiantown Gap Road, Annville, PA 17003-9618	PA	717-865-5254
815	Long Island National Cemetery	2040 Wellwood Avenue, Farmingdale, NY 11735-1211	NY	631-454-4949
816	Loudon Park National Cemetery	3445 Frederick Avenue, Baltimore, MD 21228	MD	410-644-9696

Station ID	Facility	Address	State	Phone
818	Massachusetts National Cemetery	Connery Avenue, Bourne, MA 02532	MA	508-563-7113
925	National Cemetery of the Alleghenies	1158 Morgan Road, Bridgeville, PA 15017	PA	724-746-4363
787	Philadelphia Memorial Service Network	5000 Wissahickon Avenue, Philadelphia, PA 19144	PA	215-381-3787
819	Philadelphia National Cemetery	Haines Street and Limekiln Pike, Philadelphia, PA 19138	PA	215-504-5610
872	Quantico National Cemetery	P.O. Box 10, 18424 Joplin Road, Triangle, VA 22172	VA	703-221-2183
874	Richmond National Cemetery	1701 Williamsburg Road, Richmond, VA 23231	VA	804-795-2031
878	Seven Pines National Cemetery	400 E. Williamsburg Road, Sandston, VA 23150	VA	804-795-2031
880	Staunton National Cemetery	901 Richmond Avenue, Staunton, VA 24401	VA	540-825-0027
822	Togus National Cemetery	VA Medical & Regional Office Center, Togus, ME 04330	ME	508-563-7113
926	Washington Crossing National Cemetery	830 Highland Road, Newtown, PA 18940	PA	215-504-5610
912	West Virginia National Cemetery	Route 2, Box 127, Grafton, WV 26354	WV	304-265-2044
882	Winchester National Cemetery	401 National Avenue, Winchester, VA 22601	VA	540-825-0027
824	Woodlawn National Cemetery	1825 Davis Street, Elmira, NY 14901	NY	607-664-4853

National Cemetery Administration: Atlanta Memorial Service Network

Station ID	Facility	Address	State	Phone
788	Atlanta Memorial Service Network	1700 Clairmont Road, 4th Floor, Decatur, GA 30033	GA	404-929-5899
927	Alabama National Cemetery	3133 Highway 119, Montevallo, AL 35115	AL	205-933-8101
825	Alexandria National Cemetery	209 East Shamrock Avenue, Pineville, LA 71360	LA	601-445-4981
828	Barrancas National Cemetery	Naval Air Station, 1 Cemetery Road, Pensacola, FL 32508	FL	850-453-4108
829	Baton Rouge National Cemetery	220 North 19th Street, Baton Rouge, LA 70806	LA	225-654-3767
830	Bay Pines National Cemetery	10000 Bay Pines Boulevard, North Bay Pines, FL 33708	FL	727-398-9426
831	Beaufort National Cemetery	1601 Boundary Street, Beaufort, SC 29902-3947	SC	843-524-3925
832	Biloxi National Cemetery	400 Veterans Avenue, Biloxi, MS 39535	MS	228-388-6668

835	Chattanooga National Cemetery	1200 Bailey Avenue, Chattanooga, TN 37404	TN	423-855-6590
838	Corinth National Cemetery	1551 Horton Street, Corinth, MS 38834	MS	901-386-8311
841	Danville National Cemetery	721 Lee Street, Danville, VA 24541	VA	704-636-2661
842	Fayetteville National Cemetery	700 Government Avenue, Fayetteville, AR 72701	AR	479-444-5051
843	Florence National Cemetery	803 E. National Cemetery Road, Florence, SC 29501	SC	843-669-8783
911	Florida National Cemetery	6502 S.W. 102nd Avenue, Bushnell, FL 33513	FL	352-793-7740
930	Fort Jackson National Cemetery	4170 Percival Road, Columbia, SC 29229	SC	866-577-5248
908	Fort Mitchell National Cemetery	553 Highway 165, Seale, AL 36856	AL	334-855-4731
847	Fort Smith National Cemetery	522 Garland Avenue and South 6th Street, Fort Smith, AR 72901	AR	479-783-5345
922	Georgia National Cemetery	2025 Mount Carmel Church Lane, Canton, GA 30114	GA	866-236-8159
928	Jacksonville National Cemetery	4083 Lannie Road, Jacksonville, FL 32218	FL	904-766-5222
855	Knoxville National Cemetery	939 Tyson Street, NW, Knoxville, TN 37917	TN	423-855-6590
858	Little Rock National Cemetery	2523 Confederate Boulevard, Little Rock, AR 72206	AR	501-324-6401
859	Marietta National Cemetery	500 Washington Avenue, Marietta, GA 30060	GA	770-428-3258
860	Memphis National Cemetery	3568 Townes Avenue, Memphis, TN 38122	TN	901-386-8311
862	Mobile National Cemetery	1202 Virginia Street, Mobile, AL 36604	AL	850-453-4846
864	Mountain Home National Cemetery	P.O. Box 8, VA Medical Center, Building 117, Mountain Home, TN 37684	TN	423-461-7935
865	Nashville National Cemetery	1420 Gallatin Road S, Madison, TN 37115-4619	TN	615-860-0086
866	Natchez National Cemetery	41 Cemetery Road, Natchez, MS 39120	MS	601-445-4981
868	New Bern National Cemetery	1711 National Avenue, New Bern, NC 28560	NC	252-637-2912
870	Port Hudson National Cemetery	20978 Port Hickey Road, Zachary, LA 70791	LA	225-654-3767
871	Puerto Rico National Cemetery	Avenue Cementerio Nacional #50, Barrio Hato Tejas Bayamon, PR 00960	PR	787-798-8400
873	Raleigh National Cemetery	501 Rock Quarry Road, Raleigh, NC 27610	NC	252-637-2912

876	Salisbury National Cemetery	501 Statesville Boulevard, Salisbury, NC 28144	NC	704-636-2661
931	Sarasota National Cemetery	9810 State Highway 72, Sarasota, FL 34241	FL	877-861-9840
924	South Florida National Cemetery	6501 S. State Road 7, Lake Worth, FL 33449	FL	561-649-6489
875	St. Augustine National Cemetery	104 Marine Street, St. Augustine, FL 32084	FL	352-793-7740
881	Wilmington National Cemetery	2011 Market Street, Wilmington, NC 28403	NC	910-815-4877

National Cemetery Administration: Indianapolis Memorial Service Network

Station ID	Facility	Address	State	Phone
774	Indianapolis Memorial Service Network	575 North Pennsylvania Street, Indianapolis, IN 46204	IN	317-916-3790
915	Abraham Lincoln National Cemetery	20953 W. Hoff Road, Elwood, IL 60421	IL	815-423-9958
800	Alton National Cemetery	600 Pearl Street, Alton, IL 62003	IL	314-845-8320
806	Camp Butler National Cemetery	5063 Camp Butler Road, Springfield, IL 62707-9722	IL	217-492-4070
833	Camp Nelson National Cemetery	6980 Danville Road, Nicholasville, KY 40356	KY	859-885-5727
834	Cave Hill National Cemetery	701 Baxter Avenue, Louisville, KY 40204	KY	502-893-3852
807	Crown Hill National Cemetery	700 W. 38th Street, Indianapolis, IN 46208	IN	765-674-0284
840	Danville National Cemetery	277 North First Street, Danville, KY 40442	KY	859-885-5727
809	Danville National Cemetery	1900 East Main Street, VA Medical Center, Danville, IL 61832	IL	217-554-4550
810	Dayton National Cemetery	VA Medical Center, 4100 West Third Street, Dayton, OH 45428	OH	937-262-2115
909	Fort Custer National Cemetery	15501 Dickman Road, Augusta, MI 49012	MI	269-731-4164
894	Fort Snelling National Cemetery	7601 34th Avenue South, Minneapolis, MN 55450	MN	612-726-1127
923	Great Lakes National Cemetery	4200 Belford Road, Holly, MI 48442	MI	866-348-8603
852	Jefferson Barracks National Cemetery	2900 Sheridan Road, St. Louis, MO 63125	MO	314-845-8320
853	Jefferson City National Cemetery	1024 E. McCarty Street, Jefferson City, MO 6510	MO	314-845-8320
814	Keokuk National Cemetery	1701 J Street, Keokuk, IA 52632	IA	319-524-1304

856	Lebanon National Cemetery	20 Highway 208, Lebanon, KY 40033	KY	270-692-3390
857	Lexington National Cemetery	833 West Main Street, Lexington, KY 40508	KY	859-885-5727
817	Marion National Cemetery	1700 East 38th Street, VA Medical Center Marion, IN 46952	IN	765-674-0284
861	Mill Springs National Cemetery	9044 West Highway 80, Nancy, KY 42544	KY	859-885-5727
863	Mound City National Cemetery	P.O. Box 128, Junction–Highway 37 & 51, Mound City, IL 62963	IL	314-845-8320
867	New Albany National Cemetery	1943 Ekin Avenue, New Albany, IN 47150	IN	812-948-5234
918	Ohio Western Reserve National Cemetery	P.O. Box 8, 10175 Rawiga Road, Rittman, OH 44270	OH	330-335-3069
820	Quincy National Cemetery	36th & Maine Street, Quincy, IL 62301	IL	309-782-2094
821	Rock Island National Cemetery	Building 118, Rock Island Arsenal, Rock Island, IL 61299	IL	309-782-2094
879	Springfield National Cemetery	1702 East Seminole Street, Springfield, MO 65804	MO	417-881-9499
823	Wood National Cemetery	5000 W. National Avenue, Building 1301, Milwaukee, WI 53295-4000	WI	414-382-5300
883	Zachary Taylor National Cemetery	4701 Brownsboro Road, Louisville, KY 40207	KY	502-893-3852

National Cemetery Administration: Oakland Memorial Service Network

Station ID	Facility	Address	State	Phone
775	Oakland Memorial Service Network	1301 Clay Street, Suite 1230, North Oakland, CA 94612-5209	CA	510-637-6270
929	Bakersfield National Cemetery	30338 East Bear Mountain Road, Arvin, CA 93203 Mailing Address: P.O. Box 459, Arvin, CA 93203	CA	661-867-2250 866-632-1845
906	Eagle Point National Cemetery	2763 Riley Road, Eagle Point, OR 97524	OR	541-826-2511
910	Fort Richardson National Cemetery	P.O. Box 5-498, Building 58-512, Davis Highway, Fort Richardson, AK 99505	AK	907-384-7075
892	Fort Rosecrans National Cemetery	P.O. Box 6237, Point Loma, San Diego, CA 92166	CA	619-553-2084
895	Golden Gate National Cemetery	1300 Sneath Lane, San Bruno, CA 94066	CA	650-589-7737

898	Los Angeles National Cemetery	950 S. Sepulveda Boulevard, Los Angeles, CA 90049	CA	310-268-4675
914	National Memorial Cemetery of Arizona	23029 North Cave Creek Road, Phoenix, AZ 85024	AZ	480-513-3600
899	National Memorial Cemetery of the Pacific	2177 Puowaina Drive, Honolulu, HI 96813	HI	808-532-3720
900	Prescott National Cemetery	500 Highway 89 North, Prescott, AZ 86313	AZ	520-776-6028
901	Riverside National Cemetery	22495 Van Buren Boulevard, Riverside, CA 92518	CA	951-653-8417
902	Roseburg National Cemetery	1770 Harvard Boulevard, Roseburg, OR 97470	OR	541-826-2511
921	Sacramento Valley National Cemetery	5810 Midway Road, Dixon, CA 95620	CA	707-693-2460
903	San Francisco National Cemetery	1 Lincoln Boulevard, Presidio of San Francisco, San Francisco, CA 94129	CA	650-761-1646
913	San Joaquin Valley National Cemetery	32053 W. McCabe Road, Santa Nella, CA 95332	CA	209-854-1040
905	Sitka National Cemetery	803 Sawmill Creek Road, Sitka, AK 99835 Mailing Address: P.O. Box 5-498, Fort Richardson, AK 99505	AK	907-384-7075
919	Tahoma National Cemetery	18600 SE 240th Street, Kent, WA 98042-4868	WA	425-413-9614
907	Willamette National Cemetery	11800 SE Mt. Scott Boulevard, Portland, OR 97086-6937	OR	503-273-5250

Index

active duty, 1

Air Force, 10, 32, 58, 62, 81, 157. *See also* Community College of the Air Force

anger, 38

appeals process, 242

Army, 8, 10, 32, 58, 81, 157, 255

Army Career Alumni Program (ACAP) Center, 8, 14, 15, 17, 18, 62

Army Community Service Center, 17

Army Reserve Warrior and Family Assistance Center (AR-WFAC), 241

authorized leave, 143

babies, 161

benefits, 8, 31, 46, 183

Benefits Delivery at Discharge (BDD), 8, 178

Biden, Joe, 28

burial benefits, 231; memorial benefits, 231; national cemeteries, 232

Career OneStop Center, 30, 33

Career Status Bonus (CSB), 52

Centers for Veterans Enterprise, 14, 122

Certificate of Release or Discharge, 23–24

chambers of commerce, 141

children, 4, 147

Civilian Health and Medical Program (CHAMP), 48

Coast Guard, 8, 32, 58, 62, 81, 157

Coast Guard Institute, 32

Combat-Related Special Compensation (CRSC), 55, 56

command career counselor, 22

Commercial Travel Office (CTO), 144

Common Access Card (CAC), 32

Community College of the Air Force, 32

Comprehensive Recovery Plan (CRP), 40

Concurrent Retirement and Disability Pay (CRDP), 55–56

Continued Health Care Benefit Program (CHCBP), 19, 165

CONUS, 8, 143, 178

counseling, 10, 11, 50, 63, 66, 192; pre-separation, 10, 29–30

couples, 4

Credentialing Opportunities Online (COOL), 67

Defense Accounting & Finance Services (DAFS), 32, 59

dental care, 170–71, 197

Department of Defense, 2, 3, 8, 18, 27, 41, 82; Common Access

Card (CAC), 32; job search, 17;
    Transportal, 17, 83, 180; Voluntary
    Education Program, 156
Department of Education, 157
Department of Health and Human
    Resources, 9
Department of Labor, 7, 49, 82
Department of Veterans Affairs, 7, 8,
    14, 16, 19, 38, 41
Dependents' Education Assistance
    Program, 11
depression, 38
disabilities, 201
disability benefits, 7, 43, 201, 237
disability compensation, 49, 55, 201
Disabled Transition Assistance Program
    (DTAP), 29, 41, 62, 65
disabled veterans, 43; non-service
    connected disability, 43; service-
    connected disability, 43
discharge, 25, 29; review, 25

education, 149, 157, 180; career
    assessment, 153; counseling, 153;
    DoD Voluntary Education Program,
    156; vocational services, 154
Education Center, 15
Employment Assistance Hub, 33
employment restrictions, 127
Exceptional Family Member Program
    (EFMP), 134
Expiration Term of Service (ETS), 144

family centers, 134
family records, 23
federal employment opportunities, 88;
    applying for federal jobs, 89
Federal Financial Student Aid, 153
Federal Individual Recovery Plan
    (FIRP), 9
Federal Job Opportunities Listing, 18
Federal Recovery Coordination
    Program, 8, 9, 179
Federal Recovery Coordinators (FRCs),
    9, 179

finances, 245; financial planning, 245
finding a home, 133
first-termer, 1
foreign medical care, 199
form 214, 18, 23
form 2586, 10, 23
form 2648, 1, 14, 15, 21, 30, 62
franchise ownership, 114
Fraternal Military Associations, 68

GI Bill, 7, 11, 16, 149, 150, 158, 212,
    215
Global War on Terrorism Expeditionary
    Medal, 13, 182
grieving, 38

health, 161
health care, 161–62, 184
health records, 23
Helmets to Hardhats, 67
homes, 134; buying your first home, 135;
    buying versus renting, 136; home loan
    guaranty, 219; improvement grants,
    194; mortgages, 138
housing, 145
HUBZone, 106, 109

Individual Transition Plan (ITP), 1, 2,
    15, 21, 30
insurance, 161; life, 171
insurance documents, 24
intern programs, 34

jobs, 17, 31, 34, 66, 96
Joint Transition Assistance, 7, 177

legal assistance, 59
life insurance, 46, 171

Marine Corps, 10, 32, 58, 62, 81, 157
Marine for Life, 38
marriage, 4, 5, 6
medals, 26
mental health care, 195
midcareerist, 1

Military Family Network, 38
military funerals, 27
Military OneSource, 3, 38, 163, 164
military retirement pay, 51
military spouses, 92; jobs for, 92
mortgages, 138–40
moving, 133, 146

National Center for PTSD, 3, 163
National Guard, 8, 10, 12, 13, 17, 29,
    236; National Guard Reserve, 10, 12,
    13, 17, 236
National Personnel Records Center,
    24–25, 27
National Resource Directory (NRD), 7
National Retiree Councils, 59
National Veterans Business
    Development Corporation, 97, 98,
    111, 122
Navy, 10, 22, 32, 58, 62, 81, 157;
    Command Career Counselor, 22, 63
networking, 15
nursing home care, 44, 198

Office of Personnel Management
    (OPM), 13, 182
Office of Government Contracting
    (GC), 106
on-the-job training programs, 151, 212
One-Stop Centers, 12, 181
Operation Enduring Freedom, 7, 177
Operation Iraqi Freedom, 7, 177

Patriot Express Pilot Loan Program, 98
pay, 247; separation pay, 18, 247
pension programs, 44, 45, 210
pensions, 210
Permissive Temporary Duty (PTDY), 143
Personal Identification Number (PIN), 32
Physical Examination Board (PEB), 52
post-traumatic stress disorder (PTSD),
    3, 162; National Center for PTSD,
    3, 163
predischarge program, 8, 178
preretiree, 1

Preseparation Counseling Checklist, 15,
    21, 30, 179
President Obama, 28
private employment agencies, 87
private health insurance, 189
Procurement Technical Assistance
    Centers (PTACS), 107
prosthetics, 193
Public and Community Services (PACS)
    Registry Program, 83, 84

Quick Start, 8

Recovering Service Member (RSM),
    39, 40
Reduction in Force (RIF), 12, 62
re-employment, 87, 240–41
relocation assistance, 17, 142
Relocation Assistance Program, 134
Relocation Assistance Program office,
    17, 143
Reserve, 1
Reservist, 1
resumes, 70; samples, 71

SCORE, 101, 123
self-assessment, 31
separation, 29
Service-Disabled Veterans Life
    Insurance (S-DVI), 47, 175
Servicemembers' Group Life Insurance
    (SGLI), 19, 171, 227
skills assessment, 69
Small Business Administration, 97;
    financial assistance, 102; investment
    programs, 104
Small Business Development Centers,
    100
small businesses, 14, 183
SMART, 32
Social Security, 249
Spina Bifida program, 11, 194
state employment services, 12
stress, 6, 36, 37; transition-related stress,
    37

suicide prevention, 196
supplemental health insurance, 53, 54
support, 35, 41
Survivor Benefit Plan (SBP), 15, 18, 59

Temporary Early Retirement Authority
  (TERA), 56, 84
Transfer of Entitlement (TOE), 214
transition, 1
Transition Assistance Office, 21, 30, 66
Transition Assistance program (TAP), 7,
  61, 64, 79, 177
transition benefits, 29
Transition Bulletin Board, 10, 18, 84,
  95, 179
Transition Counseling Checklist, 21,
  30
transition services, 29
Transitional Assistance Management
  Program (TAMP), 164
Traumatic Injury Protection Insurance
  (TSGLI), 172, 227
travel costs, 190
TRICARE, 17, 41, 53, 163, 164, 167–
  68; dental, 53
Troops to Teachers Program (TTT), 85,
  96
TurboTap, 3, 22, 30, 33, 35

unemployment compensation, 12, 181,
  248
Uniformed Services Employment
  and Reemployment Rights Act
  (USERRA), 81
uniforms, 25
United Services Military Apprenticeship
  Program (USMAP), 67
USAJOBS, 17

Verification of Military Experience and
  Training (VMET), 10, 23, 31, 80,
  179

Veteran Business Development Officers
  (VBDOS), 99
veteran centers, 50, 243
veterans, 1, 3
Veterans Affairs, 3, 8, 16, 41; Centers
  for Veterans Enterprise, 14;
  education benefits, 11; health care
  eligibility, 169; medical care, 168;
  medical programs, 191
Veterans Business Outreach Centers,
  99, 122
Veterans' Education Assistance
  Program (VEAP), 11
Veterans Employment Opportunities
  Act of 1998, 13, 183
Veteran Service Officer (VSO), 243
Veterans' Group Life Insurance (VGLI),
  19, 174, 226–27
Veterans' Mortgage Life Insurance
  (VMLI), 48, 175, 229
veterans' preference for federal jobs,
  12, 181
Veterans Readjustment Appointment,
  13, 182
Veterans Recruitment Appointment, 14,
  93, 183
Veterans Services Organizations, 68
Veterans Upward Bound Program
  (VUB), 159
Veterans' Workforce Investment
  Program, 11, 181
Vocational Rehabilitation and
  Employment (VR&E), 10, 11, 29,
  41, 42, 65, 178, 180
voting, 25

wills, 24
Women's Business Centers, 102
women veterans, 187
Workforce Career Centers, 12
workshops, 67
wounded warrior, 39; benefits, 46

About the Authors

Janelle Hill is the president and lead consultant of PBS Marketing/Federal Concierge LLC, a consulting provider supporting a variety of project and program needs to businesses, contractors, and the federal government. She is also a United States Marine Corps Key Volunteer and an advocate for special needs children. Her husband is a major in the USMC. She is the coauthor of *The Wounded Warrior Handbook* (2008).

Cheryl Lawhorne is an original plank holder in the Wounded Warrior Battalion West at Camp Pendleton, California. She now serves as the deputy project manager for the Recovery Care Coordination Program with the Wounded Warrior Regiment in Quantico, Virginia, under the guidance of Headquarters Marine Corps and the Office of the Secretary of Defense. She was a contributing author to *The Wounded Warrior Handbook*.

Don Philpott is the editor-in-chief of *International Homeland Security: The Quarterly Journal for Homeland Security Professionals*, and the author of more than 5,000 articles in various publications and over 90 books, including *Is America Safe: Terrorism, Homeland Security, and Emergency Preparedness* (2009) and *The Wounded Warrior Handbook*.